SPENCEr AUSTIN

Know The Score Books Limited
118 Alcester Road, Studley, Warwickshire, B80 7NT
01527 454482
info@knowthescorebooks.com
www.knowthescorebooks.com

A CIP catalogue record is available for this book from the British Library
ISBN: 978-1-84818-399-5

Jacket design by Spencer Austin

Printed by Athenaeum Press, Gateshead, Tyne & Wear, UK

To my most unexpected godchild.

1

3

5

51

80

99

115

137

139

151

introduction

IT WAS EARLY 2008.

I left Britain: sick of it. Sick to my eyeballs of its piddling rain, the nose-to-armpit overcrowded trains full of dreary, misery-gutted gits, the £4 for a Pret-a-cardboard sandwich of fat on malted and the sepia streets in which people spit, steal and stab. What a toilet. What a slagheap. I sulked like a ripe old tart, stormed out, flounced off, ran away. I sold up my TV production company, rented my flat out to someone still infested with the rat race, kept six grand for beer money on the Visa card and swanned off around the world with the defeated gait of Reggie Perrin.

At 33 years old, this East End scrotebag had been encouraged by Thatcher throughout the 80s to *want*, *earn* and then *want* again ... and by 2008, I realised that no matter how high up the career ladder, how much I earned, how many greedy trips back from John Lewis with grubby hands full of gadgets, gluten-free garibaldi biscuits dipped in gold and ironic cufflinks ... I still wanted more. It's never ending. You never get to that singular point of satisfaction; the task is never complete, life alone doesn't make you happy. I sat back and realised I'd spent my entire 12-year working life running after Maggie's golden carrot; chasing the 80s dream.

I blamed England.

I never wanted to come back; the country was dead to me. What a rip off – Maggie had gone to the dogs and taken my wallet with her. Happiness is not at the end of nine-to-five or in its associated PAYE-dented payslip. It's somewhere else, surely. But where?

And then one day, while gallivanting around the world being the dog on the other side of the door, it smacked me flat on the snout.

When Spurs beat Chelsea that day, I was in Vietnam.

Phu Quoc island, on the map, dangles suspiciously off the southern mainland as though it should belong to Cambodia. I think Cambodia probably think so too. It's a tiny, relatively untouched paradise with white sand beaches and clear waters that combine to form irresistible foregrounds for sunsets you could dip your toasted bread soldiers into while sobbing over its beauty. Where else could you cry over breakfast at sunset? I was lounging around for much of the days, drinking shrill Vietnamese beers and losing a stone a week on paltry tofu side plates, while writing up my first book *Chasing the Eighties*: a tale of my journey around North America hunting down people and places from 80s movies and TV shows – with the ultimate goal of curing nostalgia. The mission then was to stop myself from gulping the loss of that glossed-over past that had somehow become an unreal idyll, a mental construct that probably never really existed in such glory in the first place.

We found a bar to watch Spurs play Chelsea, and after that nosebleed 90 minutes, I realised that with nostalgia pretty much eliminated, it was time to look after the present, to save my now…

The Carling Cup final, Wembley Stadium. For Spurs fans everywhere: glory at last. At last. The ecstasy, the relief, the bloody treacly delicious cloud-nine-o-rama of it. There's nothing quite like the dizzy-headed reality-suspension of utter, unabated glory. Sex? Drugs? Nah. This is what it's all about; this is the *real* rock and roll. (Slight stipulation: depends on who the sex is with.) Faces everywhere were contorted with that unconditional momentary happiness (which I call the 'football-gasm').

Berbatov, penalty. Goal. Woodgate, accidentally brilliant intentional inadvertent rebound off the bonce. Goal. Two-one. Tears and sick up the walls, confused Vietnamese locals watching the riotous screen … Robbie Keane, affecting a sort of joyous sob (which, in truth, looked a bit mental), as he waved the cup in front of equally mental-with-joy fans with flags being waved at lactic acid pace. Even that death-faced Bella Lugosi Junior, Dimitar Berbatov, cracked his wretched boat open for the occasion.

All was now.

Everything was *that* moment.

Nothing else existed; past or present. Tick-tock stopped, froze; time was scrapped and the rest of the day hung in the suspended animation of Tottenham's cup glory. Of course, tomorrow was another day; the miserly clock started chiselling away at us once again. The onset of hangover and thoughts of back to work and the next match or maybe even fleeting fantasies about next year's cup ensued. But if only you could stop the clock from firing up again; keep that moment alive, maintain that feeling of invincible glory and live it as a reality. If only it could never end.

And that got me thinking.

After three months on the road (in backpacker speak, that's around four pant washes), having crossed from London to Ho Chi Minh City by train through Belgium, Germany, Poland, Belarus, Russia, Mongolia and China, I started to realise that having seen all those different cultures and their traditional idiosyncrasies, wonders and wind-ups ... we're all, after all, just human. We all have the same-shaped brains. We all love, hate, get angry, get sad and everyone, especially myself, has the propensity to annoy me. Maybe, after all, I just have a problem in general with the human brain and its universal insanities, and not necessarily just the English-shaped ones. In every culture, in every country, there's the rough and the smooth, the good and bad, the Spurs and the Arsenal. I realised that I'd spent all this time giving other countries and cultures a go, a chance to woo me, when miles and miles away is my *home*, England, and that just maybe I hadn't really given it a fair chance.

Before, I'd got so wrapped up in my own ten-mile radius, completely strangled by my Thatcher-induced greed and its relentless quest for more and bigger, that I'd lost sight of what might actually be *Great* about Britain. Maybe it was *the way* I was living my life, not necessarily *where* I was living it. And then watching that Cup final win on the telly, with those faces in that crowd and those flags and the noise and the shivers of awe running down my spine, I felt a pang of *wanting to be there*, that maybe it's where I belong, after all.

But I couldn't go back and pick up where I left off. Just *couldn't*. We needed counselling, me and England. We needed some sort of trial period, to test whether we really are compatible or not. *Come on England, let's give it another go*, I thought. *You can be a nasty bastard, but deep down I think that perhaps I love you.*

So, I had a desire to freeze that feeling of untainted glory, and an urge to reconcile my differences with England, which tangled together at once.

Hmmmm. How could I get both?

Could Spurs really *guarantee* me more glory? I've been conditioned by the recent past to think probably not: Juande Ramos, Christian Gross, Jacques Santini ... I've been hurt before, I'm like a spurned lover, like a smacked Pavlov's dog, like

1.

LEt'S BUrn
aUStin mitCHELL mP

WEDNESDAY, 23 JULY 2008.
A pub, in London. With a beer. On my own. Thinking about stuff. Particularly that this sub-heading might be too long.

As the warm, spittly dregs of a fourth pint of Fosters slope down my parched central London late-summer gullet, I can't stop thinking about that film with Gwyneth Paltrow; you know, the one directed by the bloke who played Joey Boswell in the 80s TV sitcom *Bread*. The film's called *Sliding Doors*.

I remember John Hannah in it, being about as face-punchingly smarmy as any man could without actually *being* Jeffrey Archer. Gwyneth cracks out an English accent and says 'w**ker' *really* well; to the point at which you actually fancy her just for saying 'w**ker'. But neither of those factors are why I'm thinking about *Sliding Doors*.

That slobbery, watery-tart snog-fest film was based on alternate realities that centred upon the closing doors of a tube train. What a depressing pivot to choose. They could have chosen a rollercoaster loop or monster truck teetering on its fat back wheels or that agonising decision over whether to have one more flaming sambuca shot or not. But no, they went for the black-bogey-creating London Underground. And even worse, it was the Waterloo and City Line; possibly the only train line in the world with just one single stop – across two stations – that still gets stuffed up from the dreaded scourge they fob us off with because we don't really understand it … *signal failure*. Anyway, *Sliding Doors* is about the exact moment at which two different existential tangents are born, and the film follows both possibilities as they mushroom out into totally different tales of love, loss and, as mentioned, watery-tart snogging.

Of course, in reality, every millisecond and every tiny decision we make is a *Sliding Doors* moment, from a blink to a bloody minded murder; infinite possible eventualities could sprout and head you off in numerous directions from the slightly different (like ending up with a different flavour Wine Gum), to utterly life changing (like ending up having your nose surgically replaced with a penis). It's a terrifying yet exciting thought (I mean just generally, not specifically the nose-for-penis eventuality), but it's true; every second affects the next and accumulatively, our existence weaves a delicate path through a dense forest of infinite other routes. We'll never truly know the extent to which every minute decision affects our overall course. How precarious our destiny. And I guess in *Sliding Doors*, they chose the most mundane scenario possible in order to stress that even the tiniest, boringest, rubbishest things can send you off onto completely different ever afters.

But what the flipping titflap have Gwyneth Paltrow, the Waterloo and City Line and Wine Gums got to do with my ultimate football season?

Erm.

Well. Because tonight is one of those few tangibly big fat tangent-splitting moments that I know for sure will affect my overall direction; one that will kick off a series of events that will dictate the entire course of my football season and my life thereafter. I *am* Gwyneth Paltrow and this, this is *my Sliding Doors*. Well, I'm not as fit or even half as female as The Palt, but you know what I mean. So, in accordance with the occasion, I've been nervous all day today. Hence the multiple warm jars of Fosters. Hence the frantic thought processes somehow involving nose-for-penis transplants.

The names of 92 football teams are in the Gloryhat (which is not, it turns out, a Stetson. More a flimsy joke shop top hat that probably reflects me more accurately). All ninety-two offer a different season's tangent, each with their own stories marked out ahead of them (depending how much you believe in fate); adventures, tragedies and triumphs. *Please don't let it be Arsenal. Please. Not Arsenal*, I think. I wonder if there's one team that would result in my marriage? *Please don't let her be Arsenal, please.* I wonder if there's one that'll end in my death? *Please don't let an Arsenal fan kill me, I'd rather do myself in.* Or I wonder if I'll end up with a penis for a nose? Like Wenger.

92 different odysseys, folded up on tiny bits of paper – extraordinarily disproportionate symbols of their powers – all waiting to be picked out and extrapolate,
spew out their own equally unique ten months of events, each event of which will
be dictated by the previous, and all inextricably leading back to *this* very moment,
here, with the warm Fosters and the Gwyneth Paltrow calling me a w**ker in the
back of my mind. It's bonce-bending, tonight's big draw; utterly incomprehensible,
but completely intriguing and terribly significant (to me, anyway).

The Freemason's Arms in London's trendy Covent Garden. That's where I
am. Chosen because The Football Association was formed here way back when
men wore long curly wigs and maintained an astonishing dignity regardless. No, I
don't mean the days of Waddle and Hoddle and their musical *Diamond Lights*
crime, I mean an era long before that. I figured that if it was good enough for that
bunch of clowns, it's good enough for this bunch of clown.

Just as I finish throwing Gwyneth Paltrow around my mind's bedroom, a load
of mates turn up for the occasion. By now, I've had a few drinks. Actually, I'm off my
noodle, utterly marinated. I'm dolloping out nonsense to anyone who cares to
listen and/or be pebbledashed with my five per cent proof spittle infused with
cheese and onion crisp paste. Some of my twaddle may even be in Latin for all I
know. I'm a greasy mess of worry and excitement and, it has to be said, I'm slightly
preoccupied with the prospect of abject loneliness in some hovel hotel on the
wintry outskirts of hell's nadir. While this lot go back to their flats and their partners
and their jobs and their fridges full of normal stuff that they can actually cook, I'll be
in a car on my own, heading towards a hotel room that I'll share with me and me and
my big plate and some Pot Noodles.

The ceremony begins.

First, out comes the Spurs season ticket. I stand on a chair underneath the
cabinet of discoloured Football Association memorabilia: one of those glass display
units that necessarily include a flat old brown stitch-up football, from grandad days.
I flap the ticket around, backdropped unflatteringly by tobacco-stained walls.
Everything's a sort of regal red, tainted by fags gone by. A proper old pub. Decades
of swear words and tall stories float in the air like atmospheric clouds of nostalgia.
Amid the glorious grunge and wood panelling, I hand over the season ticket to my
mate, Nick. He's got a smug look on his face which is thinly masked with a pathetic
droop of sadness to see me go. The result is a sort of smarmy grimace, like he's
farted in a lift full of posh people. *Yeah, right, smarmy chops, you've got the ticket,*

but I've got the dream, I convince myself. I crack him round the moosh with the ticket, knowing he can't really react because I could always give it away elsewhere. I have the power, albeit in a loosened, dwindling clutch.

Then I get a flood of *oh no what the hell am I doing?* booting me in the stomach with the sudden nervous jolt you get at the airport when your passport isn't in the pocket you thought it was. *Is it too late to grab the ticket back and run and run off into the night (on a stolen horse, I would have thought) and leave a pretend suicide note at the ITV reception? I could still turn up to Spurs games in a series of excellently devised personas occasionally borrowed from the likes of Dickens, Tim Burton and Grange Hill...*

No. No, no, no. Shhhh. Stop this nonsense. This is it. I'm doing it. I'm doing it, doing it, doing it.

"Woooooooooooooooo000000HHHHHH," I start a chorus, building up the frenzy to a trembling hand delving into the sacred hat of 92. My mates are excellently slow to pick up that I intend for them to join in the chorus (otherwise it's not a chorus) and leave me wooooooooohhhh-ing on my own for more beats than are comfortable. Maybe they think I'm exclaiming an incredibly slow fall. But just as my voice frays into a gargled whimper of humiliation, up comes the noise, starting with sympathy, middling with a rising sense of occasion and ending with what I'm going to call a furore; not far from an actual hullabaloo. Nick's ceremonial hand dips into the Gloryhat. *Rustle, rustle,* like a rat in a bin. I want this moment to be entirely out of my control. *Rustle, rustle.* I want to be bitch slapped into the unknown by Master Fate. *Rustle.* Faces freeze with anticipation; mine wobbles with nerves that project down to the rickety chair I'm precariously standing on. It ends up either looking a little bit like a scene starring Clive Dunn or a very bizarre execution. Maybe it is. *Please don't be Arsenal, please don't be Arsenal, please don't be Arsenal, anyone but Arsenal ... and Chelsea ... anyone but Arsenal and Chelsea ... and West Ham ... anyone but Arsenal, Chelsea and West Ham ... oh get on with it...*

Out comes the chosen piece of paper, Nick hands it over, small and wrinkled. Outside of our ringed off little area, the pub continues with its raucous bar-noise composed of over-beered suits who crank the voice up a notch on each pint and laugh a little louder at Quentin's jokes about chavs. But in this bubble, all I can hear is blood rushing around my head like one of those Argos footspas you only ever use twice.

"It's not Arsenal!!!" I scream, overjoyed, relieved; satisfied. A little bit of wee and a burp pop out; all that is evil expels itself, like a spontaneous and concise detox.

Such is my euphoria that I almost forget to let everyone know the actual name that's on the paper.

I prepare myself as everyone goggles at me, probably getting a bit annoyed that I'm milking it; they've got trains to catch, kebabs to smear on their chins; someone to get home to. And I *am* milking it. Good and proper. I'm tugging the udders as hard as I can, because this moment means so much; this is the last time for ages that my friends will congregate on my behalf, before I wander off on my own.

"Weeeeee loooovvvvveeee Grimsby, and we love Grimsby. We love Grimsby and we love Grimsby!" It's not even a football song. It just comes out with the effect of singing attached, but with no actual discernable tune. It's like when football's on the telly and dad wanders in, all in the mood, attempting to be one of the lads but getting it just a little bit wrong with something like "Come on yoooouuuu fooootballlll."

Up goes a roar, not particularly for Grimsby – I don't think anyone was sitting there thinking *let's hope for the love of Christ it's Grimsby* – it's more a sort of a snide irony, a typically English delight in perceived misfortune; that among all the best teams in the country, the one I got was Grimsby Town, and now I've got to bloody go and live there. Where is it? What division are they in? Predictably, haddock springs to mind, but above the confusion, slight derision and my ignorance, I'm thrilled.

Most would imagine I'd have been longing for the Premiership and Europe, but not really, no. That'd be no adventure, we know what lies there. Although it might still happen later in the season. But Grimsby pokes conspicuously out of the remit of my English geographical abilities and although I feel a bit of a tit in that I probably know the geography of other countries better than I do England, at least I'm doing something about it, I'm getting out there and doing what every proud Englishman should do – have a good look at the motherland. And where better to start than somewhere I'd shamefully have trouble finding on a map. And how sweet would it be if I find the glory I'm looking for, with Grimsby, in the lower leagues?

The rest of the evening passes with dutifully raucous alcoholism. I fend off discussions that begin with "I bet you're gutted," and "Unlucky," with undiminished defiance. I start to look forward to my random upheaval and want to defend the town against its sudden and senseless detractors. Although I do get a hint of concern when my friend Patrick, actually a Grimsby lad, sidles up and says,

"This is going to be interesting," with a knowing, almost Gandalf-esque wisdom infected with devilish mischief. Maybe he's going to arrange for me to get the twatting he's wanted to give me for years.

I say goodbye to friends whose lives will have moved on by the time I reappear. Marriages and births will happen while I'm away, and this is me removing myself from their lives, wandering off to maybe find a new one, or reaffirm this one or make the decision to look elsewhere for one. We part with beer glasses raised in the name of haddock and cod and this place called Grimsby, somewhere in the north.

* * * * *

Today's the day. *Oh my Christ, oh sodbuckets.* Last week was a nightmare. Back into storage went my life: my entire existence stacked up in boxes in a faceless lock-up in East London. When I sweatily heaved the last box into that room, I just stood there looking at the sum of the material evidence that I'm alive. Everything that represents who I am and what I've been: stacked up, packed away as though my existence is suspended. When I come back in ten months, perhaps me and some of the contents of that storage room might not even be compatible. Maybe I'll have a fancy moustache. Perhaps I'll be wearing dungarees and a peculiar earring. I'll open boxes and find things as I left them, waiting to carry on being used as before. But whether or not I'll want to resume my old life, I have no idea.

I leave from my parents' house. Early. I weave through the country lanes, thinking about the nine months ahead of me. I can't think too far, of course, because I simply don't know what's around the u-bend of fixtures. Unless Grimsby go the whole season undefeated. They play Rochdale in five days time: will I be moving to Rochdale or staying in Grimsby? From there on, the possibilities snowball into an unfeasible array of tangents that are so multiple that they're hardly worth considering lest you could hemorrhage trying.

The drive is a marathon. Well, a bit longer than that. It's a bit under ten marathons and there's nothing to report on the journey. Less than that, in fact. The M1 is a field-flanked carriageway of yawns and angry fast-lane drivers who press up against your bumper to get you out of the way so they can continue their hundred-mile-an-hour journey that'll get them there twenty minutes earlier. I can't be bothered with the speed. Relax. Put the radio on. Yeah baby, Lighthouse Family, Enigma, Enya, *whatever*; a lone driver is automatically awarded an iffy-music amnesty. Or you can have a leisurely shout. The car is one of the few places where you can shout and scream at the very, very top of your voice without anyone knowing. It's like space, except it's not, it's the M1. I bet they get better food in space (unless Moto have got one of their poxy over-priced shacks of turd up there too).

WELCOME TO Grimsby

For geographobes like me, Grimsby is about halfway up the country on the far right, in north-east Lincolnshire. The town supposedly gets its name from a Danish Viking called Grim and the Old Norse word for village, 'by'. Grim's Village. I'd like to see how old Grim would get on in the town centre nowadays. I suspect he'd love a good old maraud at the drinks deals down at Wetherspoons.

The town really went kaboom in the nineteenth century, when the docks expanded, the railway arrived and all sorts of stuff other than just fish came through the place. During the second World War, Grimsby didn't suffer too much damage, mainly because the Germans used the Dock Tower as a navigational landmark (which lead to discussions in government about knocking it down), and because it would have been one of the first landing points in the northern invasion.

In the 50s, Grimsby was the biggest fishing port in the world. Upon visiting the fish market, I discovered that these days, the town is known not so much for its fishing, but its fish processing and distribution. The Icelandic Cod Wars of the 50s and 70s saw a decline in the town's industry – which probably wasn't as comical as my vision of fisherman dressed in big yellow waterproof coats with hoods on throwing cod at each other from the decks of adjacent boats. Pretty much all the fish I saw at the chaotic morning market had been shipped in from Iceland, and much of the business these days is in processing at places like Young's, who sponsor Grimsby Town and then make fish fingers.

Pointless trivia includes the fact that Elton John performed a song on his 1974 album 'Caribou', called 'Grimsby'. It's terrible. But you get the sense he did it as a favour for his writing partner Bernie Taupin, who comes from the area.

These days we're looking at a population of just under 90,000. Around about a packed Wembley would take them all.

Driving into Grimsby is a bit scary. The beginning. My home for at least a week. Down the A180 I get a view of the famous Dock Tower, a big Victorian red-brick hydraulic water tower that's based on a similar one in Siena, Italy. How fancy. Although it might seem like I'm swinging on the predictable stereotype, the car starts pumping through a slightly fishy edge to the air. It may seem convenient, to say that I can smell fish, but honestly I can. And it reminds me of a girl at school called Carol.

I negotiate an implausible one-way spaghetti in the town centre and after several delirious wrong turns, park up in the St. James Hotel's car park. I somehow feel like I'm abroad, which seems a bit naughty – like when you're off sick from school but still go down the shops. I don't really know whether this is a holiday, a work assignment or just a ridiculous endeavour that keeps me the hell out of an office while everyone takes bets on whether I'll actually go through with the whole season. I'm unsure whether what I'm doing is valid or acceptably within the remits of how adults are supposed to conduct their lives, and subsequently, the separation I have from pretty much anyone I might speak to or bump into, concerns me. I'll be meeting people mostly with settled lives and jobs and routines which may well stay more or less the same for years to come. And here's me, slowly becoming unable to relate to that sort of certainty. For years now, I've had no way of predicting where I'll be or what I'll be doing this time next year. Or this time next month sometimes. There are benefits and drawbacks to that, of course; the excitement of the wanderer, the adventure and the variety. But then there's the virtual inability to concrete relationships, security and cashflow. Will this make it difficult for me to bond with the fans of the clubs? Or will the common language of football provide cohesion enough?

My travel tavern hotel room is as spitefully gloomy as you might expect. Wear and tear and bits of hundreds of other people's grime, ground into the sink and grouting. This is where I live now. This is it. Well, not exactly *just* here, but this bedroom, in countless other cities, all waiting for me to inhabit them. The bed is like a foamy ditch, with a great big human-shaped divot carved into the middle of it. I fit nicely, but there's not much scope for positional change. The sheets pull away when you lie on it, exposing the browned mattress, stained with sweat and fluids.

As I drift off to sleep, I try to get in a position so that in the night the sheets don't recede and leave me lying on the naked mattress of bygone yellowing unidentifiable residue.

* * * * *

I open the browned plastic floral curtains and peer out to my first morning as a Grimbarian. Little clumps of cloud shift swiftly across a bluish sky and it looks warm but bracing. This is the coast, after all. *Right, let's get out there.* I'm up for it. Let's get out and grab Grimsby by its balls and have a right old stare at it. I'll go down the docks, get talking to the trawlermen, watch them all come and go; I'll get down the fish market, banter with the boys, we'll end up slapping each other with haddock and traipsing down to the pub, arm in arm, for frothy local ales in tankards. I'll be deliciously saucy to the old girls in the chip shops, but not too far, I won't grab at them or anything like I usually do. I'm ready to ingest Grimsby.

Leave the room, ignore the leaky tap, door slams, entire building shudders; down in the lift, judder judder crank spank, stinks of stale pipe breath and cider dregs; squeak and clunk, the doors open ,walk past bored receptionist watching Phil and Fern, into the car park.

Video camera ... check ... tripod ... check ... notebook ... check ... sat nav ... check ... smashed car window... CHECK.

Hello Grimsby.

Nothing's gone, of course, because I wouldn't leave anything in a car that says 'ITV' all over it. But off goes my brainbox with the scenarios: some grimy buzzed up little toe rag smothered in fake Burberry and a tattoo of the name of a kid he doesn't see any more because of a row over a spliff. He's probably Jeremy 'It's not about you, it's about that child' Kyle fodder, with a pinched little prematurely-aged face and only slightly more teeth than his IQ, and he decided to take my stuff for free, regardless of how hard I've worked for whatever it is. Rage and fear smash into each other and I end up a shaking swearbox looking for the nearest chav to both twat and run away from simultaneously.

Having said that, for all I know, it could have been the local reverend.

And for all I know, it could have been a football fan. This is a scarier thought. The local press, it seems, have been reporting on my arrival already, and although I know that my quest is a harmless adventure, designed only to glorify our united love of the game, perhaps not everyone will see it that way.

'A bloody fan of a Premier League club, coming round here with his Nissan Almera and cockerney accent, I'll show that twat.' Wallop. The nutter probably did it with his head. Plunged his hooter through the window. *Oh Christ. Oh bloody hell. This is a nightmare. They're going to kill me.*

Inside the hotel, the bored receptionist lifts his head from the fashion item on *This Morning* and senses by the way I'm walking – like the Terminator with a club foot – that I've got ever so slight issues I'd like to discuss with him.

"Car. Window. Smashed. Nutter. With his head. Nose first. Probably," I manage to hiss out through my clamped jaw of fury.

"Oh, that's yours? We've called the police and got a crime report number," he replies, at which point a baggy lady emerges from the dreary looking back office, uncomfortably squeezed into the same uniform as the bloke and wearing glasses with the sort of magnification that makes you wonder whether they're those x-ray ones they used to advertise in *Marvel* comics. I assume she can see me naked and recoil appropriately.

"Why did you park it there?" What do you mean, why did I park there? It's the *car park.*

"It was the only space left."

"But it's right by the subway." *I want to hurt you.*

"Yes. But it was the only space left," I insist, with teeth so gritted that they're almost squeaking the theme tune to *Eastenders* in a sort of subconsciously pro-London, anti-north gesture. I remove myself from the reception and go to smash through the rest of my window, which, incidentally, is mildly satisfying. At least he didn't get anything to pay for his next tin of Lightning White.

Is this what I've got to come to expect? If so, maybe I should just give up right now, put that call into the Australian Embassy and say 'I'm on my way, Bruce, put the barbecue on and let's have a good old middle-east style burning of the Union Jack, along with effigies of people from Grimsby. Austin Mitchell MP, he'll do. Let's burn Austin Mitchell MP.' Balls to you, Grimsby. I seethe and rage all morning and with a coffee still floating about, caffeinating my gut, I'm a volcanic mass of spurting outrage, vibrating with fear and loathing so fast I'm probably blurred to most who see me. Like an evil, mutated *You've Been Framed* clip, I clump my way around town trying to find a branch of Autoglass.

It only takes a couple of hours to get the window fixed, with the few remaining chips of glass crystal on the floor of the car; little jewel-like mementos to remind me of how welcome I am here. Maybe I should have one set into a ring, just so I don't forget.

I don't fancy it here, I really don't.

And I start having genuine fears about the rest of the season. Am I going to be seen as a prized scalp, the ITV bloke who dared enter the home terrace with his stupid little camera and funny big face? Will I become a punchbag, at which, if you don't take a swipe, it'll somehow bring shame on your club? It's alright for the likes of Jim Rosenthal and those fat-mouthed journos in the studios, pressboxes and gantries, well out of the way, laughing at the odd cutaway of a hilariously eccentric fan. They can say and do what they like, they can't be touched. Me? I'm going to be out there among them in their own home ends, getting a camera smashed to pieces in the name of the game.

But then later I eventually think, *if that happens, it happens.* I don't know of many, if any, football programmes that have got into the crowd for an entire season and shown the game entirely from a fan's point of view. I know what I'm doing is a statement that I want to make: that football, after all, belongs to us, the fans. And I hope others can see this is an opportunity: our platform. I can only hope that others see it that way.

Oh Christ.

"Hi, is that the Samaritans? Oh, great. Well, you see, it's like this…"

WE'rE Gonna Piss on 4our fish!

SATURDAY, 9 AUGUST 2008.
Grimsby Town v Rochdale: first league game of the season.
The Imperial Pub. To those in the know: The Imp.

Baboom, goes my ticker; *baboom, baboom, kerbulge* (I think that last one was a palpitation, or maybe a bit of trapped wind). The pub's about a minute away from the ground and from the outside looks like *The Amityville Horror;* a great big stand-alone haunted house-alike. I imagine once upon a time it was packed with barnacle-encrusted old fishersods discussing their starboard bows. Now, it looks a bit like it closed down years ago and was converted into a ghost ride at the fair; run by zombies and the ne'er living, amid cobwebs, sudden frights in the banquettes and toilets overflowing with ectoplasm. Grimsby Road, upon which the pub sits, is a wide, long, spacious thoroughfare that takes you along the seafront (without actually revealing the seafront) the couple of miles between Grimsby and Cleethorpes, via the odd fish and chip shop, boarded up carcasses of pubs gone by, convenience stores and a couple of dubious looking massage joints.

I stop and wonder whether I need to be drunk *before* I go in, but realise I'd have to go into another equally daunting pub to do that. I'm entering a 'home fans only' pub like I'm orchestrating an audacious breach of security. What on earth should I expect? Will they all be in there passing around their mobile phones and laughing maniacally at photos of each other posing in the moonlight next to my broken car window? Maybe I should just steam in there like a suicidal 'Nam vet screaming, 'Give me a Stella!', sling it down my neck in one guzzle, grope the barmaid (optional extra), crack a pool cue in half over the bar and ask with a touch of the Ray Winstones, 'If that's the way it's gonna be, you two-bit mugs, then who's going first?'

Hmmm. Not so much my style.

This is daunting. I'm daunted.

Come on boys; no punching, stabbing, gouging or flesh tearing; no whacking, nutting or clumping; no spur-of-the-moment vasectomies, mastectomies or nose-ectomies; no bombing, diving or heavy petting. Please, don't drub me; I'm just a poor little cockney boy...

Baboom, baboom ... baboom ... kergrunt.

At the gates, my mind flickers into a flashback, like in *Lost* on the telly, with a big swooshing noise, into the week gone by... which, after window-gate, actually improved. Teetering on the brink of calling ITV and my publisher and grizzling out a hysterical onslaught of vitriolic resignation from the project, the country and any hereafter association with human beings ever again, *ever,* I decided the best thing to do would be to go out and binge-eat myself obese. But not a binge purely born of a depressed desperation to gain at least *some* sensual pleasure from out of the situation...

I wanted to look beyond the non-descript, stultifying Freshney Place shopping precinct surrounding the hotel. My God it's a tedious monstrosity, truly typical of the brand-laden cultural wasteland this country breeds in its city centres. It's so underwhelming and suicidally in duplicate of everywhere else; packed with Marks and Sparks's, Carphone Warehouses, Jessops's, Boots's and all the rest of those harbingers for the cultural flattening of anything traditional and uniquely English. A couple of times this week I was so spiritually bludgeoned by this world of concrete, logos and value deals that I ended up sat slumped on a bench by St. James' church, devoid of inspiration, bottom lip gormlessly hanging off my gums like a bit of peeled banana skin, sitting watching the drunks who congregate around a statue arguing over a snout. Just across the other side, inside a pub, the better off ones (i.e. the ones who'd just drawn their benefits) enjoyed their Wednesday early-afternoon disco, with a DJ, flashing lights, laboured dancing, cheap drink deals that would be rude not to and murderous karaoke (along of course with obligatory arguments over a snout). I saw the drunken slow-dance climax at 2.30pm and the hammered patrons emerge into the sun: battered, squinting and less their housekeeping for the next week.

Nope, that city centre is surely not the real Grimsby; it's just a clone of city centres anywhere and everywhere. Just a piece of generic, modern day England. I started to wonder whether the shrinkage of the fishing industry is partly to blame for robbing the place of its character and personality, its spirit. *Surely* not. So, with the will to find a bit of the *real* Grimsby, the proud Grimsby, I had some chips.

The area takes great pride in its chip shops, and is pretty famous for the quality of them – so I consulted some of the friendlier members on the internet message boards and came up with a shortlist of chippies to compete in an almighty chip-off. Seeing as the club is actually situated just about in Cleethorpes, chippies from that area were more than welcome to insert fried spud into my face too.

I wobbled and weebled through six chip shops in total. From the relatively posh Steele's, where ornately arranged but decidedly dusty, heavily-patterned curtains frame every booth in a dining area that looks like an austere but just past-it Victorian train carriage, to Seaview, a typical seaside chuck-em-in-a-bag and pack-em-off affair, to Marklews, your traditional local chippie which, so they told me, takes great pride in cleaning its fryers every day. I should bloody hope so! I had chips smothered in salt and vinegar and heaped into glistening cones of perfectly imperfectly shaped crispy good old English chips. SoRry, HoLd oN, i'M SAlivatiNG iNto THe keybOArd…

Six portions, quite possibly around six hundred chips and in the latter stages, approximately six vigorous urges from my very epicentre to expel the mass of fat and potato out of a distended, very confused gut. The gut must have been thinking that I was yet another victim of council cutbacks and had been merged with six other people's guts and franchised out to McCain. It was a silly exercise really, but the people in the chip shops were so warm, welcoming, up for it and confident that their chips were by far the greatest potato heart-attacks, that it gave me some green shoots of hope that maybe this wasn't going to be a nightmarish gauntlet of kicks, punches and appointments at outpatients to have the cast removed. Maybe you *can* have a London accent *and* visit the north *and* get free chips.

And the winner? Cleethorpes's Ernie Beckett chip shop: a good chip. Very chip-like and chippy in flavour with just that little subtle hint of, well, chip.

Walking along on the Cleethorpes seafront afterwards to help burn off the mountainous calorific catastrophe I'd just volunteered myself to digest, I finally started to relax a bit. The greyish, fag ash beach and not exactly bathwater-clear sea is what chilly English seasides are all about. Scrawny, malnourished seagulls pecked desperately at bits of last night's abandoned kebab/sick amalgam and wherever I was, the distant electronic sound of *The Birdie Song* from one of those machines you put a pound into then direct a claw to a teddy bear you don't want anyway echoed in the breeze. Posters proclaiming the arrival of Showaddywaddy at the local pavilion; the smell of sea air, salt and vinegar, freshly fatted donuts and sickly-sweet candy floss; the shrill shrieks of over-excited toddlers building their first sand castles and biting into their first Dairlylea sandwiches unavoidably contaminated with the crunch of sand. It all sparked off nostalgia for days when we went to the seaside as a family; when the hour-long drive seemed like a never-ending journey to the other side of the world, but *so* worth it when the boiled egg lunch came out wrapped in two entire rolls of Clingfilm, followed by burying dad in the sand as he pretended to be asleep while mum spent the whole day debating as to whether or not it was a bit chilly.

All along Cleethorpes front the elderly sat plumped up like mallards on hard wooden benches, chewing nothing in particular as they perhaps contemplated that this might be the last time they see the sea before they're scattered in it. There's something reassuringly, comfortably depressing about this type of English seaside town; there are no pretences, no over-expectations. You're not going to Cleethorpes to blow your mind on upside-down rollercoaster rides or get a three inch thick mahogany tan; it's always going to be just *quite pleasant*. The portions of chips will be smaller than last year, the sticks of tooth-melting rock more expensive and the tatty seafood restaurant serving frozen fish fingers will always have slow service and a draught that'll play havoc with Nan's sciatica all the way home.

"Do you want to sit down and have a cup of tea, Mam?" asked a local-sounding lady, as she walked past me down by the pier, pushing her old mum around in a basic, institution-type wheelchair; the sort that looks like it would render your bum-bum so numb that the doctors could operate on them without anaesthetic.

"I'm already bloody sitting down," replied Mam.

* * * * *

Swooosh ... flashing back to match day, I walk through the side gate at the Imp, wearing local camouflage: a Grimsby Town shirt that the club presented to me at the ground during the week. A sweet gesture, I thought. They invited the local paper down too, so there I was, on the pitch doing a photo shoot with 'Gloryhunter' on my back and a look on my face that said I still wasn't sure about all this.

As soon as I get through the gate I sense that first game of the season electricity; the sparks of that one day in the season when everybody's both joint top and joint bottom of the league, unbeaten and winless, and most fans will say they hope for 'at least the play-offs'. People look at me with an expression of vague recognition as they flick through their mental Rolodex. I jostle through the big crowd of smokers round the back, hearing the word 'Gloryhunter' being muttered here and there, and before I know it there are people telling me "You're that Gloryhunter," which I know, and then the phrase I've already heard a thousand times around town, "You'll be with us all season."

I head directly to the bar, and amid a jittery fluster manage, "A p-p-p-p-p-pint of F-F-F-F-Fosters p-p-p-p-p-pleasse," and look around for a couple of faces I might know...

* * * * *

Swooosh ... during the week, after window-gate and then having my colon molested by chips, I felt the need to start moving closer to the club and fans. I was communicating with some supporters on the web (even using the obligatory sign-off acronym to messages – UTM [Up The Mariners] – and now I felt confident enough to swoop in like a journalistic hawk and start pecking at the fleshy matter (maybe not as gruesomely as that). First I visited the ground.

'Welcome to Blundell Park' said the sign, high up on the back of the stand, at the front entrance to the ground. I could see through an open gate to the pitch, which was being run about on by footballers. Turned out the first-team were having a training session ahead of Saturday's game. I wandered in. Nobody seemed too bothered. A bloke half-heartedly pointed at my camera and accused me with a disarming smile of being a spy from Rochdale. If I was, I wouldn't be a very good spy, with my camera lofted up on a big stick. The pitch looked good. Immaculate, actually. Grimsby manager Alan Buckley sat up in the stand barking orders and protestations and four-letter slurs at anyone who put a foot a centimetre out of step. He's small, bald, slightly rotund and Idi Amin-despotic scary. I wouldn't want a pound of Buckley launched at me for slicing a cross. Jesus, the man was doing his pieces. He was reverberating; seismic. I wandered around, trying to work out the implications of the ground being the lowest in the United Kingdom. It's only two feet above sea level, and I toyed with the idea that if you dig a hole two feet under the pitch, the waves would lap up at you.

The main stand sits alone, like a Subbuteo one, plonked in amongst the archaic others. It was perched there in 1981, and paid for by Findus. *Mmmm, Crispy Pancakes.* It's tall and proud and clearly mocking the one on the other side – allegedly the oldest wooden stand in the country. It's weird that every ground seems to have something about it that's the biggest, oldest, widest, lowest, highest, fattest or crappest in the country. Who keeps these records? I'd like to start a new set of records: which ground could you fill up with the most turnips? Which ground would be best suited to Sting's style of football? Which ground has the best soil for growing beetroot? The old stand sits squat, rickety-rockety and just a little bit sorry for itself, leaning its weight against the corner edge like a tired old man half way to the shops, with a wonky visor hanging over the seats below. It is after all 107 years old; it has a right to be a little bit wonky. The home fans' 'Pontoon End' behind the goal, the only end to carry the club's black and white colours, was empty, with odd wind-forced creaks underscoring the warmongering belters from Buckley and midsport voices of men shouting as though what they were doing was of desperate, life or death proportions. If this were on radio, anyone would assume we were coming live from a riot.

A man hanging around in the bottom of the main stand was clutching a Grimsby Town mug full of tea, watching the training session. I assumed he works at the club, but it turns out he just lives across the road and brought his brew over for a quick peak. He doesn't go to the games any more because from one of his windows he can see one of the goals, and watches the rest unfold on Soccer Saturday. That must be a strange afternoon – watching one third of a football pitch from a window and having Jeff Stelling over-excitedly tell you once in a while what's going on in the other two. He was smothered in tattoos, all smudged with age and former sun-tans, and delighted in giving me a brief run down of the fights he'd had over the years and how once he was beaten to a pulp in the toilets at Wembley. We didn't arrange to see each other again.

With training coming to an end, I nipped out of the ground and around the corner to the garden of The Imperial, where the Grimsby Town Supporters' Trust AGM was due to start. What better way to familiarise myself with the mood of the fans and the type of people I might be mingling with at the match. I was a bit concerned that I was poking my hooter into business that didn't really concern me, but when I arrived there were only two or three people sitting around the patio benches nursing Cokes in which the ice had melted. A woman passer-by stopped me by the gate, clearly out of her canister on gin.

"I'm Marrrrilyyyynn Monnnnrrrrrrroe," she slurred. It was good of her to let me know.

"I can see that love, I nearly wet myself, I thought you were dead," I replied. She staggered around with a curly wave in her bleached blonde hair and a stripy low-cut top that more than suggested the goods within. She had a mischievous sort of face you can imagine once upon a time was attractive, but pruned now. She seemed harmless and drunk enough that a little indulging probably wouldn't hurt.

"I'm barrrrrred frrrrrrrrrommmm eeeeeeeeverrrry puuub arrrround here," she claimed, proudly.

"I expect that'll be people who are jealous of you being Marilyn Monroe, trying to fight you over your looks."

"No. No fighting," she said, now trying her skills at presenting down the lens of my camera, "Grimshhhby Town, don't fiiiiight. Aaaaalllllll mixshh toooogether, dooon't fffffffight aaanybody." With that she sauntered off. Like a Miss World contestant appealing for world peace: point made. She had an appointment at an off licence.

With that cultural exchange concluded, I went to wander into the pub, but was then stopped again, at the door.

Am I ever going to make it into this bloody pub?

This time it was Frank Gallagher out of *Shameless*. I don't need to describe anything else about the man, just cut and paste exactly what you remember of that character into this scenario, and badda bing, that was the man halting my righteous carriage to the bar. He started waving his season ticket at me; long, greasy, grey-flecked hair flapping over a Rolling Stones-esque line-riddled face.

"Grimsby Town," he said down the lens of the camera, probably not knowing where it's from or why it was there or that it was even a camera at all, "…are the pride of 'Umberside." And with that, he stuck two fingers up defiantly and scowled before cracking into a broad, probably formerly cheeky grin that these days veers more on the side of a grimace.

Eventually, I made it into the beer garden/car park of the pub. I was in. I met Dean, the leader of the GTST; along with his sidekick Rachel, with her finely-coiffed hairdo; Jon, the narrowest-headed man I've met in a while, and a couple of others. Dean, it turned out, is a travelling salesman and was wearing an attentively-sculpted jet-black boyband barnet, a chest-revealing v-neck t-shirt, the stubbly outline of what was or perhaps will be a goatee beard and had a touch of a late-30s version of Westlife about him that sort of fitted the bill for his profession. Dean's the mouthpiece for the Trust, which aims to raise money to help the club out with things like facilities for the youth team etc. However, there have been a few dissenting voices amongst fans of late in respect of the Trust's operation. The furore led to the calling of this grand emergency AGM shootout down the Imp, and all week they'd been telling those outspoken doubters that this was their chance to jump out in front of their keyboards and come tell it how it is. Here they were … all six of them.

I could tell Dean and the gang were a bit embarrassed that someone with an ITV platform at his disposal had come along and just six people turned up, including those with ceremonial duties.

"I've had all hope battered out of me over the last few years," said Dean, with a half smile on his face that wasn't massively convincing. "Look, we're there every week, you know, whatever the division, no matter how badly or well we do, I'm always there. I'll *never* not be there." There's more than a hint of resignation and exhaustion in Dean's demeanour.

"Do us a favour, Jake," I said to the friendly teenager who they'd just made Press Officer, "give this boy a cuddle." Jake shyly put an arm around Dean and they shared a brief, just shy of genuinely touching man-clinch, with coy grins.

But do you know what? It's just the way it goes; failure is an orphan and success has a million fathers. They'll all come flooding back when the good times roll. I'm sure Dean and co will be thinking this is *their* disease, that too many Grimsby fans are fickle and don't put their money where their keyboards are for their local club. But there'll be a thousand other meetings, a million other frustrated devotees of clubs everywhere, where exactly the same frustrations are present – and not just in football. There will be a Kabaddi club in Belgium or an Origami society in Papua New Guinea that's going through exactly the same exasperation. It's human nature: we can be fickle, and those left to pick up the pieces can feel deserted and stranded. I felt for Dean. I could tell he was maybe looking to use this meeting as a way of alleviating this burden from his busy travelling life, but he didn't even get a crowd to announce it to or pick a successor from; and he clearly loves the club too much to leave it alone.

* * * * *

Swooosh ... back to matchday. Again. I've penetrated the pub. I stand nursing my fresh pint, looking around self-consciously for any of the GTST lot for only a few minutes before a little congregation surrounds me, asking questions about what I'm doing, based on what they've heard on the radio and read in the papers. It's really odd to have people you've never met before referring to what you've been up to during the week because they've already watched me at the fish market, in the ground and nearly honking up chips on ITV.com. It's almost as though they now co-own my movements, or that they're watching me the *whole* time. Jean and Nigel are the first to approach me; a nice friendly couple who I imagine wouldn't set foot in the Imp outside of matchdays. And there's a bloke who people call Ghandi. He says he doesn't know why people call him Ghandi, but if the real Ghandi had made his protests by overeating burgers and necking Stella, then I would be able to let him know that that's why. But I suspect the only tenuous association with Mahatma is his small rounded glasses. The camera is out and recording its first matchday of the season; Ghandi, Jean and Nigel give me their predictions, as do various other people who walk past, some throwing their pound of flesh into the mix, exerting their theories about where I'll end up at the end of the season. And yeah yeah, of course they say it'll be Blundell Park, *all season*. An old boy en-route to the loo shuffles past the lens and without being asked shoves an enormous puff of toothless gummy cheek flap forward and shouts "Two nothing to Town," before waltzing past to relieve himself. I put the camera up high and ask them to sing a song for me. Ghandi steams in with a defiant "We are Grimsby Town, say we are Grimsby Town" which is briefly picked up by the rest before he's left to tail it off on his own with a self-consciously slow fade in volume.

I'm dragged around the pub to meet mates of mates of fans who put their arms around me and say, "Look, it's that Gloryhunter from that ITV." Occasionally I have to explain my mission to people who haven't heard about me, and most seem to be pleased that I drew their club out of that hat and that they'll get a little bit of exposure out of it. Many are drunk already. They've been drinking since as early as possible, to herald the new season along with all the hope that comes with a fresh start to a new campaign. Here I am, pressing the record button and having them fall over themselves to get into shot with their one-liners, songs and sometimes an utter loss for something to say other than a sort of slurred Neanderthal hunting cheer.

"I'm Andy Murray, the tennis player," slurs Andy Murray, who of course *isn't* Andy Murray the tennis player, but nonetheless *is* called Andy Murray. He's one of the drunkest blokes I've ever met. Textbook; a seamless performance. Ghandi, who's taken to calling me 'Glory supporter', tries to explain to the camera what he thinks will happen this afternoon, but is thwarted when someone jumps on him and puts their tongue in his ear. Between one o'clock and two o'clock, the relatively polite inquisition into my quest becomes a heaving mass of overexcited beer-swilling, with clumps of chanting piping up in various corners amid the chaotic din of shouted conversations about expectations of play-offs.

I'm relieved. I'm excited. I'm loving it. It's only been a week, but the build-up has felt like an arduous, daunting trek into the unknown, and now I look back at all the fretting and visualising of scenarios featuring my demise at the hands of a baying mob with pitchforks and wonder what the by-jiggedy I was thinking. They might be sloshed and shouty and a bit brash and sweary, but I'm among football people; the same sort of people I've spent Saturday afternoons with for much of my life, and they all know I'm here for the love of the game with a hand of friendship. I think they just see my journey as a bit of a novelty, a focus of mild intrigue and a welcome bit of spotlight on their club.

Through gate number 34, its pealing black paint marked with remnants of old posters from matches years ago and the red heavy metal turnstiles ... *clickety clickety clickety* ... and the Pontoon End is a boisterous kerfuffle of welcome backs and handshakes among people who haven't seen each other for a couple of months, while the rowdy singers – who affect a macho swagger to suggest there's something a little more sinister about them than there probably is – pile up to the back, proudly spread their arms out wide and proclaim Grimsby the greatest team the world has *ever* seen. As kick-off approaches, that stomach-tensing anticipation tightens itself around the saliva-bating aroma of frying burger onions and the tinny echo of the Tannoy that's just out of reach of comprehension...

GRIMSBY TOWN 0-0 ROCHDALE
Attendance 4,213

The match grinds out to a comprehensively dreary goalless draw. I don't get the first game of the season fireworks many predicted in the Imp before the game, although such a result against ambitious Rochdale isn't really to be sniffed at. Far from fireworks, it was a stinker. But my enjoyment of the day is unflapped by the quality of the game. Especially as halfway through the second half, someone digs me in the ribs and points over at the naughty corner. Half of the block at the back of the stand are on their feet, pointing in my direction.

"*One Gloryhunter, there's only one Gloryhunter, one Gloryhuuuuuuuunter, there's only one Gloryhuuuuuuuter...*"

I don't quite know where to put myself. This isn't at all what I expected. People are buying into my thing and now my name's being bounced around the rafters of the home end. This is amazing. I beam like a kid going up in front of school assembly to collect a swimming certificate; bright red with an awkward, daffy grin.

After the game, the perennial moaners, sceptics and cynics that you get at all grounds half mount their mile high horses but generally, the Imp is a happy place. People are trying to cajole me into getting on board the rest of their day's drinking programme at various pubs in various parts of town. But I've had quite enough to drink; I don't want to risk some sort of shameful drunken debacle ending with me waking up in a police cell dressed in someone else's clothes and nursing a scabby new tattoo saying 'Grimsby 'til I die'. Nope, that'll do; I'm a happy, drunk Gloryhunter.

UTM.

3.

LONDON'S CALLING

TUESDAY, 12 AUGUST 2008.
Grimsby Town v Tranmere Rovers; League Cup Round One.

The camera's rolling. "So ladies, tell me about the offside rule," I ask the two morbidly bored looking stewards wearing high-visibility jackets 30 sizes too big who would probably rather be sitting on the toilet than standing here. They appear more or less as just heads poking out of a deflated bouncy castle, indifferently guarding the entrance to Blundell Park on the way in to my second game as a Mariner. An awkward *Mastermind*-style pause ensues, where the contestants know they *should* know the answer.

"I don't know, ask her," says the one wearing a Liverpool woolly hat, as though she didn't really care in the first place. She points to the other one, who's wearing all plausible shades of make-up at the same time and has enormous hooped gold earrings that you could hula in, dangling away cheaply.

"I don't know either, I only work here," she blurts, giggling with embarrassment like an emphatic monkey. I feel a bit guilty; I kind of knew they'd struggle.

Inside, the sun starts to plop itself down onto the lid of the Pontoon End, wrapped reluctantly in indignant, clingy cloud. The first twilight game of the season: a jacket sort of evening; neither t-shirt nor coat, with both *no* rain and *some* rain probable. Blundell Park is sparsely populated tonight; a tentatively attended cup game against a team one division above. Fans are spread around the ground like strategically sewn seeds, with the ones in the corners looking conspicuous, stranded, and strangely incongruous when joining chants remotely.

"Maaarrriiiiinnnnneeerrrrs, Maaarrriiiiinnnnneeerrrrs..." sing the top left.
"One Gloryhunter..." sing the top right, sparking a reprisal of my bashful banana-shaped grin.

Wallop, one-nil. At last it's here: the first goal of the season.

I've been wondering how different this would be, compared to when I'm in the virtual mosh pit that a Spurs goal at The Lane creates. Whether the fans go more or less apoplectic; whether they kiss, cuddle, share in tender sexual congress or suddenly burst into a brilliantly choreographed musical number from the motion picture *Annie* – I've no idea. Are they a different breed, or are we all the same?

Amid the immediate knee-jerk mid-air leap and those mouth-gaping roars of the first bursts of glory ... I discover that it's *exactly* the same.

Football fans are football fans: we *like* goals. Aside from a lottery win or being led into a nightclub toilet cubicle by Cameron Diaz, there's *no* other occasion in life I can think of upon which we exhibit an entirely unedited physical manifestation of total and complete *joy*. You don't even see fathers of newborns running down the hospital corridor screaming and shouting with the incredible vigour of a midweek goal against Tranmere; not even the most joyous moment in a person's life is celebrated with such utterly uninhibited surrender of motor-neuron control as that fervour of the seconds following a simple leather ball simply hitting the back of a simple net. If only life was as simple as football, as clear cut, as black and white: goal or no goal, win or lose, *that's that.* Perhaps one of the reasons we love it is that football represents a boiled down form of life itself: a much more palatable, understandable microcosm, where success is unconditional and loss is absolute.

Formerly sitting, now bouncing next to me like a crazed Romanian orphan is Sarah, a friendly Grimsby Town Ladies FC player who invited me to sit with her during the game.

'See it from a lady's point of view,' she wrote in an email. Hardly. If it turns out that a lady's point of view is all the spit and snotted rants I've come to expect from my fellow men, then now I can see where I've been going wrong with the ladies all these years. When James Hunt stroked home that first goal, footballgasm ripped her face into a rubbery interpretation of ecstasy. Her open mouth seemed to stretch out of any sort of realistic proportion, into the realm of something in paint by Edvard Munch, as her voice scraped and grazed the side of her throat as though gargling nonsense and pebbledash.

Me? I think I'd have to be some sort of emotional prostitute for this goal to send me into an episode of human distemper. When Spurs score, the celebration is a champagne cork pop; a release of decades of pent up frustration; every defeat and every disappointment is channelled into the insanely disproportionate joy brought by one single goal. I haven't got that kind of history with Grimsby Town; there are no memories to plug into, no tragedies to eradicate.

However, seeing the momentary high that my new friends are experiencing, I can relate to them via the universal football supporter's condition; I understand what they're going through. It's like holding a mirror up and not so much seeing me (disturbingly as a female footballer called Sarah), but just every football fan across the country. And as I grow fond of this fishy, endearingly brash bunch, the focus of their passion is my pleasure by proxy. Although I don't exactly feel a *natural* part of all this – I can't quite yet bring myself to leap around with a delirium equivalent to that of having just seen Tom Huddlestone launch a nuclear volley, or even of having bagged Diaz in the bogs down Faces Nightclub – I can still raise my arms aloft and feel a genuine sense of vicarious joy.

Wallop, 2-0. Off we go again.

I try out a slightly self-conscious fist pumping celebration, which seems to go quite well. It's weird trying to celebrate a goal *and* be in control of myself. I'm used to turning into a screeching blurred mess who may well wet himself; jumping around in something close to the way dad dances at weddings. But now I'm in control and have to work out what an appropriate reaction might be. I'll stick with the fist pump for now.

"Glory, what's the score, Glory Glory what's the score?" sing the herberts up the back. I shyly hold two fingers up and a sort of ironic but affectionate cheer reverberates.

"Mate, you're famous," says a bloke covered in virtually the entire contents of the club shop – much more memorabilia than is intended for one body – standing with his friend who's holding out a camera-phone. "Can I have a photo with you?"

What? Are you having a tin bath? You want my grubby boat in a photo? This must be an elaborate dream, some sort of Truman Show *wind-up ... Even my mum once sent my school photo back with a post-it note attached, asking if any of the other kids in the class had a better one that she could have instead.*

I stand posing with my arm around a grown man, managing to squeeze out an apprehensive, confused grin; that of a harmless idiot who's also a bit embarrassed. All this is a bit difficult to process. Everywhere I go, even in Marks and Spencer's – while lavishly buying new underwear instead of finding a launderette to clean the others – people are stopping 'That Gloryhunter' with the same questions about where I think I might end up at the end of the season or, "Come on, honestly, how gutted was you when Grimsby came out of the hat?" They continue conversations with me that have never occurred. But because they've seen me making a plank of myself on the internet, they feel as though they know me a bit. Some come up and simply say "Alright?" and then just stand there, staring with an empty expectancy; as though I've got an episode of *Eastenders* being projected onto my face. I assume they're waiting for me to be that character off the web shows. It's all just a bit strange; sometimes fun-strange, sometimes sinister-strange (like Uncle Glynn).

This thing is expanding beyond my control. Don't get me wrong, I know I'm not exactly filling the pages of *Heat* magazine with airbrushed images of me with my top off holding a baby panther, but for someone so utterly ordinary and completely anonymous as me, this is much more than I bargained for. I've been on *talkSPORT* with Hawksbee and Jacobs, most of the BBC radio regions, 5Live, *FourFourTwo* magazine, the *London Paper* and all over local press. People are slagging me off, commending me and debating my movements on internet forums all over the place. Podcasts, newscasts, simulcasts and broadcasts. Even Gary Oldman is weighing in with a bit of it. Well, sort of. Some website or other in America has reported that Gary is appearing in the latest ITV adverts for their football coverage (not quite sure where Oldman becomes relevant to football coverage, but it's true, he is) and have mistakenly claimed that he is also being 'The Gloryhunter'. Somehow I can't see Oldman sitting here watching Grimsby play Tranmere in the first round of the League Cup on a brisk Tuesday night. Not without pulling out a gun and a frighteningly cool one-liner.

When I left home, I had no idea any of this would happen. The thing began as just a potentially interesting device for a book, where I would quietly travel the country digesting and interpreting ordinary experiences in the underbelly of English football. But with ITV involved and all the press kerfuffle that comes with it, suddenly I'm in Grimsby's Pontoon End at half-time, having my picture taken, being sung at and kissing the cheek of some bloke I've never met called Swanny. Oldman definitely wouldn't have kissed Swanny. I'm not sure why I did it, but there he was, looking all happy at the half-time lead and I just got the urge.

"Last season we had a bit of a tendency to concede just after half-time," imparts baldy beardy Swanny, as he grips a little flask of half-time tea and tries to brush over that the fact that the bloke with the weird camera on a stick just gave him a rather needless smacker. "If we can lose that habit, not only are we going to have a good game tonight, but we're going to have a good season," he concludes like a proper football pundit. And then out of nowhere, he plants one back on my chops.

GRIMSBY TOWN 2-0 TRANMERE ROVERS
Hunt 20
Chorley (og) 54
Attendance 1,858

And so, despite the expectation that Tranny would bundle me into the second round draw, haul me north-west and up a division, I remain a Mariner. And I like it. It's only been a bit over a week, but I'm already getting to know people; arranging to meet Ghandi down the Imp, a young lad called Leon who gave me his ticket for the game, Sarah and her footballgasm face, Swanny and our forbidden kisses...

* * * * *

SATURDAY, 15 AUGUST 2008.
Brentford v Grimsby Town, League Two.

"At the end of the road, turn right."

"Yes, I know *darling*, but I turned right before and then you got me to do a u-turn."

"Turn around when possible."

"See? There you go again. But you just asked me to turn right, you stupid, silly woman."

"Take the next left."

"Oh, we're playing that game are we? Soppy buggers, is it? It was right a minute ago, you stroppy pre-menstrual snappy little cow, this is just typical of you. Left is a bloody field, Emma."

'Emma' and I already have a strained relationship. She's a TomTom ONE Classic navigation unit with a 3.5 inch LCD touchscreen and weighs in at 148g. And apart from being a total bitch who gives me the proper run around, she's rather tragically assumed the role of my closest friend right now. She *hates* when I play loud music, but nevertheless it seems somehow right that I play *London's Calling* by The Clash as loudly as possible as I head back down the country towards the west of the capital.

As I packed up and left Grimsby this morning; hazy and convinced that maggots were eating the back of my eyes after a night drinking silly amounts of beer with some Grimsby fans (including a bloke called 'Nutty') in pubs I'd previously been too scared to go in, it hit me that I might not be coming back. It seems too early to have this stay-or-go scenario, but it's totally out of my control. This season is going to be full of the threat of sudden transience and I have to be prepared to be wrenched away from situations that are still unfolding, whether I'm ready to go or not.

The soul-destroying, nondescript A180 plunders away and after a delicious sawdust and plastic sandwich courtesy of Watford Gap, before I know it I'm getting those surges of incandescent rage that can only be induced by the grimy London North Circular Road that curls round the inside of the M25. A fatty, clogged, diseased artery of North London, lined with rows and rows of empty, boarded up houses coated in years of exhaust fumes and decorated occasionally by Christmas lights left up since 1996. I nudge my way westbound in fits of screams at both other drivers and Emma's constant nagging. London makes me want to hurt something, anything: in its eyes.

I've not been to Brentford since the late 80s, when I used to follow Leyton Orient a bit because my tiny little wallet couldn't often cope with the price of a ticket at Spurs. I remember that Orient really hated Brentford. Not sure why; there are more obvious, closer geographical targets like West Ham, but they really did hate Brentford and somehow I feel as though that residual dislike carries across with me now, as though it's laden in my genes. Back then I was too young to have even known that Brentford is the only club in the country to have pubs on all four corners of the ground. These days that sort of fact excites me more than is nutritionally advisable.

Being an East London lad, this side of town is utterly alien to me, and upon arriving I spend a good deal of time bumbling around backstreets trying to negotiate my way to one of the pubs. Then I hear it.

"Piss on your fish, we're gonna piss on your fish…" There's a writhing black and white mess smothering The Royal Oak on one of the corners of the ground. It's a belligerent hub of staggering, swearing and half-arsed conversations that nobody can understand. It's the very definition of 'drunk', and executed to a degree I've rarely seen. It's spectacular. Fabulous. I wander into the pub, which is essentially an old lady's living room that's been opened up to the public like a living museum. I gain a Fosters and go back outside, where along with the retro exterior and some of the older Grimsby fans' hairdos that haven't been updated since the 70s, the whole scene feels like a re-enactment of the 1977 Silver Jubilee street parties that took over the nation's roads for a day.

The unshaven, hops-filled posse of Grimsby Town fans bask in the afternoon sun, baking themselves dehydrated on the pavement. After a minute or two of attempted mingling, one of them recognises me. Before long they're singing louder and harder down my lens about fish and Grimsby being the centre of the universe.

"You can go all over the country and you won't find Jesus," shouts one of the fatter brigade, who's somehow got himself into a replica shirt that's so tight you'd think he's about to go scuba diving in it. He's referring to an absolute shambles of a man next to him, who I suppose could be mistaken for someone in an episode you'd call 'Jesus: The Homeless Years'. Long straggly hair infused with engine oil that in all depicts a rather more natural version of Russell Brand's self conscious attempts at unkempt. The beard is utterly out of control, totally out of order; it's growing so far over his mouth that in water I suspect it could filter out plankton. It becomes apparent that although he tolerates it, he really doesn't like being called Jesus; maybe he sees himself as more of a Lemmy from Motörhead. I remember spotting him from the other side of the ground at the last match, so distinctive is he, and now here he is on his big day out in London. He's clearly majestically dedicated to the club, but I wonder how some of these blokes can afford to go to all these away games. There's no way I could find the cash to follow Spurs all over the country every other week. Maybe he's been saving all the money he would have spent down the barber's.

"We're not quite like this lot," mouths a bloke called Bruce, who stands next to me wearing a pair of false breasts (which are actually a really nice size). He asks if I want to go with him and his mates, away from these bits of obliterated man-rubble swigging themselves senseless around us. They drag me to The Griffin, another of the corner pubs, where shortly after arriving, a Brentford fan shows me a text on his phone that says 'Gloryhunter is by the jukebox'.

I love this type of away day end-of-the-world drinking, where there's no tomorrow and only just a now.

* * * * *

The game starts and I'm still outside the ground, on Braemar Road. Waiting. As I flick through the programme, I find an entire page about me, which is nice, but it's weird reading about yourself being at a game that they then don't seem to want to let you into. They've forgotten to put my ticket on the door and can't find the bloke responsible. But perhaps it's just as well; inside the Brentford fans are going mental, totally off their noodles. I finally get through the compulsory harassment from stewards and find a spot at the back of the away terrace with the Grimsby lot. The mood goes from away day celebration to abject doom within just 45 minutes.

BRENTFORD 4-0 GRIMSBY TOWN
MacDonald 27, 45,
Elder 38, Poole 60
Attendance 4,009

Talk of play-offs recedes to that of survival, as Swanny et al harness their happy-go-lucky drunkenness into something altogether angrier. Some boys in front of me turn away from the pitch, arms folded and faces like wailing Eastern European widows; a girl in a stripy jumper, who's spent the entire day transfusing her bloodstream to 90 per cent Chardonnay, sits on the floor, slumped, suspected asleep. Brentford tonk Grimsby so profoundly that I expect some of this lot will need treatment for post-traumatic stress disorder; the players will only be identifiable by dental records. They'll be enduring harrowing flashbacks for years to come.

"*You're not Grimsby anymore, you're not Grimsby anymore,*" they sing at me just before half-time.

And that's that.

It's brutal. With the final whistle comes the first evidence that this Gloryhunting game is for bastards. All my burgeoning relationships and half plans to explore Grimsby some more come to a smacking halt. My first adventure is over.

The away end filters out in gloomy silence as the home fans wave with the sarcastic "Cheerio, cheerio, cheerio!" chant and the Town fans head off for their trains via every pub possible. I say goodbye to Bruce and Jesus and the man in the skin-tight replica shirt, and suddenly default back to the aloneness that my season started with just two weeks ago. I've only just got to a point where I can turn and talk to the people around me, but they've all gone back up north now, and standing on the empty terrace with the final echoes of victorious Brentford fans' applause fading into the ether, I once again face that daunting first few days of trying to barge in on another club's season.

I'm a Bee.

WELCOME to Brentford

Brentford actually pre-dates London. That's a fact and a half. Apparently it was a meeting place for pre-Romanic tribes long before old Julius crossed the Thames to have a big punch up down Brentford High Street. And if it's battles you're a sucker for, there was also the Battle of Brentford in 1642, in which the King tried to retake London and decided to have a chunk out of Brentford in doing so. He won the battle, but never regained London.

Famous Brentford inhabitants include Pocahontas, before she went all Disney. Brentford also became mildly famous for having the highest number of internet searches for pornography and fetishes in the country…until it was worked out that this might have been because an ISP routing centre was based in the area. So they're not *necessarily* all perverts.

In 1889, a rowing club in the area decided to start up a football team, for something to do during winter, and Brentford FC was formed. Voila.

The hotel is on Brentford High Street, but they sell it as Kew (even though Kew and its beautiful and world famous botanic gardens are technically on the other sde of the Thames), which is a bloody cheeky way to hoik the price up just over the top lip of my wallet.

"I need to extend my stay please," I tell the violently bored looking receptionist. Someone must have just made her eat a wasp. I consider explaining, in a friendly chat, that I need to extend my stay because Brentford twatted Grimsby … but somehow I doubt she'd listen to that any more than if I started to read aloud from an old Asda receipt.

"We can't take bookings at reception," she replies with cantankerous relish, forcing a smile that moves her guitar-string-tight scraped back hair and entire scalp further round the other side of her head.

"Where can I extend it then?" I say, more calmly than I thought myself capable of. They really don't make things easy, this particular chain of travel hovel.

"Online. There's an internet café in town." Unbelievable.

"How about some change for the car park?" I ask, through teeth slowly grinding themselves into stubs, almost *wanting* her to refuse me so that I can have more justification for hating her. *Breath, just breath. Do not, repeat, DO NOT bludgeon her with the fax machine.*

"No, we don't give change. We don't handle any money at reception." Well what do you handle at reception other than your own bloody internal battles with bitter depression? Off I huff on a sweary 20-minute stomp to re-book a room I'm already staying in – at an internet café – and to get some change to pay to keep my car there.

On my way down Brentford High Street, a man with a big long white beard and skin pealing off his ear lets two buses go outside Brentford Magistrates' Court because he wants to explain to me how, just as the stone obelisk in front of us says, Julius Caesar crossed the Thames nearby. He won't talk to me on camera though, because he hasn't got any front teeth.

Until now, in my brainbox, Brentford has only occupied a tiny slot, filled with merely a football team that I know lives in West London. But as I walk around town trying to get to grips with exactly where I am, it's unfolding into a little place next to Kew with a long High Street that boasts specialist stores for things such as radio controlled helicopters, or, if you're up for a really exciting afternoon, an Incontinence Centre you could pop into for a swanky new commode. There are shoddy pound stores, deep fried cafés and pubs. Plenty of pubs. It's like a slightly grubby little mirage penned in by the Thames, a picturesque lock; the big stately

Syon Park down one end and well-to-do-Kew just on the other, with, importantly, Brentford Tandoori somewhere in the middle. The High Street is a little bubble around which council flats camp: the affordable face of West London … which developers are probably waiting like evil predators to bulldoze and replace with bourgeois balconies that the overworked inhabitants will be too busy to get time to sit on.

A couple of minutes' walk from the High Street is Griffin Park, where I slip through an open gate and wander among the auras of the highs and lows, dreams and nightmares of Brentford FC's history. Empty football stadiums are disconcertingly eerie; it feels as though the world might have ended and I'm the only sod left. I stand opposite the Bill Axbey Stand, named after an old boy who supported the club for 89 years before passing away a couple of years ago. The ground was only 14 years old when Bill started coming to Griffin Park.

Tired from hotel-rage and still bleeding internally from the over-beered exertions of my final weekend as a Grimsby fan, I lie down on the pitch and spot serene criss-crossy trails in the sky as planes pass over, vibrating my belly-wobble and ensuring I don't drop off in the tranquillity of it all. As the fresh breeze tickles against my face and the smell of football rises off the turf, I wonder if I'm the first or only person ever to sunbathe on the Brentford pitch. With the occasional metallic clang from a bit of net flapping in the wind against the goalpost, hypnotising me like a new-age wind-chime, I start to drift into the wonderment of what adventures Brentford has in store for me, and whether something occurring on this very spot on the pitch will change the entire course of my journey…

* * * * *

"Well you should have been quicker," says receptionist-of-doom as I speechlessly thrust at her the parking ticket I've been issued while going to get the change to pay for parking. OK, so maybe I got waylaid somewhat, sunbathing on a football pitch, but she knew I was going to pay for the whole 24 hours anyway. "It's nothing to do with us; the car park is run by a separate company." At this point I begin to wonder whether this little ray of sunshine is actually a real person, or whether she's just an emotionally disconnected hologram installed to misinform and irritate, just so that your 'cheap' hotel experience – which once you've paid for all the extras like parking and breathing, isn't so cheap – isn't allowed to be too pleasant lest we actually enjoy life. Because for any sort of satisfaction or fulfilment, they'd probably have to charge an extra fee, and that of course would be supplied by an external company which, *of course*, laughing girl here can't take bookings for.

I start to wonder whether these hotels and my Orient-themed sourness towards Brentford might make this leg of the journey difficult.

4.

†HE COUNCiLLOr and †HE Crank

WEDNESDAY, 20 AUGUST 2008.
Outside the Princess Royal pub, Braemar Road, Brentford.
Raining abysmally. Half cut at 6pm.

"What do you want then?" huffs bang-on-time Brentford fan Luke Kirton, abruptly, and before even saying 'hello'. I reply faintly as he breezes straight past to the bar and disappears into the scrum of flat capped old sods propped up on stools. *Here we go,* I think, *this is going to be a long old night.*

Luke has half reluctantly agreed, through pressure from others in the gladiatorial word-pit that is 'The Griffin Park Grapevine' internet forum, to guide me safely through the infamous four corner pubs of Griffin Park. He's dressed up as though he's on his way to a ska convention – uniform Ben Sherman shirt, a black bomber jacket type affair, slightly overgrown gingery quiff and no messing around with such a thing as a smile. Given his opening brusqueness, I considered replying initially by making clear, right now, that of anything I do *not* want, it's his forehead colliding with the bridge of my nose. Instead I ask for a Stella, hoping it might help medicate the situation.

Luke's just a bit cagey early doors, with narrowed eyes like a way too indiscrete secret service agent. But once a pint of London Pride collapses down his throat, the eyes glass over into a more friendly, less headbutty shape, as he realises that I'm in no way astute or grubby enough to be considered 'press', or specifically the type of press that would try to coax him into saying entirely the wrong thing for my own malicious gains. He's not the first to be a bit frosty and suspicious of me to begin with. But generally, people realise soon enough that I'm *not* trying to uncover their closeted atrocities, or scandalous revelations involving their secretly snapped photos dressed in a Batman outfit and a thumping great strap-on. No. I'm way more harmless than that. Although … I wouldn't mind just having a look at those photos, if you've got them to hand.

Even further from being someone who might like to smear your face over the gutter with a sovereign-ringed knuckle collective, Luke markedly betrays the stereotypes his attire initially and probably wrongly evoked in me, and proves himself an eloquent sort of Londoner with the intellect, composure and conscience that gives a hint as to why his nickname is 'Councillor Kirton' (although after the third instalment of London Pride, a portion of said composure and a tad of the intellect seem to ebb off in the same direction as my ability to stand without leaning on one of the old sods at the bar).

"This is The Princess Royal, and my fact about this pub is that it used to be the registered office of Brentford Football Club," slurs Luke to the camera, in the first of four facts about each of the respective corner pubs – all part of my brilliantly crass plan to turn what's essentially a pub crawl beer bender into 'content' for the latest webisode. *How are ITV letting me get away with this?* But aside from pumping Luke for really naff, ill-prepared facts for the show, and making sure my debut night as a Brentford fan sets out my manifesto for the duration of my time in office as Gloryhunter of Hounslow; the plan is actually to learn more about Luke's amazing story. You see, 'Councillor Kirton' isn't *just* a nickname…

"Like all things, it started in a pub," he starts, as though I'm all tucked up in bed, ready for a fairytale. And it's not far off. Although I'm not actually in bed.

"I was part of the Independent Supporters Association, and we were fighting on two fronts," he sets out in a low, purposeful tone. "One: we were very much not happy with the current owner of the football club, Ron Noades, and wanted to do something about that. I detested the man. We were all about the local community owning its football club, as opposed to the rich person coming in and messing you about and then leaving you." It's way too easy to compare the love for a football club to the tragedy of romantic love. Jane Austen would have had a field day with Brentford. "It was about us taking responsibility for our own football club."

This was around the turn of the century, and Noades had perpetrated seemingly the ultimate ego trip by successfully evolving, like the first amphibian out of water, from club owner into club owner/first-team manager (a feat he achieved with definitely more success than American Terry Smith's bizarre reign over Chester City, in which as a virtual stranger to 'soccer', he employed American Football tactics and took players to fast food restaurants before games). Ron also played the martyr card, claiming that he'd been keeping the club alive with his own money, but it turned out he was simply stacking bank loans against Griffin Park to keep afloat. With Noades having picked the club up in a relatively healthy condition, the debt was now piling on for fun. Luke and others flipped and decided they *had* to act. So, while 'Bees United' was formed to get fans on the board to be a part of the decision-making process, and eventually wrestle power of the club off Noades, Luke joined another prong of attack.

"We weren't happy with the local authority. They had a dismissive attitude towards us, the fans. With all the sports activities that they do, Brentford are by far the biggest organisation in the borough that does that. To just dismiss that as another local business just wasn't good enough." So off he went; this local warehouseman and his mates, to stick his beak into council affairs. *Go on my sons.*

Except that the council were not at all keen on them doing that. A simple survey they sent to councillors, asking what they actually knew about the involvement the club had in the community (with the overall aim of getting the council to be more aware and back the club up on local affairs), was blocked by a senior official.

"It was war," says Luke, with the defiant touch of Edwin Starr. "We said *right* ... if they're gonna block our ability to speak to councillors, then we're going to stand. So then ... great ... standing in the local elections! Can we afford it? How much does it cost? Are we going to lose our deposit? Those of us around the table didn't have any particular knowledge of local authority. I'd been working in a warehouse. But off we went, worked out how to get it all sorted and registered our own political party." They didn't have a clue; a group of political virgins; mere football fans, opening their metaphoric legs to local authority and taking on the metaphoric towering veiny phallus that was the ruling Labour council.

By now, Luke and I have wandered around to The Royal Oak pub, the old lady's living room where I met the Grimsby fans at the weekend. With all the curtains closed, ornaments back in place gathering new dust and just a few dedicated regulars sitting around a sofa, all it needs now is the snooker playing on the telly in black and white and Nan lumped in an armchair, clacking a mint humbug around her dentures.

"The Royal Oak was a massive terrace in the ground years ago, and it was named after this pub," churns out Luke, proving that these facts aren't going to get any better. Back to the election trail…

"We put a request out for help. When you've got a crowd of 5,000 people sitting there, the breadth of skill is enormous. People stepped forward; we had a former Labour Party campaign manager, Green Party people, Conservatives, the whole spectrum all come forward. We only stood one in each ward, with the idea being that we weren't there to stand *against* anybody. You could still vote for your party; we were just standing for what we believed in. Just give us one of your votes; a vote for a future for Brentford football club in your community. I was one of between 15 and 20 candidates in Hounslow and said I wanted to stand in Brentford, the ward that the football club is in, the ward where I live. I've got a passion about the town and I wanted to stand." He flips back briefly to that punk-nutter face; nobody was going to stop him going for the ward central to their campaign.

They set up a team of five specifically for the Brentford ward and steam-rollered the bloody thing. They swamped and spasticated all over the opposition – in the streets they put stickers over the top of theirs, mobbed the rivals' leafletters, decorated cars and even had an open-top bus. They worked their nuts off.

"I was particularly determined that I was going to get voted in. They didn't like it. They were threatened," he says dramatically, stoically; voice raised and with eyes staring off into a heroic distance where the scenes are probably replaying themselves like a scratchy cinefilm.

"But where did the money come from for all this?"

"Fans. We did bucket collections. A couple of fans gave us a bit more than others, but it was all from fans."

It's here that I start to reflect on my narrowed, withering vision of England; the cynicism I've allowed to creep in with the late trains and abject rudeness in the streets … and I begin to feel a bit of warmth, a sense that we can pull together. Until, that is, we wander around to the New Inn Pub, the only Irish pub of the four corners.

We're outside on the pavement when the landlord comes wheezing out like an unfit Blakey, claiming he'd seen me earlier, prancing around with my camera and that I should have asked him first. It's true, I was nearby, but I didn't film the pub and really it's got nothing to do with him. I tersely let him know exactly my stance. It goes from being a re-enactment of the scary Irish man scene in *Withnail and I* ("perfumed ponce!"), to him backing the flip off and insisting upon showing me his garden – just in case I want to use it as a film location one day. I won't.

The New Inn is a Celtic pub, which doesn't seem quite right, considering where it is, and while we're inside this snug, homely gaff, the landlord stands on the other side of the bar, eyeballing me like a jealous optician. He hates me. I'm not especially keen on him either. Let's leave it there.

"My fact about this pub is that it's one of the pubs on the four corners of Griffin Park," stutters Luke, genuinely thinking he'll get away with it. If the other facts were dubious, this one is just a complete rip off. What a con.

"Is that seriously your fact for this pub?"

"I couldn't think of anything else."

"Right, it's your round."

The campaign trail went down to the wire...

"I tell you, that was a weird experience, going in and voting for myself. There I was, on the ballot paper. It makes it real, because before that time, politics had never really been real to me. I came bounding out of the polling station." I imagine Luke emerging from a school hall, grinning like Rusty Lee, doing that Madness-style robotic conga along with probably a bit of pogoing, underscored by *One Step Beyond*.

"On the night, word started going round that it was close. We could see Labour coming out of the counting room; sweating, nervous, worried. There were some real arguments going on. A couple of our people were standing there, minding their own business and just getting abused: 'You lot don't f***ing know what you're doing, la la la la.' We had to separate them from these people. This just increased our expectation; they're resorting to that? They *must* be in trouble. The results came in and our guys were standing up there; we were cheering them for getting any votes at all really, but none of them got in. One by one they came in, and Brentford was still ticking away. Eventually, the agents got called up and were told there was 13 votes difference. *13*. I won. I got 883 votes, but the Labour party said they wanted a recount. So off we went. Started all over again." Right now, he's talking from the very centre of the moment; his eyes following each emotion, flicking through the whole mental tape.

"Three o'clock in the morning. Some of the Labour party brought their flasks along, and what was in their flasks? They were stumbling about ... oh, it was shocking. Finally, finally, finally, the candidate from the Labour Party I was up against came up to me and conceded defeat. No more recounts." A broad grin widens his whole head. "The crowd was going mental and I was up on the podium with me arms in the air, and then I'm coming down and getting pats and people were trying to pick me up ... I had no idea what was going on." Beaming; eyes glinting; hasn't even swigged his beer for a few minutes. This was his moment and always will be.

"Emotional? Was it like a goal going in?"

"Very emotional. If it was a goal going in to win an FA Cup final or promotion, I think, yeah. But really, it's just something completely different. I don't think I cried. Or I might have. Me mum was there, saying 'I don't know what he's gonna do now, he hasn't even got a mobile phone, he hasn't got a computer'." Laughing now. "My poor mum had to put up with it all, because our house became the HQ; people stomping in and out all the time."

"Did you get her vote?"

"I hope so!"

Here he is, a warehouseman living with his mum in a little gaff in Brentford, twatting a Labour candidate out of office. Brilliant. In these times where we're plagued by political indifference, exasperation and mistrust, here's a story of someone just like you or I, who got out there and did something.

"I was just at the front of what hundreds of people achieved," he adds, a humble caveat that's doubtlessly required to do justice to everyone else who worked to make it happen.

Once installed as councillor, Luke worked with the Bees United members who'd by now got onto the board of the football club, and to cut a long story short, they improved ties to an extent that the council ended up lending them the money to give Ron Noades the one single pound he wanted for the club and took on the debt he left behind.

"And the rest, as they say, is history."

Luke ends his fairytale, sitting on the top step leading to a plain looking upstairs room at our final corner pub, The Griffin. His final fact here is that this is the pub where it all started; where Luke and his mates decided they were going to take matters into their own hands and bring the football club back to the fans.

With job done, the club saved, Luke finished his four years as a councillor and now works for a charity with young people within the borough. His experiences awoke him to his calling; working in and for the community. But given his success as an independent amid the domination of bureaucratic party politics, did he consider moving into that world full time?

"They're in it for themselves, local politicians. Ego boosts, power trips, all the wrong reasons. I wouldn't piss on them if they were on fire."

That'll be a no then.

* * * * *

Saturday 22nd August
Brentford. In the beginning.

I clamber, grunting, out of my creaky travel pit bed and blearily, without any real sense of co-ordination, start hunting for clothes that won't be damaged by the parcel-tape. I've got to meet a load of Brentford fans at the train station in about half an hour to go through the pre-match ritual of being bound by the tape and made to play chicken with a train. *Rummage, rummage.* I decide upon on a singlet, but can't quite find one. *Where are my singlets...?*

Hold on.

I haven't got a singlet. Why would I have a singlet? I'd *never* wear a singlet.

Hold on.

Parcel tape?

Train?

Sometimes, my dreams seep nonsensically through to the initial few moments of wakefulness. Once, I dreamt I murdered Bruce Forsyth. I can't remember why I did it, but most of the night was spent on the run in the countryside. When I woke, I spent a good ten minutes gasping out of my wits, petrified that the police were about to arrive and say 'nice to see you, to see you...'

It's not hard to work out, with my first match as a Brentford fan approaching, where the anxieties that caused the parcel-tape dream might have come from. Although this week I do seem to have been gathering at least as strong a bunch of supporters as I have detractors in that centrifugal gathering point of minds (and mindless), the Griffin Park Grapevine (hereafter, GPG). So much is decided and undecided; derided and demonised on this anonymous forum where only a few know who each other are in real life. Its power in shaping a collective view, along with underlining the shouts of the dissenting few cannot be underestimated. And the same is happening all over the country with other clubs. The anonymity worries me; you can be a borderline illegal racist bully under the pseudonym of 'Nigel69LovesArses', or whomever you chose to be on any particular day, and get away with it. And people do.

With summer clinging onto August, throwing up a deep blue sky like it's the last summer ever, Underhill is awash with the red and white type of Bee. I didn't expect this charmingly tin-pot old ground to be nestled among tranquil rolling green hills. The texture of the word 'Barnet' just doesn't sound like that; it sounds more like a freezing rainy Tuesday night stuck at traffic lights on the A406. It sounds of concrete. Brentford have commandeered most of the ground and by the look of it, have twice as many away fans as the listless home bunch who after two games, already look battered into submission, like the opponent at the end of a Rocky film. But for Brentford, it's a London derby; everyone's drunk on sun and sun-coloured beer and subsequently no-one can any longer say the word 'Constantinople'. Not that they need to.

However, 20 minutes into the game, I'm still outside the ground. Again. No ticket. I also would have trouble with saying 'Constantinople', although I may as well be there.

"No, sorry love," she says, eye-goggling me over silver framed mum-glasses with thumb prints all over the lenses, "there's nothing in the pile under your name. Who are you again? Oh, you're not The Gloryhunter, are you?"

I'm not really into the idea of calling myself 'The' anything. I certainly wouldn't go up to a counter and like some naff superhero announce with my chest puffed out and a handsomely raised single eyebrow that 'The Gloryhunter. Has. Arrived'.

"Yes. Yes, I am," I admit meekly, as though owning up to something heinous. I feel a right tit. The problem is that I can't go around telling everyone that calling myself this name is tongue-in-cheek and not a replacement for my real name. I know I'm not Batman, nor Batman wearing a thumping great strap-on.

Or perhaps I should just swallow it, run into it ego-first and introduce myself as simply 'The', with a mysteriously aloof snoot.

Meanwhile, inside, Brentford have of course scored without me; a goal that kicks off a blur of almost extremist-type celebrative behaviour akin to that of the crazed burning of effigies in the streets of Islamabad. As I arrive in the away end, kids writhe and wrestle over each other to get on camera, pulling faces full of grizzly glory and grabbing each other by the nostrils like cattle.

"*Too big for this league…*" they sing. Right now, it feels like they're right.

"There's only one Gloryhunter..." they sing, pointing at the camera after I've stuck the stick thing to its fullest extent, so it hangs over them like a sinister tentacle in *War of the Worlds*.

With my first chant, gone is that supposed hatred that my Orient days suggested I should retain. It's just not relevant now, 20 years later. Very quickly, I feel a part of this lot. Maybe it's the London thing, maybe they just enjoy a bit of spotlight on their club, but they've welcomed me with open arms and those few who've been cynical haven't been brave enough or bothered enough to come any closer to me than their keyboards. Even the one who suggested they should all set light to me. The only problem is that they drink. A lot. And they drink it fast. And then when they go back to the bar, they buy me one too; often accompanied by not so much a cheeky as an obligatory sambuca. I've hardly had to crack my wallet open, which as a Spurs fan, successfully complies with all sorts of vile racial stereotypes.

Luke and I have worked out early doors that we're dangerously compatible drinkers, but now I'm meeting new ones all the time; there's a tiny little bloke called Smiffy, who resembles a sort of monkey-like version of Kiefer Sutherland in the latter stages of a particularly taxing series of 24. Being in his late 30s, he's dangerously, nut-achingly single and after a few drinks, enjoys exploring the more surreal suburbs of reality.

"I love the penis," he says to camera, after accidentally brushing my crotch with his hand, in the scruffy post-match bar-clamber.

Later, he goes on the GPG and claims profusely that he said 'peanuts'.

BARNET 0-1 BRENTFORD
Poole (pen) 10
Attendance 2,815

The whole thing bleeds alcoholically through from match to match, Saturday to Saturday, and before I know it, I'm getting sunburned aubergine on the Ealing Road Terrace at Brentford's home game against Rotherham, listening to my first single being played over the Tannoy.

Have things come that far that I'm releasing a single? Not really, no.

During the week, I discovered that back in the mid-90s, a band of Brentford fans recorded a song about the club called *Red on White*, and ended up selling a thousand copies. So I had the idea, on reflection a pretty dicky one, to interview them and re-record the song with my vocals on it. Can I sing? Not really, no.

Steve Hedge was the drummer of the band One Touch To Go, and at the bottom of the garden of his home in a pleasant, non-descript Crawley road, he has a recording studio. 'The Wash Room Studio' is a little bit of solace; sound doesn't come in or go out and the trains creep by on the other side of the fence without us or them knowing. The pictures inside seem to be all from around the mid-90s; there's one of Goldie Hawn from when you could call her 'sexy' without it being a weird near-necrophilia fetish, all from back when One Touch To Go had their day, and I get the sense things just didn't get any better than that.

Now, Steve is approaching middle-age and this week he sat at his little mixing desk, probably wearing slightly stronger lenses in his glasses than back then, while I emitted noises only partially recognisable to the human ear. Apparently, the song went down a smash with dogs, mermaids and viewers of *See Hear*. But for Brentford fans generally, it's not quite the rage. Although I really did enjoy getting to hold my headphones like a popstar while I sung, just like Glenn Hoddle did on *Diamond Lights*.

I've quickly had my status among the Brentford lot lifted to that of some kind of talisman of success – it's pretty obvious that while I'm here, it means they're winning – and even though I've been signing people's programmes, having pictures done with them and getting used to and in a weird way actually enjoying the attention, surely anyone could see that bringing out a single was not really the natural progression. And now I realise that, as the song echoes and rattles around the ground like a ton of gravel pouring into a skip. I stand on the terrace next to a bloke called Twiggy, who's on his stag do and has already been the mascot on the pitch – wearing a Brentford shirt from his youth, which thousands of beers later now looks more like a skimpy bra-top – and even he, with that gear on, looks at me with pity.

On my Facebook page, I've offered the single up to anyone who wants it, as long as they donate something to the club. Sales this time around were only down by nine hundred and ninety-nine. Actually, more like a thousand, because the one bloke who asked for it never got back to me with his email address.

iTunes haven't been in touch, either.

BRENTFORD 0-0 ROTHERHAM UNITED
Attendance 4,381

* * * * *

"Hello there. I am one of the Swebees," says Sven, a curious looking Scandinavian bloke in a plinky plonky sort of accent in which the vowels of 'Swebees' are pronounced about two furlongs longer than you'd expect.

Outside the Griffin pub, with his tiny Mongolian wife in tow, he's wearing a Brentford shirt covered in autographs and a stiff white shirt collar poking out the top. He has mannerisms like a caricature of something I can't quite put my finger on. Perhaps a character Jim Henson would fashion. Maybe he's just a unique oddity: tall and knobbly with the stance of a giant triffid caught perpetually in a hurricane. "We are 200 supporters in Sweden for the Brentford. And I will be here again," he promises, wangling a gangly index finger at the camera. "I want to see them win." He giggles out of the blue, like a little girl after her first spliff.

It transpires that Sven has spent £1200 to come all the way over from Stockholm to watch the Rotherham game – possibly one of the most profoundly toe-twitchingly dull matches ever. And now off he goes, back to Heathrow, over a grand lighter.

I wonder whether he's enjoyed himself. I wonder whether the Mongolian wife had any idea what was going on. I wonder what compels 200 Swedes to become Brentford fanatics...

* * * * *

"What are you expecting, Luke?" I ask Councillor Kirton, as we're getting on the plane, on our way to probably his first ever diplomatic conference overseas. Luke has no idea. Compared to his days in office, this is way off the remit. Ricky and 'Top Cat' haven't a clue either – the other Brentford fans who I've cajoled into coming with me to Stockholm, to visit The Swebees.

Sven – and gawd knows what other little gems they've got lurking over there in Sweden – has unwittingly been playing silly buggers with my curiosity muscle all week. I really feel like I need to get to the bottom of what the Swebees are all about. After all, they have no geographical or genetic reasons to support Brentford and still, they spend silly amounts of money shipping themselves and their moose meat (Sven always hands out moose meat in The Griffin) all the way over to little old Brentford. A constantly shameless promoter of the Swebees, Sven leapt so fast at my email asking if a visit was possible that he almost crashed through my monitor with his wangly finger. At first, amid the excitement of it all, he declared that we were all going to be staying at his home in some sort of international red and white orgy. I suspect that was until the missus found out, and then he downgraded it to just sorting out a hotel for us. Which then turned into a hostel.

"I'm nervous, mate, nervous. Come all this way to visit some Brentford fans … oh, hello … here he is!" Luke spots Sven in the distance at a bus stop, wearing a very long-looking suit, an incongruous flared Brentford scarf and carrying a briefcase, which – because of the perpetual hurricane he looks as though he's walking through – is flapping all over the place, almost causing an urban outrage. Sven spots us and exacts a very peculiar move; he crouches down, only slightly, and points at us with the full length of his three-feet arms and again cocks the finger, holding the pose there and looking down his shoulder as if to aim. And he's not smiling while doing this. Not one bit.

"Errrrrrr … we have some problems…" Sven announces gravely after the initial greetings, which are a bit like foreign dignitaries getting off a plane in the Middle East. I think for a second that our problem might be that the Swedish QPR fans are about to jump us, but it turns out Sven hasn't booked all the rooms and seems a bit annoyed with me for adding an extra one late doors. It feels a little tense at this point.

"But now … we go straight to the pub," he concludes, clearly the answer to the problem. I look over at Luke and immediately he opens his arms out in joy and mouths "Yeessssss!!!" We'd had visions of being dragged on some sort of cultural bus tour around the origins of the Swebees founder members. We're not up for that; we want the pub, and we want it now.

On the bus, my eyeballs are out on stalks. Swedish women. Lordy lordy. Blondey ones, dark haired ones… for a man alone on the road, this is like flicking through a catalogue of dreams. "How can I get myself a Swedish girlfriend, Sven?"

"Errrrrrr…" the pause goes on longer than the question warrants "…you can't," he replies eventually, succinctly and in all seriousness, with a face as straight as if he's just told me I've got cancer. No explanation. Quite simply, I can't.

'Dovas' says the sign. Just an ordinary looking bar on the corner of somewhere, wherever, in the middle of Stockholm. Are we to expect the full gamut of Swebees in here? Surely 200 of them won't fit in? Passing through the door, we find a whole glass-cased noticeboard full of Swebees business, including a picture of Ralph, the landlord of The Griffin. He's pulling his customary mardy face that's infused with a touch of the long-suffering husband which he affects for comic gains.

And then there's one of *me*, holding a pint. I have my picture up in a Swedish pub. If only that's as bizarre as it gets…

The bar has a smattering of sepia-stained Brentford memorabilia pinned precariously to the walls, and on one of the tables Sven proudly attaches a pennant to a metal frame so that it dangles. The Swebees are now in session. And we quickly work out what 'in session' means. The closer you get to the mahogany bar, the stronger the aroma of urine gets. There are three half-cut middle-aged Swedish men perched on stools, dressed up as last week, arms folded across the sticky dark wood surface and staring at the wondrous bottles facing them. These are the Swebees. We're introduced briefly, without pomp or particular over-friendliness and rather than tell us their names, they simply go by their Swebee membership numbers. So, for the record, we meet numbers 4, 13 and 53. In fact, it turns out that wherever you go around the pub, people have a number.

"Would you ever go to a game at Brentford?" I ask number 72, a smartly dressed lady sitting on a stool on her own, away from the main clump.

"No. I don't."

From what I can work out, the main men are either jobless or just enjoy drinking, *a lot*. They've told me how one day they were discussing the idea of supporting a small, random English club just for fun and somehow, over a few beers and hours poring over a dribble-laden map, they picked out my West London friends. But subsequently, *200* of them? Huh? It seems Sven is very keen to recruit more. They are like an inane and harmless Al Qaeda. They'll recruit whether they like it or not, and probably the vast majority are either drunk regulars or drunks passing through who wake up in the morning with a freshly-laminated membership card in their wallets that they have no recollection of acquiring. The Swebees, really, is simply the folly of a few drinkers who thought it would be quirky and a little bit 'crazy' (grrrrr) to support a lower league English team.

That's not to say we're not enjoying this fascinating, intoxicating cultural exchange. Every so often, me, Luke, Ricky and Top Cat exchange looks and a few words that all approximate '*what on earth are we doing here?*', in a way that's appreciative of the glory of this stunning randomness. If I was thinking that my ten-month endeavour was going to be generally peculiar, then this particular episode is stratospherically random.

We exchange all manner of tat, from football shirts to pin badges and the like, all of which the boys brought along from their own personal collections of rubbish, and all of which are received with surprising lack of excitement from Sven. In fact, he looks a little bit disappointed by it all; maybe he was expecting fancy velvet robes or one of the current manager's children. With that underwhelming ceremony plodded through, we get down to the serious business of the international language of beer. Across the course of the evening, we all get cornered individually by Sven, who confides in us his frustration at being number 11. He says he does it all, the magazines, the membership cards, the website … and he's only number 11? He wants to be number 1. More beers later, he changes his number to two hundred and something; almost an act of self-harm, a cry for help, a poignant dig at old number 4 over there. It's here that we get the first inkling that all is not well in the Swebee ranks.

But then out comes his mobile phone. You see, Sven writes and records his own songs about Brentford. What must his wife think? He plays his latest single over the phone's loudspeaker and mimes for my camera. I really do hope that he's not deluded enough to think that this sounds anything other than brilliantly appalling (and I say that even after my own musical catastrophe).

Brentford our favourites,
We will beat them all,
Bees will be there at the top,
We love our wonderful Brentford…

All in glorious monotone, without any semblance of discernable tune other than the Bontempi orchestra electronically stumping up what minimally detectable musical order there is. He doesn't play it just once. We have various reprisals at almost half-hourly interludes. And each time he hits 'play' on the phone again, we're expected to quietly listen to the entire thing.

The more the Swebees drink, the friendlier they get and within three hours, we're all arm in arm as number 68 declares he's going to sing us a song. He's a mammoth of a man, like a Scandinavian Hulk Hogan with a shiny bald head and moustache you could use on the front of your bike to Brighton. I expect him to knock out a Swedish standard or maybe, I racistly anticipate, a bit of Abba...

"Maybe it's because I'm a Londoner, that I love London Town..."

He does the entire ditty with a near-passable cockney accent in an utterly in-tune operatic boom. The whole pub is transfixed. I simply can't believe what's happening. Suddenly the whole weirdness of it all slaps me sober. Is this for real? I look briefly for hidden cameras, but no. His crescendo is greeted like a cup final; our cultural intercourse has just reached its climax.

"Are you crying?" I ask number 4; an unshaven travesty of a man who's been drinking since way before we got here, and by that, I mean our births.

"Yes. Because I love this guy. He's got such a beautiful voice." The tears crash down his cheeks and get lost somewhere in the undergrowth of his beard.

This whole conference has been exhausting, but somehow, for a simple night on the lash in a pub, amazing.

"How has it been for you, Top Cat?"

"Well, you know, we're in Stockport..." He stops to think about what he's just said, "...Stockport?"

Clearly, they're utterly bonkers. But good for them; why not? In a strange way, I admire Sven and how he gets so much out of his little parallel Brentford world. But on the way home, I start thinking beyond Sven (number 11) and the Swebees (numbers 1 to 200) and more about all the others who support teams that are technically outside their geographical relevance, such as the infamous 'Surrey Manchester United Fan Club', who are always held up as the example. Where does their passion actually come from? I grew up two miles from Tottenham and on occasion, because of the closeness to my origin, can find almost as much heart for Orient as I can Spurs. But what else, other than geography, attracts you to a team? Is it just affection for the glory?

When I go to Spurs, I'm cheering for my part of London and the boys representing us. Unfortunately, the influx of foreign players takes the shine off my argument slightly, but there's nothing I can do about the commercial juggernaut that's bulldozed our top league. So, what *really* are these people cheering for? Each to their own, it's up to them, but I don't really get where they're coming from. *They* are the real gloryhunters; I'm just a pretender. And as this journey unfolds, I realise more and more that my bastardly Gloryhunter front is really an ironic jab at those people, because the ones I'm actually featuring in the show week-in week-out are the most dedicated fans – of their local team – that you could hope for.

And I salute them.

5.

A BET WITH BOWLES

WEDNESDAY, 2 SEPTEMBER 2008.
The boardroom toilets, Griffin Park, Brentford.

I wonder if Greg Dyke did it. Hmmm. Been looking a bit shifty all evening, the old Dykester. When I go back out there, I'll be watching you, Dyke; I've got my eyes on you, sunshine.

You don't expect to be invited into the diamond-slung opulence of the Brentford boardroom, rubbing shoulders and swapping a mixture of over-firm and wringing wet mackerel-like handshakes, to then go to the toilets and find a floater winking up at you from the pan.

Just an ickle brown marbled nugget; a sphere of poop, bobbing happily under the deluge of my Budweiser byproduct. It's not that I came in here scouting for floaters, please don't think that of me. I wouldn't even have come in here at all if one of the more mischievous Bees United board members hadn't raced out of the trap excitedly to alert me of its presence. He really was quite keen that I come in here with my camera and get some live floater action on tape. So here I am, filming someone else's poo.

I wash my hands, although nothing could truly rid me of the filth I've just shrouded myself in, and head tentatively back into the boardroom – where it's more like a working men's club than the Saddam Hussein-style gold-leaf-coated den of erotic indulgence that an outsider might imagine of the mysterious inner sanctum of a football club. Shepherd's pie that stinks of school dinners (along with that ominous feeling of dread that came with them) steams away in the corner like a freshly heaped cow pat, as the occasional ruddy-cheeked director – or friend of a friend of a director – puffs open the lid and scoops a supersize portion, half dolloped onto his plate and half onto a tie that looks like it's only just been scraped free of last week's catering. They ooze essence de local businessman; risen from the ashes of the state school system, 'against all the odds', to rule the roost when it comes to fitted kitchens or building supplies.

Being the only one who's dared enter the hall of righteous power dressed in a mere commoner's football shirt – mainly because I haven't owned anything approaching a suit since 1998 – they all seem to know who I am, and most of them in turn recite their own slightly different version of the quip that suggests I'll be here all season. One of the Bees directors reveals to me in a whispery conspiracy, huddled underneath former goalkeeper Graham Benstead's framed shirt, that a visiting Yeovil director has asked discretely whether they gave me the replica Brentford shirt with 'Gloryhunter' printed on the back, or whether I had to pay for it. Clearly, they're bracing themselves for the sideshow freak to hit town.

I feel dreadfully out of place. Eternally grateful, of course, to have been invited into this world for a one-game glimpse – the club have been the utmost in supportive and co-operative – but these people in here are a different breed to me. They actually have a defined purpose in life; they have businesses and children and cars with leather interiors and reverse parking sensors, and this stuff called money. All I have is whim and dreams, all frothed up in bubbles that over the years burst, one by one. They're out of my league; they occupy another dimension, one called reality. However relatively you use the term, these are achievers, and standing here beside them, as some sort of novel court jester, dressed almost identically as I did in 1993, I feel like a child; one of life's dawdlers.

Outside, it's my second evening game of the season. It's a chilly twilight following a custard sunset, and from the director's seating area, which oddly gives only enough leg room for a double amputee, I can see the bundled together Ealing Road Terrace lot donning their first jackets of the impending autumn; warbling out their Brentford adaptation of *Hey Jude* and trying their best to muster enthusiasm for a midweek Johnstone's Paint Trophy tie against Yeovil Town.

Yet again, no sign of Gary Oldman.

In truth, it's expected by many that *this is it*; this is my reluctant carriage away, up west, to adventures in League One. This thing is after all designed with exactly such shameless league-clambering in mind, but now it's actually come to the moment where it might happen, I feel as though I'd rather not, thank you. Somehow looking up, from down here, the once-so-familiar Premier League looms distantly; a gigantic money-chomping beast that would just chew me up like fleshy bubble gum and leave me wandering around its vast gut alone and lost. I've got my feet under the table here and this experience at Brentford, and Grimsby before, is just more real, more relevant. This is football as I remember it, the football I fell in love with; played by players I can actually relate to.

I sit with the two Bees United chaps who invited me, Dave and Jon, with an empty seat to my left that I can turn into legroom and enable at least a trickle of bloodflow to my tingling feet slabs. But just as we approach kick-off, almost as dramatically as a Siegfried and Roy puff-of-smoke illusion revealing a camp tiger, he ghosts up and magics himself into that very precious leg-space: the suspected Demon Floater Layer of Old London Town: Greg Dyke.*

Non-executive Chairman and local boy Greg Dyke has almost come full circle; from nearby Hayes Grammar School he flitted briefly through the world of politics and into the debauched champagne slagheap of television, where he made a fortune from the sale of my old employer, London Weekend Television, and occupied ever so important roles at various companies before hoisting up to his career's pinnacle: Director General of the BBC. *La de da*. But after successfully steaming in, upping morale among workers and winning a lot of supporters along the way, the dodgy death of government weapons expert Dr David Kelly and the subsequent Hutton Enquiry ended with career hari-kari: his resignation. As well as various subsequent books and TV documentaries, Dyke returned to Brentford to take up his non-executive role. And here he is, being all non-executive, sitting next to me; complaining that my stick thing is digging into his ribs. It isn't, he's lying. I don't know why he's lying, but I also don't argue, I'm too scared; he's The Dyke.

* * * * *

It's been quite a week for mingling with the upper echelons of Brentford Football Club. Although I'm not sure an upper echelon is a place Stan Bowles would feel very

---

*For legal and moral reasons, I should point out that Dyke probably *didn't* heave out that floater. Although he *might* have. But probably didn't. Although…

comfortable sitting in. He'd probably storm off from an echelon and then slag it off, drunk.

"Hello?" croaks a slow, gravel-swilling voice with a Manchester edge on the other end of the phone. Then there's some scrabbling around that sounds like crisp packets in a tumble drier.

"Stan?"

"Yeah … Yeah … hello?"

"Have I just woken you up, Stan? Are you tumble-drying crisp packets?"

"No, no, it's alright, I've just got back from Spain. Who is it?"

I explain to Stan Bowles who I am, what I'm doing and that I've got 50 notes for him if he'll meet me down his local, The Royal Oak/Nan's living room, to do a quick interview over a pint.

"That'd be the cheapest job I've ever done," he complains, as though I've just stabbed his dog.

"Listen Stan, I'm offering you 50 quid in cash to have a pint down your local. That's not bad work if you can get it." Stan concedes that he might as well go along with it.

Stan Bowles is one of your archetypal 70s footballers, with the dodgy bouffant barnet to boot. He's known as much for his boozing and betting as for his dribbling genius on the pitch. 'Maverick', 'colourful character' and (the worst) 'hellraiser' are overworked clichés the press sling on him – but for football managers, 'occasional liability' would also join the list. My dad would probably call him a 'cowson'. He's best known for his days at QPR, for whom he played between 1972 and 1979, and was recently voted the club's best ever player. Brentford didn't come until the very end of his career, and seeing as Rangers and Bees are sworn enemies, that didn't necessarily sit well with everyone.

"Yeah, Brentford days, I was more or less retiring then, really," says Stan in his naturally shifty manner, eyes darting around everywhere, largely expressionless, as he settles down with the pint of ale I've just shouted him. He's looking sharp; silver hair more controlled than previous eras and still bearing this morning's comb-tracks, along with a suit worn immaculately in the manner his father taught him.

"So you weren't really trying then?" I tease, testing the waters to see whether this stone-cold seriousness is flexible or permanently set to droopy-chopped deadpan.

"Oh I was trying alright, don't worry about that. I was still liking the game, yeah." He propels a wheezy chuckle with the splutters of an old Cessna starting up, curiously trying to keep his lips as together as possible; maybe to cover dental irregularities. I detect with relief that he's up for a laugh. "That was pretty easy for me out there. Except for the pace, it was a lot quicker. We had a good group of lads then; Chris Kamara was one of them, the one with the loud mouth and tash off Sky. Eventually, when Frank McLintock became the manager, I could have stayed for another season, but you know, I'd just had enough. I'd played for 17 and a half years. Some people think I only played for QPR!"

"Stan," I interject with faux irritation, "you mustn't mention the 'Q' word around here."

"Oh, I know, but they know me around here. A lot of the supporters don't like me because I played for QPR," he says with a trace of incredulity.

"Really? Do you get any abuse?"

"Occasionally, but I've always got someone wrapped round me, do you understand?" His eyes flash out of the window and across the pub furtively, and with a little sniff his face goes blank and unreadable again. He loves it, old Stan, a bit of needle, or at least the suggestion of it. Always has. Even with his own teammates, he's never stomached anything or anyone he didn't fancy.

"I was quite fiery in those days, especially at QPR, you know, we had a blinding side," – arguably Rangers' best side *ever* in fact – "but I didn't think some people were up to scratch. When I wrote my book, I actually realised that they was a lot better than I thought." He giggles cheekily, with an air of knowing he could get away with saying more or less anything. He is, after all, 'Stan Bowles: maverick'.

"So did you feel a bit guilty?"

"Not really," he sharply replies with conscious arrogance. Not only can he get away with anything, but balls to 'em as well.

"There was Ralph Coates; he was at Orient with me. He had squiffy hair like Bobby Charlton. He wasn't a good player; all he used to do was run up and down the line. The worst player we had a QPR was Brian ... Brian someone ... came from f**cking up north. Well, I come from up north..." he falters, confusing himself with the obvious hypocrisy, "...but ... he never stopped moaning. Brian Williams. And he had a big black beard. He came in one day at half-time and said 'you never passed the ball to me'. I said 'you're a decoy, now keep running up and down that line'. It's pointless giving these types of people the ball because they just lose it again. They take somebody with them, one of the opposing side, so they're handy for *something.*" All said in the present tense. I wonder how much of Stan's life these days is lived in or in the spirit of the past.

"Have any of them come back at you afterwards?"

"Yeah, I've had arguments. I had a fight with Frank McLintock. I bit his ear on the training ground," he boasts. Lovely.

As we speak, Stan works hard at keeping only half-engaged, the attention of his cold blue eyes split between the mundane goings on in the empty pub and our conversation. It might just be that for 50 quid, this is all you get; he's said it all before, anyway. But it strikes me that he's something of a contradiction in all this. In one sense he portrays such gigantic self-regard that he thinks nothing of belittling former team-mates in a way the unspoken code of footballers' unity doesn't often allow; on the other hand he's spent years persistently seeming to sabotage himself and his career with the booze and the betting and the controversial storm-outs.

"I can go back to when I walked out on England," he confirms defiantly, referring to his reaction at being substituted in a game against Northern Ireland. "Mick Channon was my room mate. He said 'you can't walk out on England'. I opened the window..." (he reaches up and pulls open the pub's dusty net curtain next to us), "...and I said 'see that motor there? That's taking me right back to London'." Not just honest, but proud of his stand against the holiness of the England set-up, he sits back down again and re-scans the empty room.

I wonder if all this is just a front, cordoning off the insecurities that come with being a natural, creative footballing genius. It's no surprise that Stan was a great friend and a famed drinking partner of the late George Best, a similarly destructive character who eventually succeeded in betraying his gift to death. Could Stan really have gone *so* far in the game with a genuinely immense chip of indifference carved out of his shoulder?

"You wouldn't really call yourself a football man, would you Stan?" I posit with chance, putting the cross in for him to head home the ultimate sin.

"No, no," he confirms without a second's thought. "Playing it was alright, it was the buzz, the crowd. At Man City, when I made my debut there was f**cking 70,000 people there. When I made me debut for Notts Forest; 120,000 in the Neu Camp; Kenny Burns, Martin O'Neill there, all going like that, between their knees..." – he leans over and mimes honking up – "I wasn't really interested in football. My father pushed me to get into it, at Manchester City, where I started off. I played with some good players there, but I got the sack," (for missing a flight to an away game at Ajax). "I was getting more money running around for people in Manchester, illegal bets, with the Quality Street gang. We were notorious in Manchester. So I was never going training. I think my first wage packet was seven pound. I've known these people for years, you know, they're my type of people. I like characters."

"But what about Cloughie?" I ask, knowing that here's one 'character' he *didn't* like.

"What about him? We just didn't get on. You know, I went there [Nottingham Forest] because of the European Cup, and because of the money as well. I walked out on the European Cup final. I would have had a medal. That would have been worth 20 grand now," he spits ruefully. The only open shows of regret for his actions seem to come when discussing money. "It's just the way I am, I just do things on the spur of the moment. He [Clough] didn't really do anything, for me. He didn't do the training you know; there was two trainers, Jimmy Gordon and I can't remember the other bloke's name now, and they just walked their dogs down the Trent, him and Peter Taylor. He'd join in the training on a Friday, when it was all over, basically. So for me, I thought where the f*ck's he coming from? He had something about him, but tactics? There was no tactics. Just keep giving the ball to a red shirt!" He bursts out laughing, not just at this example, but seemingly, by his tone, at the whole Brian Clough tribute circus.

Stan seems to enjoy sticking in the knife into things other people covet; Cloughie, England, and ultimately football itself. He even once knocked the FA Cup Trophy off a display table with a ball while playing away at Sunderland (who had just famously beaten Leeds in the 1973 final). It caused uproar. For me, I can't help thinking it's a form of self-defence, rather than genuine contempt or disregard. Surely, someone as successful as Stan *had* to care. In fact, I wonder whether Stan Bowles cares *so* much that he feels he can't expose his vulnerability to the outside world, especially the worlds that he's walked in, and so he tarnishes everything with the protective gloss of 'whatever', just in case. It's just so hard to tell with a man so tanked up on exterior displays of indifference.

"So after you finished playing, you stayed in Brentford. Why was that? You're a Manc!"

"Well I liked it round here. I bought a house. The *News of the World* put in the paper that I was bankrupt. I went to Martin Lange [Brentford director at the time] and said I've never been bankrupt. So they sued them, I got the money and that's how I got the house in Braemar Road. And it's just gone for about 280 grand!" Money, regret, money, regret, money...

"So you literally used to walk across the road to play?"

"I did. And Terry Hurlock was facing the ground in Braemar Road as well."

"Were you ever late to a game?"

"No, no. Terry was. I wasn't as bad as I was at QPR; I used to go there ten minutes before kick-off. To me it was just like a Sunday morning game, you know, get your kit on and away you go. But at Brentford, probably 20 minutes before kick-off, I used to be down the betting shop on the corner; people would say 'are you playing today?' and I'd say 'yeah, don't worry; I'll get there in a minute. I'll catch up with you.'"

Talking of bets; I explain to Stan that I've been asking the Brentford fans on the GPG to tell me what their greatest ever Brentford season was. Overwhelmingly, they've come back with glorious nostalgic rhetoric about their Third Division promotion winning side of 91/92. Under the steer of manager Phil Holder, Bees went up as champions in a barnstorming climax, winning the last six games of the season and pipping Birmingham to the top spot.

"What odds would you give me on finding 11 members of that squad, and getting a photo with each, within the week?" I ask, hoping to get a bet on with the Bowles. He thinks about it hard, with that gambler's twinkle, that utter inability to refuse a wager.

"I'd say all of 10/1," he eventually returns, with the serious caginess that's compulsory when striking up a bet.

"Alright," I start, slowly and with equable cage, "I'm gonna put a fiver on it."

Pause. Pause. Pause...

"That's 50 quid then."

Pause. Pause...

"Yeah," he confirms, "I'm working all the time now, so you'll get paid."

"Right, let's do it."

We shake hands. It's game on.

* * * * *

After 120 minutes (plus stoppage time) of JPT magic, Brentford and Yeovil share four goals between them and prepare to commence a penalty shoot-out that will – most importantly for me at least – decide which hotel I stay at tomorrow night.

"So *what* is it you're doing?" asks Greg Dyke almost convincingly interested, as he momentarily flits his noticeably erratic attention in the direction of my camera and the stick he reckons is trying to penetrate his rib cage. About three words into my answer, he drifts off to another point in the distance, on other side of the stadium. Probably a pigeon or something. I consider finishing my sentence with a spectacular array of expletives, because he wouldn't be listening anyway, but before I get that far, a hellish screeching, a frenzy of high pitched bleating like an amplified ZX Spectrum loading up 'Manic Miner' sodomises my ear drums from behind. It's Greg Dyke's daughter. I've been talking to her and she seems nice, so this racket is sudden, and quite a surprise.

Brentford have taken the lead in the shootout…

Surrounded by the Dykes, with their combined scary importance and shrillness, it's difficult to concentrate on the enormous implications of what's happening on the pitch. There's probably more at stake out there for me than there is for any of those players, which is a strange thought. I manage to drag my focus onto Sebastien Brown, the 19-year-old debutant goalkeeper keeping guard of my tenure at Brentford. Whether or not I move up a division, and the course of my entire next nine months, is entirely in his hands. He has no idea and probably wouldn't give much of a toss, but it's down to him … *Go on Seb, it's all you mate, go on son…*

"He's a hero!" shouts Dyke with a Jonathan Ross 'r' and arms punching the air, as Dyke Junior once again raises her vocal siren above the roar of the crowd and beyond health and safety regulations. Sebastien Brown – rookie goalkeeper – makes the penalty save that sends Brentford through to the next round and me to reception to tell fancy face that I'm extending my stay at the travel tavern. Seb runs across the pitch, lifts up his keeper's jersey and reveals a t-shirt emblazoned with the words 'Gloryhunter is a Bee'…

…well, no, he doesn't. It would have been a nice gesture though. But suddenly, the buzz these ties often lack explodes out of remission, and one of the Bees United guys next to me, in all the excitement, simply can't stop himself from a mid-40s body popping display. At least I think it's body popping, or maybe it's a serious convulsion that requires immediate medical attention. He's smiling though, so until he actually stops breathing we'll assume it's just an unwieldy b-boy move.

> BRENTFORD 2-2 YEOVIL TOWN
> Poole (pen) 28   Bircham 39
> O'Connor 37   Tomlin (pen) 77
> Brentford win 4-2 on penalties
> *Attendance 1,339*

And so again, the glamorous Johnstone's Paint Trophy fails to pull me out of League Two. My Brentford days are un-numbered, and I narrow my attention to Operation Bowles...

* * * * *

Bet With Bowles: Day One

Marcus Gayle, Keith Millen, Ashley Bayes, Terry Evans, Graham Benstead, Jamie Bates, Gary Blissett, Bob Booker, Simon Ratcliffe, Paul Buckle, Les Sealey, Detzi Kruszynski, Richard Cadette, Lee Luscombe, Brian Statham, Billy Manuel, Chris Hughton, Neil Smillie, Kevin Godfrey, Dean Holdsworth ... where the bloody hell are you all?

I've gone OCD over this; sweaty and obsessed. It's taken control of me: hot flushes, hives and whispery muttering in public places, probably in Latin. Four days to find eleven men – who, it turns out, are either scattered all over the country or just plain hiding from me – just to win £50 off old Bowlesy. The tank of petrol to get to Newport has cost £50 in itself. What am I doing? And Newport? How did all of this land me up at Newport?

Walking around with an hour to spare in the samey city centre of Newport (the one in south Wales not on the Isle of Wight), I've got that nervous edge that comes with needing a wee. Although in the past I've moaned about all the chain stores homogenising our city centres, now, with pangs of on-the-road loneliness and Bowles-infused frustration, exactly all I actually want right now *is* a homogenised city centre; the gentle hand of Subway, the cuddle of Burger King, the bosom of McDonalds. Am I now a victim? A convert? A capitalist freak? Perhaps it's just this constant awayness, leaving me clinging to anything familiar. Watch it mum, much more of this and I'll be back on the teet.

"I've Googled you on the internet," booms pot-bellied Dean Holdsworth knowingly, a few seconds after his aftershave curled around the corner before him. With a little look that suggests he's maybe discovered we're both from the jewel of East London, Walthamstow, he shakes my hand like a Boa and does that towering domination thing that footballers do even if they're shorter than you. He's undoubtedly likeable right from the off, but looks a million miles away from the pretty-boy footballer who fronted Top Man campaigns and cracked out an extra-marital with fleshy glamour-breast Linsey Dawn Mckenzie. And if all that malarkey didn't quite overshadow a very decent football career that included being one of the infamous 'Crazy Gang' collective of top-league thugs at Wimbledon, he recently appeared in reality TV shows *Deadline* and the classic *Cirque de Celebrité* to ensure that the public's enduring images of him will be mainly of his various dalliances in the media. Which is why it seems odd now to drive over to Wales and find him in a distinctly un-*Celebrité* little office at Newport County.

For Dean, Brentford came before the footballing peaks, personal lows and shameless televisual sell-outs, and I can tell that he has real affection for those innocent days and virgin glories; especially as the 91/92 promotion year was his last at the club – he left in a blaze of victory with a sweet taste in his mouth (which wasn't yet Linsey Dawn Mckenzie).

"Oh, it was fantastic. Great team. The whole season just gelled together. First game of the season I scored a hat-trick against the Orient, we won 4-3." This was the game at Griffin Park I was at, all those years ago. "I actually had a bet on myself to score a hat-trick." He flashes the grin that must have buckled the patellae of hundreds of kiss-and-tell wannabes up China Whites down the years. "It was a fantastic team for me to play in. I enjoyed every minute of it and obviously I had my sights set on playing higher. I got to Wimbledon; then I went to Bolton and then Coventry, and then on to Rushden and then hung around the non-league for a while. And now I find myself in the manager's job here at Newport County."

"Do you keep in contact with the others?"

"Well me and Gayley [Marcus Gayle] speak a lot on the phone, he's at AFC Wimbledon." He immediately gets the mobile out and leaves Marcus a message to contact me. This is going to be how I win this bet – harnessing the address books of the players I meet.

"Gary Blissett, I think he's now playing in goal in Germany, believe it or not." *Balls*. With my budget blown on those Swedish nutters; there's no way I'll get over there. Still, it's a big squad.

"What about Paul Buckle?" I ask. Dean laughs to himself.

"Buckle…" He shakes his head and I can't work out whether he's being disparaging or remembering crazy, crazy times...

* * * * *

Bet With Bowles: Day Two

Crack of sparrow's, and I arrive, as instructed, at Newton Abbot Racecourse, near Torquay. There are no horses; in fact, no people either. It's desolate and soulless, just a big damp green expanse flanked by white racetrack rails and smothered in litres of early-morning dew that's slowly soaking its way up my trouser leg and into my bones. As instructed, I continue to make my way to a run-down little hut slap in the middle of the racecourse. This can't be right. I feel like I'm taking part in a roleplaying adventure game; wandering according to cryptic clues to this decrepit dwelling built for a Middle Earth hairy-toed tiny person … the next roll of a 12-sided dice might see me attacked by an emerging goblin with special powers and a sickle. I knock on the door and a little blonde man in his pants, with eyes looking in slightly different directions, opens the door. Maybe this *is* Dungeons and Dragons after all.

"Paul?" I probe tentatively, wondering if goblins speak English.

"Yes, hello!" he replies, without any sign of a Tolkien accent or clutching of a wand. This is Paul Buckle, manager of Torquay United and a midfielder in the Brentford fans' favourite promotion-winning side. And far from being Goblinish, he quickly adds clothing and stands in front of a sign in his miniature office that says 'Fail to prepare, prepare to fail'. Now smartly kitted out in pristine training gear with thinning hair precisely modelled in gel, he greets me with enthusiasm. After small talk in which he mentions something about former manager Dave Webb in the same sentence as a word starting with 'c', we set up ready for an interview and decide to go for the 'entering the door' bit again, for the sake of television magic.

"Paul Buckley!" I exclaim upon my faux-discovery.

"Buckle. Go again," he sharply returns, giggling like a soap actor in an *It'll Be Alright on the Night* clip. Way to go, GH.

"Why am I at Newton Abbot racecourse?"

"I'm manager of Torquay United now, and we train here." *Ohhhhhhhh.*

"That Brentford team was a long time ago now."

"What do you remember of your team-mates?"

"Strong characters. Unforgiving," he says, with a wry smile. Along with Holdsworth's reaction yesterday, I get a sense that a young Buckle was maybe a little bit of a whipping boy for the older lads at Brentford. And now?

"I still look at the results at Brentford, and hopefully, you know, one day I might come back as manager." A different sort of wry smile spreads across his face, this one less playful. Perhaps his desire to manage Brentford is not such a joke.

Buckle feeds me some more phone numbers, I get his name wrong again, and then race off to Ashton Gate, home of Bristol City Football Club. That's two of eleven done. A slow start; Bowles will be rubbing his hands.

* * * * *

"Blaaaaaagggggghhhhhhhhh!!!!!!!!!!"

I spontaneously nearly sick up a lung while half of my spleen instantly dissolves into something like sauerkraut and propels itself towards the opposite end.

"You stupid little sod," is all I can bark at the tracksuited youth team player, as soon as I've re-swallowed vital organs and dragged my breathing back from not-at-all to the normal pattern of in-out. You wouldn't expect opening the door to the players' tunnel at Bristol City Football Club to evoke hell itself. The bleeder scared the living twat out of me and now he looks just as shocked; I think he had visions of being up on a manslaughter charge.

"Sorry mate, I thought you were someone else." Damn right you did you tit-faced little slag.

Composure regained, relatively, I stand on the side of the Ashton Gate pitch, looking out at an impressive stadium. They're not mucking around, this lot, they're clearly ambitious. Keith Millen – a towering, dependable, no-nonsense lower-division central defender and stalwart in the promotion team – seems a little non-plussed; perhaps he's looking at the full film crew interviewing someone else next to us, and then back at my poxy little video-wasp-on-a-stick and feels like you do when you end up with the fat mate.

"I've tracked you down, Mr Millen, what are you up to?"

"You have. I am assistant manager here at Bristol City." Keith doesn't say much more than the obvious, really: "great side", "brilliant experience", "mixture of age and youth"; all that stuff. It's that modern day Alan Shearer-style media interview, a concoction of a variety of different clichés that approximate pretty much nothing. But then again, I was only here to get a picture. Snap. Millen done; three down, eight to go.

Heading back to London, I'm totally Bowlesed out; I'm knackered, feeling like I've driven myself bloody on motorways that are starting to look like a crap computer game which I'm bored of playing. I stop off in Woking, as you do, to catch a few minutes with former goalkeeper Graham Benstead, who's the first of the squad I've met that's no longer working in the game, and also the only one who bears more than a passing resemblance to former *Neighbours* character Jim Robinson.

"Jim … er … I mean Graham … why are we outside Woking Football Club?" I ask, perched up against the car in the baron car park, resisting the urge to ask what *West Wing* was like compared to *Neighbours*.

"Why? Because I live down here." He's wearing old paint-splattered clothes and gesticulates with enormous great flapping hands that look like baseball mitts painted in flesh.

"Nothing to do with the football club?"

"No. In fact I've been here 20-odd years and never played for them. I just wanted to concentrate on my painting and decorating business really. It's gone from strength to strength." He seems to feel the need to validate his opting out of the game, the limelight, by marking his success; as though I was ready to judge it a cop out or a failure. "People say to me what were your best times, Norwich or Sheffield United, but for me it's Brentford. They've got one of my shirts in the bar there, I dunno why." He laughs humbly.

"Any messages for your team-mates from that squad?"

"Well. I think Jamie Bates still owes me a bob or two for food on the coach on the way back…"

* * * * *

Bet With Bowles: Day Three

With only four of eleven players caught and two days to go, I frantically email, text, phone, smoke-signal *anyone* who's even stood in a queue in the Post Office with the players. I may as well be whipping myself naked in the streets of Stranraer, because all I'm getting back is nothing.

I'm facing humiliation among the fans who've been looking forward to seeing their old idols on screen again. I'm letting them down. Come on Gloryhunter, you've got to do better than this. I decide to pace around the hotel room a bit. That'll help.

The phone rings (*ring ring, ring ring* – like that).

"What? You're outside the hotel? Now? Here? Outside?" It's Jamie Bates, returning my call at last. I dash out of the room, past old smiley chops on reception and out to the rainy, grey Brentford High Street; into the smell of wet pavement and the sound of lorry wheels throwing puddles into the air. On the way down to the corner, I remember Paul Buckle saying something about Jamie Bates and a saucy newspaper scandal involving his wife. I haven't had a chance to look into it; all my searches on Jamie so far have thrown up is a quote from a website that says of the promotion year:

"'…sent off after a tussle with Jamie Bates,' is the most used phrase of the season.'

Sitting all snug and dry in his white delivery van, Jamie's wearing a standard courier company polo shirt and goatee beard surrounded by stubble. He kind of looks like Neil Ruddock without the extraordinary weight gain. As I get in and sit on the passenger's seat with all the dockets and food wrappers, he's got a big happy-go-lucky grin on his face that suggests all is well and he's enjoying the novelty of being on camera again. Jamie was a hard, dedicated partner in central defence with Keith Millen.

"I quit football in 2001, saved me knee, saved me ankles, quit a bit early maybe but I enjoyed meself. I took a couple of years off to spend time with the family, built me house and became a postman for three years." It's funny that although I don't remember Jamie as a player at all, I'm always fascinated to know what players do next, once the spotlight has faded and they're once again 'just' one of us. "And now I'm just a courier driver, for Rainbow." He cheekily raises his shirt breast to show the logo and giggles.

"Still in touch with any of your team-mates?"

"Big Tel [captain Terry Evans], yeah, he's been ringing me saying 'go to Benidorm soon for the boys' bender.' Might get round to it if the wife lets me.

Keith Millen, Dean Holdsworth – all doing well. Would be good to see them one day ... have a game one day..." he finishes, with a look of pensive reflection. In the way he describes himself as 'just' a courier, and with the references to how well the other boys are doing, I get the feeling Jamie considers himself a little left behind; that he's let life overtake him. I don't ask about the 'scandal'. I'm sure, whatever it was, he's lived enough of that. To drive over to meet me as a favour and have that stuff sicked up in his white van, in the rain on a Thursday afternoon outside a travel tavern, probably isn't what he needs, and neither really do I.

Before I know it, Jamie's put me on to Terry Evans, who directs me to a sports ground not too far away. *I'm on a roll. Coming at ya', Stan.* Terry's my sixth of eleven. Although when I arrive, I wonder if it's a wind-up; something Stan's done to throw me off the scent. There are a load of giants kicking egg-balls through funny looking goal things.

"Rugby?" I ask walking manatee Terry Evans, having worked out that 'Big Tel' is indeed at this arena of strange sport. The former defender and captain is huge and hairless and as far as handshakes go, this is definitely a rugby one; around three times the deadly clasp that footballers inflict. As I try to work out whether my little finger has permanently welded to my ring finger, Terry explains: "I'm a conditioner here at Wasps now. I do the fitness, look after the lads and really enjoy it. As soon as I finished football, I got a season ticket to watch Wasps, followed them for eight years and it's just sort of taken over now." But what about my fingers?

And of the promotion year? "You'd sit and look around the dressing room and you'd have so much trust with each other. That was the ingredient for success I think." Yes, *but what about my bloody fingers?*

With time tick-tocking, I run away from Terry and rush over to Tower Bridge, rearranging my fingers back to their traditional hand-style shape, and have a little think back to some of my old days watching Spurs.

On the shelf, it's packed. Grandad's brought a crab sandwich with him, it stinks. The bloke in front keeps letting one go, it stinks, and all I can see is his head; I hate his head. When the crowd sways though, I get a peak through the rows of bonces and catch flashy glimpses of skinny little Paul Moran dashing through to score the winner to finish off Watford ... up we jump, come on you Spurs; glory glory hallelujah, crab sandwich everywhere; accidentally catch the bloke in front's head with my elbow – shame that – and Paul Moran revels, young and full of hope, in the celebration...

The last I heard was unsubstantiated reports that Paul Moran was working as a painter and decorator in Enfield … but out there celebrating with him on that New Year's day in 1988 was stocky Spurs full-back, Brian Statham. I hadn't actually realised that he ended up with Brentford, and as I stand waiting for him in the reception of an office block just by the Tower of London, I get the little tingles that I imagine Brentford fans will get when they see my video of their former idols.

His handshake exacerbates the metacarpal carnage Evans started.

"I went to Gillingham and then retired, after which it was about trying to find a new career. I had a lot of friends in the city and that's where I am now." Yup, you are, slap bang in the middle of it. I'm not as nervous as I thought I would be; he's quite disarming, this Mr Statham. "Just set up a company called CSS Investments with two colleagues of mine. Message for Brentford fans – if you need some advice, call me! Always pleased to help in this current climate." The transition has clearly been made, sitting here in the lobby of the plush office block, next to the obligatory under-watered indoor spider plant; he's now a suited and booted slippery-spoken shameless businessman for whom football probably seems another lifetime ago. I wonder for a moment whether he thinks about those days more or less than Jamie Bates.

"You preferred it at Spurs, though – didn't you," I coax, sneakily, expecting a smoothly diplomatic return.

"Oh, absolutely." *Yeeesssssss, go on my son, you beautiful, beautiful stocky little full-backy man.* "Yeah, I think I played 30-odd games under Terry Venables. Got injured and was sold to Brentford." *I love you, Brian Statham, you delicious Spurs-flavoured human,* I think, and of course, all this remains unsaid, in a manly, Spurs sort of way, and we leave it there with a firm handshake and well wishes.

* * * * *

Bet With Bowles: Day Four
"Der der der der der, der der der der der der der … BOOKER!" sings much travelled striker Bob Booker shyly, through a goofy grin in reply to my question as to whether the fans had a song for him. He didn't mention that another song, sung by the Sheffield United fans when he was there – 'Ooh Ahh Bob Booker' – was subsequently, possibly, arguably, stolen and adapted to the now famous 'Ooh Ahh Cantona'.

It's a nice gaff here in Brighton, where the Albion first-team train at a leafy, secluded university campus. Bob has a banana on his desk, and for some reason my brain keeps saying *Bob Booker's banana* to itself. The strain of this is perhaps getting to me. Or maybe I just fancy a banana.

"They call you the Gloryhunter? Dunno what you're doing down here," he says with a silliness-lined chuckle.

"I still look through me scrapbooks at all the times we had. Great times," he says mistily.

I have a good chat with Bob, mainly along the lines of all the rest of them, how great it was and how brilliant it all felt. We get the picture taken and I slowly make my way to Brighton Beach for a deep breath and too many donuts. No rush now. The writing's on the wall.

I stroll along the promenade as blue sky struggles through blustery gaps; wondering if at some point I'll get a team like Brighton, on the coast, so I can live next to this noisy wave-fest for a while. That'd be nice. I check my phone: zero messages, zero texts … and realise, it's over. It's just all too late. I use the names Gayle, Bayes, Cadette and Godfrey in the same breath as other, more obscene words, while donut oil streaks down my chin. I've left messages and messages and texts and short of sending in the KGB with balaclavas and threats of assassination, I've done as much as I can.

I know that keeper Ashley Bayes is now at Stevenage, because my old mate from Walthamstow, Chris Day (formerly of Spurs), is keeping him out of the side there. Chris said he'd have a word for me, but Bayes didn't get in touch. Maybe those two times I flimsily tried to punch Chris with drunk fists like bags of custard (once outside Faces Nightclub and once in just pants at Butlins) have come back to haunt me and he's not passed on the message. Who knows? Of the rest, Les Sealey's dead, so that's a non-starter. AFC Wimbledon said they'd ask Marcus Gayle "if he'd like to take part" (in my two-second photo) and Kevin Godfrey is apparently driving a van locally … but that's as close as I can get. Oh, sod the lot of it.

Meeting these players has been a bit of a lesson in itself though really. A lesson in how people carry on with their lives regardless, even when probably the best moments they'll ever experience have already come and gone before the age of forty. All that adulation and attention, and now they've got buggered knees and an occasional geek chasing after them for an ITV internet show to show for it. It must seem at first that their peaks and troughs are now only troughs, and it must be tough to deal with – just suddenly being tossed onto a scrapheap, forced to carve something new out of what's left of yourself. But they've carried on, kept at it – some with more gusto and hunger than others, but they're all hanging in there.

I take a deep, poignant breath, and like a stodgily emotional scene in *Dawson's Creek*, concede a teary defeat. I don't *actually* cry; I've just got a bit of something in my eye. Honest. Only eight players found: game, set and match to Stanley Bowles.

I consider sending Stan's fiver along to The Royal Oak in an envelope containing the Swedish loose change I've still got from the visit to Stockholm. But I bottle that, in case he sees it as some sort of gangland message and suddenly I've got Terry Hurlock sticking an axe through my hotel room door.

He'll get his fiver somehow. It's probably the first bet he's ever actually won.

6.

LOGAN'S RUNT

TUESDAY, 7 OCTOBER 2008.
Trapped in the rowdy travesty that is Yates's Wine Lodge, Luton.

> ✉ TEXT MESSAGE
> FROM: TOM ESPN
> That's the single most horrible
> thing I've ever seen.

The entire ESPN Star Sports Asia crew have had to walk out; they just couldn't bear it. They've seen some things in their time, while filming 'crazy' stories around the surreal edges of global football, but when they came to film me on my quest for glory, they didn't expect to walk into a Yates's Wine Lodge and find *this*; this most appalling of human unions since sex was invented...

A 22-year-old man, snogging – no, devouring ... nay, consuming – a woman who must be in her mid-to-late 60s.

And it's all my fault.

I'm not doing very well with bets, and now look; I've created a monster. But the thing is, I didn't even stipulate that the woman had to be someone's Great Grandmother. He's so depraved, so willing to win the bet, any old how, that he actually *chose* this relic; and now he's showboating, exacting the equivalent of a frivolous overhead kick on the football pitch with this decrepit strumpet. That's the mark of the man they call 'Tidy'.

I'd been waiting for them to get here for a while, among the flotsam that queue outside Yates's all morning waiting for it to open. You know the ones. I worry about this country. Actually, no, I worry about *me* in this country – that lot can look after themselves, albeit on my tax coin. But do I really want to be around them, within even a country's breadth of them? My doubts about whether this journey will produce a positive outcome – in terms of me fleeing the country or not – at moments like these swing me decidedly towards the jumbo jet side of the conundrum. Anyplace, anywhere, other than here; paying for these toothless drunken shell-suited benefit-botherers to sit in a pub all day while Eastern Europeans are being shipped in illegally to fill the jobs this lot consider themselves too good for. Even for a bloke from Walthamstow, am I being a snooty twonk? Have we an underclass so far beneath *even me*, that *I'm actually* concerned about appearing snotty? What's going on, people? Is it not our duty, as citizens, to point a finger at those who aren't doing their bit while the rest of us work ourselves naked to keep the country going?

Move on. *Breathe, GH, breathe.*

Nick Logan, a surprisingly gentle man underneath that template of the laddish front, has enormous eyeballs and a belly only slightly bigger, and is the sambuca-peddling Brentford fan who invited me to meet them here ahead of the Johnstone's Paint Trophy tie away at Luton. I like Nick. He's a quick-witted brainy man who enjoys subduing such with booze as much as I do. When they finally turn up, or fall over the threshold, the infamous Tidy is among the little hard-drinking brat-pack, and while Nick opts to call him 'Shergar' – in reference to his apparently racehorse-esque teeth – I would just as easily pair him with a hundred other look-alikes ranging from Buzz Lightyear through Ted Danson to Herman Munster; he's just got one of those faces. And he's not short on confidence either; a proper wide-boy cockney chancer who, like a lot of fans, when he isn't working down the nearby Heathrow airport, is all about the bets and the birds and the beers. While they all try to knock Tidy down a peg or two with the relentless name-calling, he shamelessly counteracts by bigging himself up to an alarmingly verbose extent – specifically regarding his alleged prowess with the ladies.

"With looks like this, you can't go wrong, know what I mean?" he humbly professes with a wink and a flash of the gnashers.

I couldn't possibly let an opportunity like this pass me by. So, I offer him a simple £20 bet:

Snog someone, by the end of the match.

Proper snogging, mind, with tongues and closed eyes and all that stuff – romantic and that.

My £20 says he won't manage it. Easy, I think. I can erase that whole Stan Bowles debacle – this one is mine. All mine. There's no-one around in the pub that I can imagine him snogging, and beyond that, who ever pulls in a football ground? I just can't see where she'll come from, this potential kiss-ee. Unless Nick goes through with his threat to do the unthinkable with Tidy and do it himself for a share of the money, *this one's in the bag,* I think.

36 minutes and 12 seconds later, from the urinals I hear wild giggles of incredulity and outraged jeering mixed with the gargly bile sloshes of gag reflex among bystanders. Upon emerging, I see right into the middle of the pub, a *Saturday Night Fever* type circle formed around the scene of the crime. Fresh from a tray of bargain flavoured shots, Tidy's renowned teeth are penetrating the prune-lipped, bedentured mouth of the random lady some 40 years his senior – hand-selected from among Yates's ever-present dregs.

This is unbelievable; there must be laws against this. Someone … do something … call the police, the RSPCA … anything … please. These people are *not* for snogging.

He doesn't just do the bare minimum to win the bet, either. He takes his ten pound of flesh from the situation. They're at it for a good two minutes, rolling their booze-marinated tongues around each other's mouths while hands go wandering tentatively in all the traditionally taboo areas. I could go all *Mills & Boon,* but I fear that you'd vomit over your book and have to buy a replacement. Hmmm, not such a bad idea, commercially. Maximise profits by inducing vomit and repeat purchases. OK, so…

… his hands fumble rampantly, with wanton urgency over each roll of her sumptuous flab, as she in turn cups his backside with her sun-damaged, spindly old hands and chipped two-week-old nail varnish – occasionally wincing with clenches of lust when his tongue forages deeper and deeper into her mouth and towards her very soul … the chorus to Come On Eileen *wafts over the pub speakers, not that either of them are aware of anything other than their desire for each other. "Come on, Eileen, da do dar ray…" whispers Tidy as his thronging shaft fills with love blood…*

… sorry, have to stop there; worrying things are happening in my gut.

"I feel a bit bilious," agrees Nick Logan, who's suddenly gone off his beer for the first time since 1993.

"It was all right actually," shouts Tidy victoriously, now retrieved from the clutches of the Steradent Queen.

Oh, Tidy. Tidy, Tidy, Tidy. It was horrendously awful, it truly was … but football culture can't survive without people like you making it something to talk about for years to come. I think, despite the current revulsion, we'll be friends, me and Tidy.

I decide, however, to withhold payment of the £20. For now. I don't feel as though morally this act deserves immediate reward, lest something in his brain begins to consider what he did is OK. And it definitely is *not* OK. It's therefore my societal duty to leave the payment for a month or two (which also happens to suit my wallet just fine), in order that the semantic link in Tidy's mind – between snogging old ladies and monetary reward – is well and truly broken.

There's a kind of shell-shocked hush, an embarrassed silence, as we walk through town towards Kenilworth Road. Apart from Tidy, who really would prefer to have his £20 now. Right now.

* * * * *

Incidents such as denture-gate above are testament to how settled I've become at Brentford. Being here is a way of life now, I can't imagine it any different – it's almost as though I've forgotten about the whole Gloryhunter thing, because the team doesn't look anywhere near losing and even old Giggling Gertrude at the travel tavern has started cracking the odd pained smile at me. It's been an amazing few weeks of social growth amid weird situations, and the games have just been flying by.

BRENTFORD 2-1 DAGENHAM AND REDBRIDGE
Elder 23   Saunders 50
MacDonald 34
Attendance 4,519

WYCOMBE WANDERERS 0-0 BRENTFORD
Attendance 5,799

BRENTFORD 1-1 LINCOLN CITY
Elder 24   Patulea 30
Attendance 4,557

CHESTERFIELD 0-1 BRENTFORD
                 Bean 7
Attendance 3,188

BRENTFORD 1-0 MACCLESFIELD TOWN
MacDonald 15
Attendance 4,773

* * * * *

Wycombe ... 27 miles away.
It's the ankles that go first. Then a thing round the back of the knee that I didn't know I had. Whatever it is, it's now like a dislodged, stretched old fan belt. And then the brain goes – not that it was especially there in first place – on around 22 miles; it starts making me talk about Bourbon biscuits and the hits of Genesis. Top Cat (if you'll remember, one of my fellow Swebee adventurers), who has this natural propensity to laugh just a little bit too hard at only moderately funny things, walks with legs so bowed they may be medically considered boomerangs. And on around 23 miles the laugh slowly evolves into a psychotic sob-chuckle. How he'll finish these 27 miles from Braemar Road to Adams Park – walking like he's hovering over a long-drop toilet – I'll never know.

With the constant pressure on me to deliver interesting and varied content for the webshow, I haven't been able to just sit in cafés and pubs, hanging around lampposts theorising like a long-bearded sociologist. I've been creating some ridiculous ways of immersing myself into (not literally) the people of Brentford, and walking to Wycombe (continuing the Brentford fans' recent fad of walking inordinately long distances to games in order to raise cash for the club) is one way I can force a few fans to spend quite some hours with me without being able to walk off. Because we're already walking off. One of the Brentford fans, Perry, said to me the other day of my silly endeavours, that through them I'm bringing some people together who've only previous met on the GPG or seen each other as nameless faces on the other side of the pub. I'm creating a little focal point away from the football that's actually pulling some fans closer. That's a satisfying world away from the silent observer I'd originally planned to be.

When we leave from the club at five in the morning, it's still dark; the sort of dark that belongs to the clinking milkmen and the cats patrolling their territory with distant yelps and ominous meows aimed at sparrows. There's a slight bite in the air that sparks all those conversational quips along the lines of, 'can we go back to bed'. Along the way, I get talking more to Top Cat (real name Tim). During one of our philosophical silences (or a gap where we can't think of anything to say), I consider how weird it is to call a grown man 'Top Cat', and decide to use Tim from now on. For a nearly 50-year-old beer drinker, Tim is surprisingly rakish and frail, a sensitive single soul who's taking an unusually late gap year from work. For now, he does what he likes and goes where he likes, which is why it's surprising he's bothering to sling his awkward and by no means pain-free boomerangs on this particular bout of nonsense. But the club is his lifeblood; he lives nearby and most of his social interaction surrounds the matches and the bits before and after. One of the other guys, Chris, is the same. A dedicated supporter, he's just got off a flight from Spain without any sleep, straight to us for the walk. He looks like someone's just shovelled him up and then cracked him one with the spade. Around 16 miles in, he foolishly reveals on camera that his groinal erogenous zone has started to bleed. *Actually bleed.* I secretly wonder whether this is really due to walk-based chafing, or whether in fact his holiday to Spain was more vigorous than he's letting on. I don't ask.

These people breathe football, more than I ever have, and I can't help but admire them.

We traipse through the darkness of Southall and Uxbridge, and it's like an untidy version of *28 Days Later* or *Shaun of the Dead* – in any case, long after the crux of the apocalypse has passed. Desolate and dirty with identikit rows of grubby moribund shops; even the local stores have the same homogenised signs sponsored by the likely candidates. It's like their souls have been ripped out and fed to Coca Cola. Nothing about it makes me think *Yes, I could settle here.* There are old grey roundabouts that they've actually bothered to name and the same graffiti tags reappear on underpasses and fences … even graffiti has been levelled out into some sort of chain vandalism; I can guarantee that after reading this, you'll notice the name 'Tox' tagged all over London – one of the serial taggers trying to brand the entire capital. Closer to Wycombe, I stop to photograph what could be considered a symbol of twenty-first century England: a shopping trolley in a ditch. While humming the national anthem I think about how torn I am at the moment – between the ground-in cynicism that tempts me to seek out negative evidence like this, to confirm to myself that England is on its deathbed, and the fresh, more positive evidence: hope, gathered from my experiences among the warm and supportive football communities. I just don't know which voice to listen to.

Hold on … I'm hearing voices? Uh-oh.

Adams Park is one of those new grounds set amid tranquil hills on one side and an end-of-the-world industrial estate on the other. As we limp and moan like extras from *Thriller*, past the infamous strippers pub on the main road (resisting the temptation), down through the corridor of identical industrial units and into the stadium, a standing ovation rings around the packed away end. *We did it. Oh the glory.* I lap up the applause while wandering along filming the crowd … *it's rapturous, it's rousing, my toes are humming but my heart is singing above them…*

"You can't film here…" That is until a steward stops me and does the usual overly-parental routine. I produce the necessary press pass, which seems to hurt his ego a little; I think he wanted to be right. He grabs at my arm and says,

"Well, you can't stand here," determined to get me somehow.

"Why?" I ask, careful not to display any signs of annoyance. I'm tired, bristly and probably a little taken with my own heroism. But I don't want to play into his hands.

"BECAUSE I SAID SO," he shouts, a bit of spittle hooking onto my eyelid with a brief dangle, his face as close as you can be to another without committing to some sort of kiss. I can't help but laugh at this great puffing clown, so pathetic is his desperation to feed the ego with this outrageously aggressive pulling of power. This is what I'm having to get used to; what football fans all over the country are being subjected to every week these days.

Stewards are becoming a real problem, for all of us. It's not so much what they're asking us to do, although that in itself is often ludicrous; it's the manner in which they do it. I've worked out that the worst ones are those from agencies, who don't understand the temperature of a situation, or the extent to which a football crowd can police itself without needing them to come wading in and make it much worse. The ones who are fans of the club itself, who are there every week and know when a situation really needs attention, are usually better. But even then, like this moron trying to transfuse his spit into my bloodstream, you get the ones who only do the job to fulfil a desire for power that they've probably failed to acquire in the real world. They make my blood boil, they're a disgrace; I'm panting with rage even as I type. Many of them will complain that they've been given directives from beyond the club and much higher, and that the rules regarding the policing of a crowd are a whole different debate – the constantly being forced to sit down and the ejections for incredibly minor offenders are all part of it – but with all of that *and* some of them harbouring ravenous egos, it's getting out of control. And here he is in front of me, a tremblingly, bitter, wrinkled up f**cking failure, a bullied-at-school tit who's decided he wants *me* to pay for all of his own under-achievements.

I think I should say at this point, that there *are* good stewards – and to you I apologise for my generality and sympathise that you have to work with these prats. I also acknowledge that football fans can often be a horrendous, drunk handful and perhaps that's why the behaviour of some stewards gets calibrated on the aggressive side. But for the well-behaved decent ones like me, the heavy-handedness is an insult to our entrance fee. You wouldn't pay £40 to go to the opera and expect to be talked to like something off someone's shoe. Is a football fan's money worth any less?

Anyway, spitty here really doesn't like me laughing at him, with threats being thrown in the air and the walkie-talkie of power being clutched close to his face as one of them. So I limp up into the stand making sure I laugh even more on the way, despite the back of my knee making me want to collapse into a heap and signal with Ronaldo-esque drama for the physio.

The game plays out to a goalless draw, while the walkers sit dozily in the stand trying to understand what our legs are saying.

* * * * *

I wake up with a body filled with concrete, layered on a ballast of knackeredness. Someone *must* have beaten me up in my sleep, repeatedly, until every sinew has been pulped and I'm just a breathing bag of offal with advanced rigor mortis.

That walk has decimated me. If I was in a *Monty Python* parrot-type sketch, they'd be saying that this Gloryhunter is no more, that I've ceased to be, gone to meet my glorymaker.

Surely just walking alone can't do this to a human body. I try to get out of bed and just sort of clank onto the floor like a bag of leftovers from a self-assembly IKEA nightmare. I feel my age, and somebody else's added on. I wonder whether Tim has even made it through the night.

I need help.

I found out the other day that Brentford's resident physiotherapist is a guy called Dave Appanah. The name immediately clunked a Big Ben-sized bell in my memory and I realised that this must be the same Dave Appanah who played for the same ramshackle Sunday league team of generally hungover carcasses as me at least ten years ago. I remember that Dave was training to be a physio at the time; it must be him. And so with my legs in such disarray that I can't even bring myself to look at the snidey things, and most other muscles shrunk back to around a third of their normal size, I know I just have to go and find my old friend for some help in somehow re-lengthening my constituent parts...

* * * * *

Brentford's training ground isn't so far away, in Osterley: proud home of the stunning A4. The players' muddy car park is rammed with Fiat Pandas and battered Vauxhall efforts. Such is the vehicular morbidity around me that it feels as though I've turned up at a Lithuanian car auction circa 1978, and the Glorywagon – itself a humble Nissan Almera – makes me feel like I've driven here straight from an episode of *Pimp My Ride* in a disgustingly lavish, blinged up dream machine. I don't know what these players earn, but the car display is poor.

I approach the pavilion, and following my ride being comparatively pimped, I now confidently don one of those fake limps that rappers affect. I find myself in front of something that looks just like the sports ground changing rooms I remember for cold P.E. showers and the clattering of football studs on cold stone floor, perpetually ringing around the walls, even when empty. It's the type of place where the wafting smell of deep heat triggers anticipation for the battle; a growl that courses through your veins as soon as the sound of shinpad Velcro rips open, the moment you've wrestled your favourite shirt off the other bloke who also fancies himself as a number eight. There's always a single tap dripping, bits of shredded tape, broken off ankle straps, empty Lucozade bottles and always a lone pair of forgotten or abandoned Y-fronts. Relics from the wars. Relative treasures. I immediately miss my playing days: now that was *real* football, and these hubs of true soccerites are the reason why them lot of prancers up there are known as The Premiersh*te.

Hanging around, possibly lurking, outside the pavilion are some Brentford-scarved strays; one bloke who says he comes straight down every day after his night shift, another who just pops down occasionally (although I suspect that's an under-statement) and another who looks like he's not even sure he's here. The players are training miles away in the distance; specks of men with the occasional distant bark of manager Andy Scott. I'm just not sure what these blokes get from coming here. Just to be a part of it all? It seems really quite sad. And then I realise that I'm here too. A bit freaked that I might be turning into one of this lot, I quickly check:

- Face, for wispy tash. Check – no wispy tash.
- Teeth, for an unfeasible caking of tartar. Check – no caked tartar.
- Jacked-up trousers with white socks. Check – not present.

I conclude the geek-threat alert is currently at a low level. Although I do have a kagool in my bag.

Inside the pavilion, I find a rummaging Dave Carter, the kit manager who's alone, trying to make some sense out of the fallout from the pre-training melee, while checking his courgettes. Dave also doubles up as the canteen chef, so as well as washing dirty pants, he also single-handedly makes all the players' dinners. He's a gruff, hard sort of a bloke and one of the least likely candidates to happen upon toiling over a giant lasagne in the kitchen. He clearly loves the club, and looks after the boys well, but speaks out of the corner of his mouth about how footballers can be self-centred and mercenary. Well there's a shocker. He also warns me about the Luton lot, who, he claims, behaved appallingly when they won promotion down at Griffin Park. Luton are currently handcuffed to the very bottom of the entire foot-ball league; I can't see me ending up with that lot anyway.

Dave points out a caravan-thing just to the side of the pavilion – it's the phys-iotherapy caravan-thing where Mr Appanah operates. It doesn't look like the cutting edge of sports science is being practised in there, unless old man Steptoe recently qualified. Before heading over, I'm suddenly caught in a torrent of foot-ballers; they've finished morning training and appear all around me, chirping and ribbing and swearing and mock fighting. A few of them nod and wink and say hello;

I don't know if they've seen what I've been doing and I sort of hope not. For some reason I don't want them to think for a second I'd be a football sycophant, a hanger on, gawping in awe at their mere presence. It's probably my own pathetic ego rearing up in defence at me not being able to make it to where they are; my jealously not wanting to concede to them the upper hand. I tell myself off for being such a tit. But with egos aplenty and ruthless competition for places in the team, the lasagne-flavoured canteen is pumped with testosterone, it honks of maleness. I think about how the politics of their social pecking order must be a bloody minefield.

These are men who are worshipped by other men three times their age (something I've always been a little bit uncomfortable with), men who've been unwittingly dictating my course for the last two months. With the power they seem to hold, somehow you build them up in your mind as proper grown-ups, responsible professionals who take everything very seriously. But really, they're none of that. They're not necessarily the opposite, but what I mean is that *they're just kids*. All of them are younger than *me*. Here in the canteen, they look smaller and younger than their manners on the pitch suggest. Nathan Elder plays darts against John Halls as a gaggle of them stand around watching, jeering, probably constantly re-jigging their mental pecking orders in accordance to little digs and minor personal victories. One of the others sits quietly reading *Nuts* magazine like the lonely kid at wet-playtime, as Charlie MacDonald, an older head, analyses the fitness routine they're doing this afternoon, maybe wondering if he'll get through it … I think about how these young lads carry such great expectation (and the destiny of a Gloryhunter) on their backs. Most of them these days won't have any history of supporting Brentford and suddenly, this club's heritage, pride, reputation and future – the hopes and fears of supporters who've been following the club all their lives – are resting precariously on their young shoulders. It seems an awful lot for them to bear, but from what I can see, there's no outwardly obvious evidence of the pressures upon them. Perhaps they learn early on to cope with it – as I did when sitting in a gallery messing up a live TV show – as we all do in our relative callings. Or maybe they go home and sob their little guts out into pillows every night, releasing all the tensions that are covered up all day by machismo and bravado.

I wander over to Dave's den of physiotherapy, a hospital-scented cabin full of charts and whiteboards with notes about people's knees, and the tables where all the healing magic happens. And there he is. Ten years later, he doesn't look any different. I think his family's from Mauritius, and his dark tanned skin looks no wrinklier than I remember. He's still a slight fellow, was always a quick footballer, and has an unassuming manner that puts you immediately at ease. I expect he's thinking exactly all the opposites of me – fatter, older, balder and generally more obnoxious. Anyhow, we choose an unemotional but enthusiastic reunion; it's really good to see Dave again and reminisce about all my glaring misses from point-blank range.

He sets about getting his thumbs into my broken body and tries to loosen it up into something that can bend again. I feel like a slab of Kobe beef. While he's at it, I try to get a bit of an insight into the lesser spoken-of world of the club physio – via the obvious questions that are too irresistible not to ask.

"What's the worst injury you've ever seen?" Now that, folks, is quality journalism. No sensationalism here. But Dave doesn't seem to mind.

"When I was at Orient," – which is how he ended up here, following Andy Scott across London from the O's – "one of the goalkeepers went up in the air for the ball, got hit by one of our defenders, flipped over and landed on his head." He tries to express the horror with his hands, which doesn't quite suffice. "Slap bang on his head; his whole body then jackknifed over his neck." Sounds like the time Nan tripped over the dog. "He ended up unconscious. I got to him and all his mouth was foaming, but he came round in the end was fine." You can catch rabies from falling over now?

"Do you get any players coming in here faking it?" Come on, don't tell me you wouldn't like to ask the same thing…?

"I wouldn't say faking it as such," he starts, with predictable diplomacy. "Everybody is slightly different with their pain perceptions. You'll get one guy who'll come in with a knock and soldier on; and another guy who'll come in and it's the end of the world. I'm not naming names; it's more than my job's worth." Doh.

"What's your favourite injury?" Don't these questions just get better and better?

"My favourite is no injury at all, but ankles are quite nice. I like knees as well. With footballers you get more or less the same problems."

I can't help but think there *must* be something in a physio that gets a tiny bit moist when a big juicy cruciate ligament comes in, or a nice bleedy head wound.

"What's the weirdest? Has someone done an earlobe or something?" I ask, hoping for something way too gruesome and perverted to print here.

"You get a few strange finger ones that you can't really tell people how they did it." Fingers. The mind boggles. Really it does. Fingers?

"You've got the neck of a 70-year-old," he finally concludes having played with most of my muscles like frozen Plasticine. "Try and move that for me now, mate," he asks, after utterly raping my neck. *Clunk*, it goes, like a ballsed up old lawn mower. "You've made it worse!" I jokingly exclaim, although secretly, not joking at all. Dave doesn't fix me. To be fair, he had as much chance of conditioning my anomaly of medical science back to working order as some of those players' cars outside have of passing an MOT. I hobble and creak back to the travel tavern, not bothering to explain my crab-like movements to smiler on reception, hoping she'll think I've been off starring in a porn film.

* * * * *

"Yes, it's true, I did defecate on a public highway..." admits Smiffy with a curious half-smile that gives him a sinister edge, as we stand in the shadeless away end at Chesterfield, being lightly tickled by an autumn sun that glares harder than it singes. From the outside, Saltergate, set among a quiet housing area that looks out to an expanse of picturesque green hills, is a bit like a foreign legion outpost that should be in the desert, with its big towering sand-coloured walls with momentous cracks running from top to bottom. Inside, we all try not to look at the teenage cheer-leaders, in fear of ill-gained reputations.

"...but no-one saw," continues Smiffy, with an addendum that I think is sup-posed to somehow morally validate his dirty protest in the streets of Sheffield.

I was invited by a few fans – Smiffy, Jonesy, Stu, Perry and Jacob – to come up north a day early; not so much to poo all over the streets of Sheffield, but to perpe-trate a night out of Tony Adams proportions. In the car, I'm barraged (and in truth dish out a fair share of such barrage) by a beery festival of West-Londonified cock-neyisms that Jacob has lifted directly from every football gangster movie ever made. Raucous dance music plays alongside the banter, swearing and swollen promises about tonight's drinking performance. They also seem to be into brutally cracking each other on the top of the head with really clenched fists every so often, along with boys-only humour about dead mums and the like that I left at school. Welcome to a Brentford away-day.

Because I'm an absolute clothing disaster, they decide to do me up like a boy band member (the ugly one, on the third reunion gig, twenty years later, down Walthamstow Assembly Hall), hair spiked into unfeasible angles and a skinny black tie. But I don't last all that long in my suspiciously school uniform type garb before tequila provokes the homing mechanism to kick in – that moment which arrives at the apex of drunkenness, whereby all senses are missing other than the innate ability to find your hotel room among the ruthless scrabble of a big city. It seems Smiffy did the same, except he was caught short – which considering the size of the man must have been *very* short – and ended up using his Calvins to wipe, then laying them on top of the dung like an undergarment wreath, in honour of the meal which created it.

Even above Marcus Bean's early winner – which is greeted by the smattering of Brentford fans more like a boundary at the cricket than a promotion-chasing goal – none of us can still quite get over the fact that Smiffy would admit on camera to such an atrocity, such a dire breach of public decency. Are we going to have to start taking a pooper scooper to games now?

"Some of the Brentford fans do let the side down," he goes on to claim with bracing gall, and not in reference to himself in the least. "They're ugly, scruffy and thick." Pots and kettles, all black. But then from Smiffy I've come to expect that sort of mysterious subversive statement, designed to cause outrage or offence for his own amusement.

Later on, after we've got back to London and my curry is recently ingested, I settle down to *Antiques Roadshow*, and my phone beeps.

> ☒ TEXT MESSAGE
> FROM: SMIFFY BRENTFORD
> Can you use your show to help
> me find a girlfriend?

With such gruesome revelations still fresh, it's no surprise that after Smiffy sent me that text on the way home, and I put an appeal out on the webshow ... we had no takers. Not a single desperate fatty or shameless self-publicist emerged for this man's waxed torso (it also emerged that Smiffy regularly has full-body waxes, because he's no less hairy than a mountain gorilla). Who'd have thought it – not a single faeces-and-hairy-back fetishist among all those thousands of Brentford regulars.

So I schemed up a plan, which as most have come to learn by now, is ominous. *Half-time speed-dating*. Ta da! As if the home game against Macclesfield Town couldn't be any more exciting, we'll also have a mini crescendo of the little monkey boy running around terrorising female patrons at the break.

Before we start though, I get to asking Smiffy about his previous romantic escapades.

"Four years ago. It was a very messy break up," he reflects, with a moment of genuine feeling. Although I paint him as this surreal hairy midget, there's something very giving about Smiffy. He runs the supporters' football team at great expense to his time and takes a hefty whack of mickey-taking and stick in the process. As I get this little glimpse into his reality, I also see that all this strangeness and subversion is his little way of subtly taking the mickey himself, a sort of lofty humour that he enjoys exclusively from his own perch. I think behind that facade, he's a caring bloke and beyond this silly dating thing – essentially designed to have a laugh at his feeble chat-up attempts – I think he deserves to find someone.

Then he goes and ruins my burgeoning goodwill by saying, "I like to be hit by women, I might as well say that up front," followed by an impish grin that's around 36 years younger than him, dominated by a protruding bottom lip, goofy kind of teeth and a toddlerish gawp that's incongruously framed by an overhanging axe-murderer brow that could easily have been transplanted from Lou Ferrigno. That's the walking juxtaposition that is Smiffy.

He's not exactly gone to town on the style side of things; a bobbly bogey-green fleece that says 'Petroleum' on the front and, ironically, oily dirty-blonde hair that's been allowed to form a spiky mistake. Maybe that's why the first candidate/victim he nervously approaches – Nicky, an attractive girl with tight ringleted blonde poodle-ish hair who's queuing up for a pie – claims to have a boyfriend, which I'm not totally convinced isn't a polite way of saying *not on your nelly, chimp boy*.

"It's a *little* no," she says quietly, nose wrinkled into a cute wince that she hopes will soften the blow. However, he gets a compassionate hug out of it (from her) and seems thrilled with the brief moment of physical contact. Buoyed by not being slapped and reported to the police, we wander around the forecourt, Smiffy still emanating a nervous hesitance that's probably to be expected of someone charged with smoothly wooing a lady on camera and risking having the mother of smackdowns recorded for all to see.

The next girls he approaches are way too young. Embarrassingly young. Pay them a pound to wash the car – yes; ask them out on a date – borderline illegal. I extract him from that scenario before it becomes beyond wrong and we head over to a face he recognises, one of the girls who works behind the bar at The Griffin, Fraulein. Fraulein? That's a title, not a name, no? No. That's her name. Fraulein.

"How are you doing?" says Smiffy with all the formality of a trip to the embassy. "Are you enjoying your Bovril?" Oh yeah Smiffy, you smooth old sod; the stuff of Jackie Collins, worthy of Casanova, James Bond, Steve Jones. How could she resist opening patter like that? Fraulein giggles reluctantly into her steaming watery beef beverage – *not* a euphemism – half trying to cover her face with the paper cup to avoid the embarrassment. My toes curl themselves into a toe-ball; there's no two ways about it, this whole thing feels dreadfully awkward.

"One of the last girls I went out with had chronic bad breath," he confides clumsily. I'm not sure that Fraulein's Bovril is exactly going to lace her oral output with roses, but he soldiers on regardless.

"I'm looking for a girlfriend, would you know of anyone that might be able to fit that description?" he trudges on, mystifyingly drawing an imaginary box in the air with his fingers. Fraulein keeps the paper cup firmly at her lips; allowing strands of blonde hair to cover her face. Did I mention that this is just a little awkward? I have to jump in. We need to get to the point before the whole situation grows mould.

"How about you Fraulein, would you go on a date with Smiffy?" Her big brown eyes bulge incredulously at the idea. Then she pauses, thinks about it and among subsequent giggles and red cheeks, says: "He's sweet, yeah. I'd have a drink wid him," coyly, in her English/Irish crossbred accent. We cheer. He's sweet! He's in!

"That's made me quite excited," confirms Smiffy slyly with a grin the width of Neil Ruddock. With his arm around her, mainly to keep her standing amid the laughing fit she's embarked upon, he kisses her cheek and gives a thumbs up to the camera, which seems more like he's just caught a prize cod on a fishing trip than secured a date with a nice lady.

Then, for reasons better known to himself, he licks the lens of my camera.

The game passes with a one-nil win for Brentford ... but yeah yeah, whatever, that's just what seems to happen most weeks at the moment; it never even crossed my mind that I'd be leaving tomorrow. So, I escort Smiffy through the waves of happy fans marching away from the ground in their glow of glory, around to The Royal Oak for his partially televised date with Fraulein.

"It could go either way, it's a game of two halves," he romantically muses on the short walk to the corner pub.

20 minutes later.

"There's no-one in the garden," Smiffy confirms morbidly.

"You've looked all over the pub; she's not here is she?" I add coaxingly, secretly hoping he'll cry on camera. Come on, I'm a TV producer, I'm scum and I want tears.

"No. No she's not. I've searched everywhere. I'll just wait by the women's toilets for a bit." *No you won't.* I rule that pervy plot out straight away and drag him to the bar for a sharpener. Even if she is in there, she won't want him loitering outside the door, getting glimpses of whatever magic goes on in the ladies toilets. But she's not in there anyway. She hasn't turned up.

"Like a dying octopus, laid out on the beach, wanting to get back in the sea," he reflects oddly into his beer, face collapsed into the very definition of *stood up.* Even when sat in the stinking pit of filthy misery, Smiffy can manage to be weird.

Smiffy and Fraulein: it's over. Official.

* * * * *

"*Andy Andy Scott, Andy Scott, Andy Andy Scott... na na na na na na na na na...*" sings Tidy, to the tune of KC and the Sunshine Band's *Give It Up.* Constantly. For 120 minutes. In fact the only time he stops is when the steward helps him off the ground because he's so drunk that he decides to lie down on it for ten minutes. This Johnstone's Paint Trophy really is getting its pound of my flesh.

At 2-0, Brentford are cruising into the next round and I do my interview with the Star Sports Asia crew with only half an eye on the game, which now seems a formality.

"In the 90s, I was actually part of a pop band called Take That," I tell them, in a childish plot to get as many untruths into the interview as possible. It's more interesting than *how I grew up in Walthamstow ... blah blah blah...*

"I actually single-handedly freed Nelson Mandela."

Luton pull one back; it's 2-1.

"I once stabbed TV personality Bruce Forsyth in the face."

Luton equalise. 2-2. Extra-time.

"I used to be the heavyweight boxing champion of the World."

End of extra-time. Penalties.

Hats off to Luton, if you'll pardon the pun (their nickname being 'the Hatters'); they've fought back from two-nil down to take the tie to extra-time and now the catch-ability of the last train home is threatened by penalties. Maybe it's the drink, but even now I don't consider the possibility of leaving Brentford a real one. It's been two and a half months. Almost a quarter of a year; it's like Brentford is where I live now.

But it *does* happen.

Luton win on penalties.

"I wouldn't wish this on my worst enemy," says Luke, six times.

LUTON TOWN 2-2 BRENTFORD
Hall 39   Poole 18
Martin 55   Williams 37
Luton win 4-3 on penalties
Attendance 2,029

A roar explodes in the other end of the ground like a distant thunder clap as the PA starts echoing with victory rhetoric for the Hatters. I'm now a Luton fan. I support Luton. I smile briefly at the irony surrounding the name 'Gloryhunter' and my being at the very *very* bottom of the English Football League, before looking across to the home crowd, my new fellow fans; a daunting mob, pointing and singing angrily. *This is going to be interesting,* I think.

I say my quivery goodbyes, handshakes and hugs, and with a pallid, shell-shocked face, I stay in the away end as I did at Griffin Park when the Grimsby lot trudged out dejectedly, eeking out my last moments as a Bee; thinking about my last two and a half months.

I think about that walk down Braemar Road to the ground, the smell of burgers and onions and pies interweaving with that tangible air of excitement. That's what this project is all about, the football experience, mainly before and after. People have a different walk in the streets surrounding the ground – it's springier, it has relish; they're on their way to somewhere they *really* want to be. It's not a lunchtime amble down the road to get a Boots meal deal, it's a skippy stride – perhaps one or two pints influenced – that's taking them to 90 minutes of sheer escape. When you join a football crowd, you leave yourself at the turnstile; you're part of the mass now, a mere soldier among many. Although that's not entirely true for me, however. I've briefly been a 'face' here. I think of sultry evening drinks, The Griffin garden in twilight with laughs and singing – the distant sound of '*One Gloryhunter*' coming towards us from the other end of Braemar road – and curries that I only know I've had because of the stains I discover on my shirt in the morning.

I watch my new mates and those memories filter down the stairs and out of my life. I'll miss them. Luke, Smiffy, Perry, Top Cat Tim, Logan and Tidy ... gone.

Alone again.

7.

Good Morning Britain

WEDNESDAY, 8 OCTOBER 2008.
The tiniest, icklest hotel room in the world, Luton.

The guitar-twangy *Hollyoaks* theme music pounds out of the left-on-telly and rudely jars me into something approximate to consciousness. On the screen, Mandy is flirting with me, again, the same way she does every Sunday. Slut. An internal search party discovers most of my wrecked body twisted to a malformed foetal spasm, dry-mouthed and confused, with smeary blurs and flashes of sepia-toned memories featuring last night's transferral of allegiance, flickering away in my subconscious like someone else's rubbish home video. I squint around the room; the walls are closer than I'd like. Phone goes off; a text, someone telling me that as they walked away from the ground last night, after leaving me in there alone, Nick Logan had a little man-cry. Am I still asleep? My attention flits back to the walls, and then the ceiling; it's all way too near. *Back off, room.* Am I dead? *No,* I think, *you can't get texts or Hollyoaks or headaches the size of Angola when you're dead.* Or am I suddenly Gulliver, or on the set of *The Borrowers?* Because something in here, spatially, is totally up the pictures. I stand up and crack my already ruined bonce on a slanted ceiling that tapers down to Jimmy Krankie height near the window; a clever trick of perspective, a guaranteed head mistake.

Day one of the rest of my season. God, I'm confused.

After abusing caffeine to thrombosis proportions, I come to terms with my new coffin-style hotel room and the different brand of mini-soaps that come with it, and hook up to the internet. Time to do a bit of background research on Luton Town; time to get my hands dirty. A new day, a new dawn.

My Luton memories are mainly of their top flight years in the 80s; when Raddy Antic scored a late winner to keep them up and David Pleat danced a biologically implausible skippy jig across the pitch – an act that I suspect sparked the trend of emotionally cauterised managers in recent years, all of them too scared to emote, lest they tumble into Pleatsville. I've tried to recreate it, but as I said, it's impossible. I looked like a trifle. I remember Luton's disposal of Arsenal in the delicious last ten minutes of the 1988 League Cup final, when keeper Andy Dibble saved a pen and Brian Stein won it with the last kick of the game. It was a thing of beauty. I remember players like Steve Foster, Kingsley Black, the late David Preece, the Stein brothers and Mick Harford. I remember 1985, when they became one of the few clubs to take part in the bizarre plastic pitch experiment, and their ban on away supporters in the same year after Millwall fans rioted (along with, as it turned out, fans from a host of other clubs). It may well have warranted such extreme action, but during that time The Ken was plastic and partisan ... and a daunting visit for away sides.

But it's all gone wrong since then. Horribly wrong. Completely bottom of the Football League and 30 points deducted is about as wrong as it can get. And after a quick Google I get the immediate sense that the fans, as you might imagine, feel like the whole world is against them. Well, probably not Switzerland. But definitely, apparently, me and my Angolan headache.

RE: ITV GLORYHUNTER
Hatman
Your [sic] not welcome around ear [sic] pal.
Nutter
I hope he gets his f*cking head kicked in.

I know, I know, I know by now I should have learned to keep off the internet forums and leave these people to rant bile and fester in their own juices, but when it's about *you*, you can't help but want to make it right, however futile; it's like picking at a scab, squeezing a spot, Googling *Hollyoaks* actresses to find out if they're single: it's irresistible albeit ultimately pointless. It turns out that 'Nutter' is still upset at the ITV Digital collapse in 2002 that plunged many lower league teams into difficulties, because they'd budgeted for the money it would have brought in. I try to let him know that, as a football fan, I wasn't very pleased about that business either, that I'm not actually a proper employee of ITV and that I was nowhere near any of it. He doesn't care: 'I stand by what I said,' he writes defiantly. It seems once you've wished a head-kicking upon someone, there's no going back. You can't retract a head-kicking, oh no, the said head really must be kicked. Personally, I really don't want my head kicked in, for all sorts of practical reasons, including the pain and the blood. Plus, last night's sambuca has already kicked it in enough.

Is it going to be like this every time I change club? And what should I do – still just swan into the home end and start lunging my camera at people's faces, hoping not to unwittingly shove it in a potential head-kicker's direction? I'm not the bravest of men by any stretch – definitely in the Shaggy slice of the *Scooby Doo* Venn diagram – but surely these sorts of faceless threats would unnerve most? If only I was *actually* Gary Oldman, I'd one-liner them into submission. No matter who I speak to, they all encourage me to ignore, dismiss what's said on internet forums as the idle blither of people inflated, turned into keyboard superheroes by the almighty shield of internet anonymity. But they're not sat where I am; a man alone in a Rubik's Cube-sized room with way too many hours to think himself filthy – into epic daymares featuring head-kicking and beyond. In one of the daymares, I get raped, for crying out loud. And then at the end of a week's toiling over maybes, what-ifs and writing a will, I have to actually get out there among the stars of these forums and daymares and try to weld myself onto it all. Is this really what I want? Is this my outrageous, silly journey of thrills and spills, or is it plain suicidal?

WELCOME TO LUTON

It began as clump of scattered farmsteads near the Roman town of *Durocobrivis*, or Dunstable as we know it now, 32 miles north of London. Skip forward just a little bit and we have the M1 motorway and Luton Town FC, who are known as The Hatters because, guess what Sherlock, the town has a history of hat-making that began in the seventeenth century – although in more recent times, locals have been more likely to work at Vauxhall Motors than build a fancy bowler for a toff. At last count, 184,000 people live in Luton (although I didn't count them personally), and at birth, custard-throated 'Senza Una Donna' singer Paul Young was one of them.

For two days I try not to check back at the forum to see what the next angry wave of vitriolic slagging consists of, but still I find myself shakily pressing refresh to uncover the next instalment of how they'd prefer my demise to look and how I really should stay away. I seriously begin to wonder whether I should put a stop to this whole thing now and get a flight out of the country. I really do. I briefly check cheap flight websites and consider the idea of finishing the book with a blistering tirade from a beach anywhere else in the world. Maybe running off with ITV's money would elevate my status with 'Nutter'; perhaps I could get my head downgraded to just a slap. Who needs this load of balls, in the name of a game of football? Why put myself through it?

But before I get so far as visas and malaria tablets that make you go mental, more welcoming emails unexpectedly start to trickle in; notably from Gary Sweet, the Managing Director of the club and Liam Day, the chairman of the trust – pretty important people in the recent history of the club. I get emails from Jane Ledsom, a Hatters mad singer who's recently made a single to help raise funds for the club, and a bloke called Jeff who, importantly, is willing to nurse me through a game. In fact, eventually, I get an even warmer online welcome than the original light frost from some corners at Brentford.

I scale back my extrapolated fears, put the wild-west forums to one side and begin to employ some perspective, reasoning to myself that with the club in such crisis, there's bound to be the extreme tangents of high emotion spewing all over the place like scorching molten emotional lava. It's all pretty raw for them lot, and people deal with things in different ways; some want to lash out at (and kick the heads of) whoever's in front of them, while others grab onto any help, any positive they can get. They may well *all* think I'm a prat, but there may be some who, despite that, can see I could bring a little attention their way.

So with some positive thoughts in mind – that I could put a spotlight on Luton's point of view, give them a platform, however small – I set about finding exactly what's been going on and why everybody's so boilingly, stinkingly angry.

* * * * *

I wander onto the side of the pitch, in the light of day and without trace of a sambuca filter – instantly more awestruck than I have been all season by an utterly empty ground. How tragic I am. It creaks and groans like a proud old galleon that's seen wars and been twatted by cannonballs. There's no true stillness in here, it seems to breathe and occasionally gasp. A pigeon bothers around the rafters some-where. *Don't poo on me, ratwings.* A fat man in a suit clumps up the main stand stairs like an echoey final ascent to St. Peter's gate. This old place has seen some big matches, big players, good times and bad times since 1905, and the various renova-tions down the years have left it a hotchpotch of different ideas melded eccentrically together. Kenilworth Road is one of those places you'll love or hate, depending upon whether you prefer enormous characterless concrete beer forecourts and TV screens above each urinal telling you not to shag slags without rubber; or whether you can appreciate a sense of football history, revel in the weird and sometimes inexplicable imperfections of a crumbling old ground. Personally, I'll go for the latter. And *then* the slags.

I walk down the side of what used to be the Bobbers Stand, now an entire length of squat executive boxes that are quite possibly retirement bungalows trans-planted from Eastbourne – large-windowed for those with time to watch stuff – with a huge net installed above to prevent lower league inaccuracies losing too many balls. It shimmies peacefully in the breeze, seeming occasionally to bulge in practice. I walk round to the Oak Road end, where my favourite bit is the away fans' entrance that you enter from the street of squashed up terraced houses. There's lit-erally a gap between and under the crowded houses, and then it's a walk under people's bathrooms and bedrooms that bridge the staircase leading up into the stand. On the way out you can see directly into the windows – shower gels and the like on the sills, proclaiming to the people of a different town each week that this household enjoys Imperial Leather and Timotei as its shower-room combo. One has just a lone toilet roll. I would just love to hear the estate agent's patter on these gaffs; how could you possibly make a virtue of living in a flat that's dragged through the zoo-like ordeal of 2,000 people from various parts of the country staring into the windows once a week? I just can't understand how it came to be like this, like an over-the-top Dickens theatre set that's gone so far in attempting 'quaint', that its angles alone would render the houses virtually uninhabitable.

Like Brentford, here's a club slap in the middle of a community – from pub to terrace in minutes; although these days, Kenilworth Road is embedded deeply in an Asian area of Luton, and I'm not sure how far the club and the local community have come in coaxing its neighbours into the ground. Outside, Asian kids play what looks like the mother of all street football matches. A lawless ruck of grazed knees, almighty hollers of warmongering tackles on him from next door that'll result in not talking to each other for a week; a ball collides to snap the wing mirror off a Vauxhall Nova. It's lovely to see, I didn't think kids played football in the street anymore because of paedophiles and court cases over broken wing mirrors. I try to join in, the briefest of stabby toe punts, but am shouted back through the gate into the ground. Something about "you're f***ing s**t," they say.

I clack up the old wooden main stand and it makes me sound like a 50-stone carbohydrate monster after a bread binge; every footstep is so exaggerated, taken so seriously by the rickety boards, that I struggle not to take offence. Inside, there are tight rat run corridors in yellowed white gloss and oddly shaped rooms that branch off and smell of pensioners found dead at the library. For about half an hour I wander confusedly around the inner offices. With no-one at reception and the only indication of life being the distant squealing of opening and closing doors, I feel like I'm lost in a ghostly maze from sometime yesteryear. Eventually, I run into press officer John Buttle, buttling around, trying to get matchday organised seemingly in the aforementioned yesteryear. John's age is concealed in the fact that he came to his first game at the club in 1946. Press officers tend to be younger these days, and John, with his emails that read like formal telegrams sent to foreign dignitaries, gives the sense that Luton Town is a traditional sort of club. Club secretary Cherry Newbery has been here since 1978 (I don't mean constantly, I assume she goes home most nights). Again, older than you'd expect, though she isn't half as abrasive as she was on the phone the other day. I thought I'd accidentally called a dominatrix fetish line when she first got her acidic diphthongs all over me, but here in the flesh, she's still stern and no-nonsense, but as nice as (cherry) pie and in a matronly fashion arranges for me to get a replica shirt on the house.

Cherry's a very important player in the current situation with Luton Town. It was Cherry who feared for the club's well being when she discovered financial irregularities and decided to blow the whistle. She went to the FA and came clean, probably thinking that her honesty would limit the inevitable damage in the long run. A sensational series of stranger-than-fiction events, really, and a brave move on her part. She risked everything – her job, her reputation and respect among fans.

The outrageous tenure of former owner, property businessman John Gurney is where I'll pick up the bizarre story. Gurney took over in 2003 and immediately, controversially, cleared out the popular management team of Joe Kinnear and Mick Harford. Having already incurred the wrath of the fans, he then at one point asked them to vote for whom they wanted as manager on a premium rate phone line, which as you can imagine, wasn't particularly popular either. Gurney left the club in administration and financial tatters in 2004.

Former used car dealer Bill Tomlins then swept in and the club climbed into the Championship. However, after selling the best players, such as Steve Howard and Kevin Nicholls, and not bringing too many replacements in, they were relegated and managers Mike Newell – unhappy for a long list of reasons – and then Kevin Blackwell were casualties, before the fans turned on Tomlins, asking 'where's the money gone?' Well, £160,000 of it went to agents via the club's holding company, and badda bing, there's ten of this season's point deduction right there.

Under the cloud of the charges, out went old Bill and in came Luton fan and British Touring Car racer, David Pinkney. Shortly after he arrived, the club went into administration, again, despite a bid from fans' consortium Luton 2020 to buy it shortly beforehand. 2020's purchase would have avoided administration and the penalties it incurred, but Pinkney turned the offer down.

That's when Gary Sweet, Stephen Browne and former *Good Morning Britain* host Nick Owen – along with the help of many other fans of the club – came through and Luton 2020 finally got the club out of administration and under their control. But now they were carrying ten of Tomlin's deducted points, ten of Pinkney's and another ten for good luck that'll be explained shortly.

We sit in the director's box up in the empty stand, looking out to a freshly mowed pitch; a crow pecking whimsically at the centre spot as nonsensical test messages rattle the Tannoy. Nick Owen, sitting opposite me, cuts the perfect, caddish gentleman.

"Hello old boy," he offers with charming warmth. If 'Nigel Havers' were an adjective, I'd be inserting it here, in shouty italics. This is quite a nostalgic moment for me; I grew up with Nick and Anne Diamond, greeting me of a morning in the 80s on my beaten up ghosting black and white along with Roland Rat, Mad Lizzie, Ulrika Jonsson, Gordon Honeycombe and the rest of the gang on groundbreaking breakfast show *TVAM*. Before *TVAM* came along there weren't any programmes on telly as early as that – just a selection of wildly dull looped pages from teletext. Nick was definitely better then teletext, which is more than I can say for Andrew Castle on *GMTV*.

And here he is, sitting in front of me, now in his 60s. A retreated, worry-grey hairline is neatly where once that immaculate jet-black side-parting perched, and a slight jowl has submitted to the relentless drag of age and gravity. But he's definitely survived the ravages of time better than Anne Diamond; still with that friendly twinkle shining through the wrinkles, still speaking in the way that reached out of the screen at me; avuncular, conspiratorial, making you feel as though it's you and he versus the world. I conclude that it's scientifically impossible to dislike Nick Owen. Right now though, he's seething. But then, he even manages to seeth smoothly, like a *very* English Fonz.

"We've had a hell of a challenge to cope with, right from the start of the season," he starts slowly, quietly, calmly, with a serious edge; a careful performance that conveys peace and war all at once. "Everyone I speak to, fans across the country – and I meet loads of them – they are all appalled by what happened to us. All right, you expect some sort of sanction for our misdemeanors, which are not as bad, I don't think, as they've been painted. The severity of it is so hard to take." His eyes narrow into a loathing disbelief; the eyes of a victim.

I ask what exactly happened, and he explains that when you come out of administration, you need to get a Company Voluntary Arrangement (CVA) with creditors. It's a binding agreement concerning how a company's debts and liabilities will be dealt with, and it allows the directors to retain control of their company. Luton had their application for a CVA rejected – and that's what cost Luton the final ten points of their deducted thirty.

"It strikes me that it is impossible to get that these days. You'll never get one." His voice raises a smidgen, as the perceived injustice sinks its way around his bloodstream once again. "Therefore, how can you be expected to do anything other than fail to get one, and therefore get that penalty? The Football League have got to sort that out. Bear in mind that you get ten points deducted when you go into administration, so purely from that we had 20 points deducted. Then we had ten points from the Football Association for something that happened two years ago, and that was paying agents through a holding company of Luton Town, not Luton Town FC itself." This is where Tomlins, Newell, Cherry

Newbery et al came into it. "A technicality, involving only £160,000. Nothing illegal, no corruption, no bungs."

It's hard not to see their point. There are lots of football fans I've spoken to who think Luton Town got all they deserved, and to some extent I agree that football has to punish clubs who've lived beyond their means and ended up in administration. While they were winning games and promotions, other clubs who played by the rules will almost certainly have been disadvantaged at some point. But I'm not sure all those people realise that the club is being punished for much more than just the administration and perhaps haven't considered whether the extent of those further sanctions are fair.

It must be so hard to swallow for the new owners, who are certainly living within their means but still taking the hit for the disastrous management before them.

"Well, it's harsh," Nick continues, "a very daunting challenge; persuading players to come here to play for a team that looks doomed. All the people who work for the club, what does it do to their morale? The fans: how unfair is it on them? And it's got nothing to do with them. The fans are obviously the lifeblood of the football club. Football is basically there for the benefit of the fans. So, we think it's harsh, very harsh. Lord Mawhinney [the Chairman of the Football League] said they imposed the 20 points on us to preserve the integrity of the Football League. Well, that's his way of looking at it, but I don't think it does. It has been suggested that it's demolished the integrity of the Football League."

Integrity? The competition has been so subsided by sanctions made for stuff occurring off the pitch that you get to a scenario where teams who deserve relegation will be staying up and teams who deserve promotion will be thwarted, and where's the competitive integrity in that? What sort of competition is it, when the best aren't the best and the worst aren't the worst? These points deductions – however deserved – if they continue to escalate, will totally strip the competition of balance. There has to be a more sensible way. 30 points isn't just a disadvantage, it's basically relegation without the guts to say 'you're relegated'. Pure torture. Of course Nick can't admit it, but in truth Luton don't really stand a chance; so why would Mawhinney want to put everyone through such a slow and painful death? If he really wanted to punish Luton Town so severely, why not do it while maintaining the equilibrium and integrity of the Football League that he apparently cherishes, by relegating them straight away? I'm not saying they deserve that, but at least the fans and the club could move on and start rebuilding on the straight and narrow immediately, instead of having to go through this farce of a season that serves only to relegate them in a prolonged state of humiliation and agony. That's what, in my opinion, makes this punishment so cruel. Do the fans of any football club deserve that?

"It's a very tough situation to cope with," rallies Nick, "but we are coping well. We've accepted it, stopped complaining about it and are just carrying on. The immediate aim is obviously survival. But when you start the season on minus 30, that is a daunting challenge. I think we'll do it because we have put together a pretty good team." Nick makes a good show of resilience, belief and hope, but I can just tell that deep down behind the showbiz iris-sparkle, he knows what's coming. And I get an even stronger sense of that when we get to talking about his history with the club, which he describes with a wistful fondness, as though reminiscing about someone who's slipped into a coma; alive but only in body.

"I've been coming to this ground for 50 years. 50 years ago last month was my first game. I sat over there in the main stand." He points across with a gooey romantic smile, rusty mental images probably rushing through his mind. "In the old days when I used to stand behind the goal, when we were in the fourth division in the mid 60s, I was very much part of it, if not leading it sometimes. Getting a song going and it spreading, that's a wonderful feeling." He starts singing a tune that sounds a bit like a flat *Addams Family* theme, followed by a little chant: "*We're gonna win division four.*" I somehow can't imagine cornflake lothario Nick Owen running things behind the goal, it just all feels like it'd look a bit Alan Partridge.

"Were you in the firm?" I ask, exploring this whole new side of Nick I didn't imagine ever existed.

"No," he confirms, grinning in a way that I don't quite know how to take. Is he grinning because the idea of him being a brawling runner with a firm of thugs is ridiculous, or is he grinning because he was a bit naughty but won't admit it? I try to envision him headbutting some mug and then holding his arms out wide, shouting 'Come on then you f***ing c**t,' but my brain simply refuses to play that mental movie and instead it shows him doing an airy Fred Astaire tap-dance, before can-celling the whole thought because it's got too weird.

"The passion gets worse with every passing week," he reflects, sinking deeper into flowery rhetoric. "I was passionate enough as a little boy of 10, now I'm 61 and it is agony at times. If we lose, it takes me until Sunday night to emerge. I try my best to keep spirits up but there's a big sort of cloud." He looks off around the ground, breathing it in, absorbing its presence. "I've been lucky enough to cover football all over Europe, hosted the World Cup for ITV in 1990. I've been to some magnificent stadiums. But, the buzz, the burst of adrenalin and the stomach churn you get just coming into Kenilworth Road far outweighs all that stuff. Even presenting a pro-gramme live in front of fifteen million people from Wembley, you get pretty keyed up doing that, but it doesn't compare with walking through the door here. It really doesn't. And it's so full of memories for me." That wistful smile returns as he retracts to a dramatic whisper. "This place is just full of charisma. It's heaven for me being in here, I just love walking in, I love everything about it. You can feel the old heart going, but if you're a real football fan, that's how it is. The only thing I'd change is I'd like to win every week." Amen.

* * * * *

"Thirty points, who gives a f*ck,
we're Luton Town and we're staying up."

"We'll never die, we'll never die,
we're Luton Town, we'll never die.
A hundred years of history,
a Luton fan I'm proud to be."

A mass of hands raised high, leaping up and down with disparate timing like a death-metal mosh pit, bunched in the corner of the main stand with voices ranging from celebration to accusation, non-stop for almost the entire half. When Darlington go into the lead and the fans in black and white below us wriggle in glory like an ant nest with a kettle of boiling water poured on top, the Luton fans sing louder, prouder, defiant and somehow, no matter how terrible the situation looks, tri-umphantly. At one point they take their shoes off and hold them in the air. A man who received a stray brick to the head at last week's away game proudly pushes forth his stitches to the camera. I meet Kev, a fan and member of the Trust, with a curious 1940s hairstyle and a 1980s Luton shirt, who says pretty much all the stuff Nick Owen did earlier on, but with all the frothy-spitty anger that Nick conveyed only implicitly.

"I hope every single one of them goes to prison," he shouts, pointing down the lens of the camera. "After what they've done to this club I hope that we hunt them down until the day they die." And amid the swaying, pushing, shoving and jumping, I lose track of whether he's talking about the previous owners of the club or the Football League, or whether he's just venting spleen on anybody who might be held accountable for anything.

One-all.

"F***ing yes! F***ing yes! F***ing yes!!!" screeches one of the fans, more breath than voice, bounding in childish vertical springs, clasping two mates in a headlock who in turn have others in headlocks. It's like the last goal ever scored; bodies tumble over the old wooden seats while others cling onto each other and whoever else is in reach like they're wearing Velcro skin. This is more than a cheer, this goal means more than that, it could be one more point closer to zero.

There's not a moment spent off of my tip-toes, an entire match of sharp intakes of breath, it's a spectacular display of loyalty and passion and community. All of my previous fears dissolve as I come to understand where they're coming from.

"We've been to war for this club, ain't we?" says a chirpy little round-faced bloke in a cap and a cab-driver's voice. "We're in a deep dark place, but I feel like our club's been reborn. You're seeing the beginning of life outside the Premiership, where it's all about community clubs going back to the community." And he's right, if those 30 points have done anything, it's summoned the sort of spirit among these fans that some clubs in the Premiership would love to be able to drum up week-in week-out. It's such a shame that the harnessing factor for that spirit is one of anger and resentment and pain.

No matter how much he disputes it, and he does, vehemently, Jeff looks like Minty out of *Eastenders*. Maybe he felt sorry for me, but the only way I was going to come into this stand was if I had a 'face' to vouch for me, and Jeff seems to be as respected a fan as any. As we walked in at the start of the game, a group of blokes passing us under the stand muttered, "Shall we hit him?" I think Jeff heard it too, but neither of us said anything.

"Absolutely dire," Jeff says of their predicament inside the ground, "but to be honest, we've just got to get on with it, there's no point in moaning anymore." Suddenly, his eyes flick to the next block. "That's the bloke." He points out one of the Luton fans in the stand.

So … that's him.

That's the guy who wanted my head kicked in. I thought I'd feel differently the first time I came face to face with one of my online tormentors; angry or scared or at least *something*. But I don't feel anything at all. He's probably mid-20s, baseball cap, jeans; a pretty normal looking football fan who doesn't look as though he's concealing a pickaxe behind his back. Jeff introduces me as that bloke from ITV. A look of embarrassed recognition passes across the bloke's face and settles into one of indifference.

"Oh, alright?" he says flatly and then looks away dismissively; carefully loading the whole action with unconvincing disgust.

"Are you going to kick my head in?" I ask with a conciliatory, slightly mocking grin, pulling his eyes back from the other side of the stand. Sod it, I might as well hit it between the eyes; confront him with the chance to unleash that same vitriol to my face.

"Nah." He turns away. And that's the end of that.

If only he knew. If only he knew what a few simple words from behind the cloak of internet anonymity can do. At half-time he surprisingly joins me and Jeff at the bar and while Jeff bundles into the beer queue, he sidles up to me.

"Don't take any notice of that stuff on the internet," he says quietly; neither a gesture of apology nor one of war. Not that I expected, desired or required either to close the case – I've already found enough among Jeff and the people I've met to convince me that I'm pleased to be here. Fair play to him though, for being man enough to say *something*, however tokenistic it may have been. Later on, he even does a quick interview on camera and all those amplified concerns that bounced around the travel tavern's tight walls disappear as quickly as they were conjured.

When Darlington score a winner in the very last minute, finally, Luton's brooding energy for the fight snaps off and puffs out into the rafters. The Darlo fans' taunts wash over them as heads either hang low or look to the sky, asking for divine inspiration for what more they can do to support their club.

"It's just another day being a Luton fan," resigns the taxi driver voice guy, with a smile of someone who knows he can't win.

"The world's against us," says a deflated Jeff. "We've just got to do all we can." He's not surprised though; he's seen it all with Luton Town.

In the boardroom, the only floaters this time are those pacing aimlessly around the room, trying somehow to walk off the disappointment. I find Nick perched on a table in the corner, already submerged in the cloud he says he may emerge from some time tomorrow night. I thank him and Gary Sweet – who'd offered help in finding digs and some work during my stay – for their kindness, and for a taste of the Luton experience. As I wish them all the best I feel guilty that they're left in this mire, and I'm flouncing off with my stupid novel format of whim and self indulgence. As I reluctantly leave Kenilworth Road, I feel like a proper scumbag Gloryhunter, and not proud of it.

"See you old boy," says Nick, minus some of the glow he had this morning.

LUTON TOWN 1-2 DARLINGTON

Gnakpa 31   Clarke 15
                             Blundell 90
Attendance 5,560

Back at the pub, we drink just as hard as if it had been a victory. It's all Luton fans can do, savour every moment the Football League has to offer. Jane Ledsom, the attractive dark-haired actress and singer tells me of her own internet issues and how she had to pull some teenage boys aside for posting incredibly lewd messages about her and their masturbatory practises. I talk to a lot of the fans, who are open and friendly and for what my transient words are worth, I try to offer support and express how genuinely disappointed I am not to stay. This is a special season for Luton fans, one that's generated an atmosphere I've never really experienced. Every game is a cup final, every point is a victory and despite the morbid prospects of survival, there's plenty to enjoy and gain heart from. 'Jane Ledsom and The Shouty Boys' – who really are just a bunch of very shouty lads picked from among the fans, and Jane – sing a slurry rendition of their song *Thirty Down to Zero* for my camera, and I leave them in the height of their drunken defiance, but still a way off zero.

I go and sit on my own in a takeaway curry place opposite Kenilworth Road, slurping down dhansak with a naan and thinking of all the things I could have done with the Luton fans. Jeff might just have been reluctantly persuaded to meet Minty from *Eastenders* for a Minty-off, I might have got Jane to sing a Gloryhunter theme tune, I'd have tried to have a shower in one of those bathrooms overlooking the away end entrance, or I might even have moved into one of the executive boxes/retirement homes on the Bobbers side for a week. But more than any of that, I would have loved to have been a part of this Luton crowd for a bit longer, to show everyone in football what they're going through and how admirably they're dealing with it.

I finish my curry and wander back up the darkness of Dunstable Road, passing flashing kebab shop signs and women in elegantly patterned saris – the football crowd long gone and the area reverted back to Asia. I stumble past shops that smell of incense and get a sweet paan, a wrapped up betel leaf full of spices to aid digestion. I could be in Mumbai; how lucky, I think, that we can experience so many cultures within minutes, within yards.

And to the shoebox hotel room, yet again wondering what awaits me, this time in the north-east.

8.

free the gloryhunter 1

WEDNESDAY, 15 OCTOBER 2008.
The Darlington Arena, Darlington.
Standing over former Premiership referee Jeff Winter, who's lying across some seats
in the press box, fast asleep...

I used to want to grab hold of his poxy little goatee beard and swing him around, wrestle him like a big fat crocodile until he sicked up anything he'd eaten in the last year and then make him eat it back up again on toast. Granary. It was that bad. I couldn't stand the smug look on his face; that self-satisfied relish when he gave a penalty; revelling resolutely in all the glorious attention: 'Look at me; I'm the star of the show!' I imagined him theatrically proclaiming with camp vowels.

Jeff bloody Winter.

We've all thought ill of referees at some point (maybe not as far as the bit about the sick, sorry about that), but *Jeff bloody Winter.* Second only, I thought, to Uriah Rennie, in the list of referees who appear to be as much about self-publicity and ego-promotion as they are devoted to officiating our precious game. Whether or not any of my angry, heat-of-the-moment cynical snap-judgments about Winter were ever in any way true, I don't know, but now in the empty Darlington Arena I have the bizarre task of trying to wake him up and perhaps finding out.

Look at him, lying there, breathing like a sea lion with a cold, basking across the padded seats of the press box in an old tracksuit that's either just baggy or piled up with loose flab.

"Are you alright mate?" I gently enquire. He stirs groggily, a bewildered debacle of a head pops up and the goatee beard bears itself full frontal at me; now grey-flecked and converged upon by cheek fat. Oh Jeff, Jeff, Jeff. What happened, Jeff?

"Times haven't been that easy since I lost the money being a referee," he admits with a sorrowful look and a north-east accent that's one of the more decipherable I've experienced so far, "so in between games I just tend to get me head down at one of the local clubs. Here or the Riverside, or Hartlepool; that's the coldest with the wind coming off the North Sea. But Darlington's probably the most comfortable. Look, the seats are quality." He prods at one of the spongy cushions that have left an imprint of faux leather grain on his temple. Not so smug now, Jeff. From refereeing his first Premiership game at the City Ground in Nottingham to his swansong in the 2004 FA Cup final and now to this: homeless and destitute, living off the kindness of local groundsmen.

Joking, of course. Another hilarious set-up for the Gloryhunter camera. Oh the fun. But when I came along to the Darlo stadium for the first time to meet him – and be interviewed on the radio station he's now presenting for – I didn't expect to be getting up to such high jinks with a man at whom I've shouted groundbreaking obscenities and whole new annexes of verbal evils that probably haven't even been logged as official swears yet.

WELCOME to darlington

Darlington, the gateway to the Tees Valley, has a population of just under 100,000, which means that around 3 per cent of them turn out to watch the Quakers.

The 'Quakers' nickname comes from the Quaker religious movement which hit town in the eighteenth century.

The town is known for its association with the railways, and a brick sculpture of a train by David March went up in 1997. It cost £760,000, which is astonishing, just for a lifesize brick train just off the A66 which, to be honest, is a bit rubbish.

Vic Reeves comes from Darlington. Fact.

The stadium sits prone to a gusty biting breeze that sweeps into its bowl a mixture of chill and rain-spit; gone are the late-summer beer-garden Saturdays. But the reception up here has been warm, as legend will have you believe is the norm for people of the north-east. And Jeff's radio show is just one of a heap of local press I've been doing in the first few days, including TV with Sky Sports News, Setanta and ITV Local. I've had to say the same old blurb over and over again and actually don't get even a teensy bit of bellygut nerves anymore. I go into *rabbit-rabbit* autopilot and just switch adjectives once in a while with the ease and arrogance of a fairground waltzer operator. I'm not exactly a natural, I doubt my performances have turned Steve Ryder into a quivering wreck of 'I just can't compete with this', but I think I just about get away with it as a novel 'and finally' oddity. The fans have been sending messages about the delights of the local area and I'm glad to be here. Darlo are another club with a chequered financial history whose fans *deserve* a bit of success, and this season is looking a bit alright for them so far – sitting in ninth, just outside the play-off zone with that healthy bubbling amalgam of hope and its steadying yang of history-weary cynicism.

I desperately don't *want* to like Jeff Winter, because that would make me feel guilty about the abuse I've dished out to him. But unfortunately he seems nice enough and I get a sudden jolting realisation that shouting myself raw at Jeff Winter from the anonymous comfort of a sea of fans back then was no different to that Luton bloke shoving online gunpowder enemas up me from his keyboard. For all my whining and self-piteous philosophising in Luton, it turns out that I'm guilty of the same crime. With that thought nagging at me like vindaloo diarrhoea, I try to find if my acidic assumptions were wrong; whether the picture of a self-important bighead people paint of Jeff Winter is mistaken.

What's he been doing since giving up reffing? Because until this week, I'd actually allowed any memory of him to dissipate entirely.

"Well, putting on a couple of stone to be quite honest, which I've found far too easy to do." I tilt the camera gut-wards. Yup. "But I've been working in the area with local radio. A couple of shows every Saturday, before and after the game; covering Middlesbrough, Hartlepool and Darlington. So I'm usually in here on a Saturday afternoon, dressed a little more smartly and not asleep." He speaks slowly and carefully, as though I'm a retard, but I think that's just his way.

He must have had some horrendous things said and done to him down the years, on and off the pitch. Is there vulnerability there, did our shouts get to him, or do referees really have metre-thick rhino-skin and actually enjoy spotlight in whatever form they can get it?

"Probably the *worst* thing that happened to me was when Dean Windass twatted me on the back of the head with a ball that he claimed he wasn't directly kicking at me, after I'd given a penalty against Bradford City. That did hurt a bit. But unlike Paolo Di Canio's push on Paul Alcock, I didn't hit the deck, you know, I'm a big lad. But if you really want to know what they said to me, get a copy of *Who's the B*****d in the Black?* by Jeff Winter." He opens his mouth wide and laughs at the gall of his shameless plug. Well, the self-publicist bit may be true after all and having read some of the reviews of the book, the self-importance is still bundled in with it. But still, how does anyone cope with verbal barrages and come out of it still managing to appear self-important? It would *destroy* me.

"Most of it is in the heat of the moment, out there on the football pitch. You give a penalty against a player, they're not gonna ask you round for tea. There were a few choice words coming my way, but there were a few choice words going back the other way and to be honest I think that was a damn site more effective than a yellow card." It takes a certain personality to do what Jeff did, and whatever that is, it definitely isn't me or anything I can imagine myself being. And for that, perhaps he deserves credit. But I get the sense Jeff doesn't take it all as seriously as maybe the rest of us do, that he sees himself as a sort of theatrical pantomime villain. How else is a referee going to forge a celebrity status in this country (if that's what he really desires)? The public are never going to take a referee to heart through his loveable charm so the only way he can shout above the rest is by playing on the villainous officious character that we pinned to him in the first place. If you think about it, in the long run, Jeff wins: while I stood there barking hatred at him, little did I know that all that stick was *creating the character*, feeding the myth that's now providing him with a brand and a living beyond his refereeing career. The scary thing will be if Uriah Rennie follows in his post-career footsteps.

Whatever role in creating this Jeff Winter media figure us fans had (and maybe he even has us to actually thank), on a personal level, man-to-man in an empty arena, the hypocrisy I am utterly guilty of is stinking out my mental alleyways, and I feel as though I somehow want to come clean to him about what I did – tidy my soul – maybe in the same way the Luton bloke did when he came up to me in the bar. I want to get it out in the open and admit I was up there with the vilest.

"OK Jeff, which referee do you think I've shouted the most obscenities at. Is it:

A: You...

B: You..."

(At this point his face shows that he's clocked what I'm doing and accepts what C will be. I say it anyway.)

"Or C: You...?"

"You see I was thinking it had to be Graham Poll. I can't think of any reason why you would shout things at me, because I think I was superb really, I don't think I made a mistake in my career..." There it is; out pops the shameless pantomime villain, recycling the negative and feeding it back to me as the brand. "But having thought it through, logically, probably the one that got on your tits most was me, Jeff Winter." And he smiles smugly, not in the least affected or hurt by it. Water off a duck's back. It's just a game; this is his bread and butter now.

* * * * *

MONDAY, 20 OCTOBER 2008.
9.30pm, Scotch Corner motorway services.
Things were going so well...

Darlington FC has a strange way of dealing with stuff. To contact them, you have to go through a separate PR company, who work from different offices elsewhere in Darlington. But that seemed all fine earlier in the day when they OK'd me to film at the ground and I set off on my 250-mile journey to make the evening home game against Bradford City.

Now: I'm drinking lukewarm, puddle-flavoured 'coffee' in the car; rain collapsing on the windscreen like the bottom end of a water flume ride, smearing the neon glows of a KFC sign in front of me at the most depressing motorway services I've ever been to. And that's going some. They should dole out lithium at the entrance, just to make sure the toilets aren't clogged with people trying to end it all next to the chewable toothbrush dispenser. I could go and sit in my hotel room ten yards away, but it's less damp in here. I've never ever imagined myself longing for the warmth of the crowd at a Darlington versus Bradford City fixture, which, incidentally, is still going on ten miles down the road.

OK then, let me just unplug the hosepipe leading from the exhaust to the car window for a moment, and I'll tell you about the mess I've got myself into. Since I was Jeff Wintered at the ground, I've been all the way down south and back up again ...

* * * * *

SATURDAY, 18 OCTOBER 2008. Two days earlier.
Adams Park, Wycombe

My first game as a Darlo fan: away at Wycombe – my second visit to Adams Park of the season, this time not by foot. Before the game I find myself caught in the players' tunnel, standing next to Wanderers manager Peter Taylor as they prepare to enter the arena. Because I've spent so long in the bar, telling Darlington fans who their celebrity look-alikes are (we had a Mario from *Big Brother* and a David Walliams), at 2.55 the usual entrance for those with a press pass – the players' tunnel – is sort of being used, by, erm, the players. Tiny Peter Taylor, probably unwittingly, throws me a look as if to say 'I don't remember signing *that*', sneering through a leather face that looks like it's just got back from a shrinking by the tribes of Papua New Guinea. Studs-a-clattering like a concrete equine disaster, players barking unrecognisable football generics, the smell of oils and adrenalin ... for a moment I allow myself to believe I'm about to run out and play. The little butter-flies kick off in the stomach, the hamstring flags up its concerns and I look down the line of players to see which Wycombe player I'll pile into first with my traditional early doors warning: *I can't tackle but if I'm going down, I'm taking you with me, John.* I choose Scott McGleish. I follow them down the tunnel, the applause starts with the first man but it's for me, all for me ... and as they enter the war zone, I allow my pretence to continue right to the chalk-dust, before peeling off with the security guy and down towards the away end.

I meet with Simon, a pleasant London-based Quaker, his well-coiffed mate DJ and a perpetually laughing off-duty policeman with an ironic flat cap. I like these people. After the break, Jason Kennedy scores to give Darlo the lead; the laughing policeman is thrown into the air like a punctured inflatable; a man with a club crest tattooed on his breasts brandishes his mooby floppers at me; dreadlocked Deano throws his way-too-small novelty London policeman's helmet in the air and little drummer boy Andy wallops the wotsit out of his snare ... It's funny though; it seems when I start with a new club, I re-grow my football hymen, and it takes a bit of time, gentle coaxing and a bond with my partners before I can really enjoy a goal going in. Sorry, this metaphor is vile. I guess what I'm saying is that I haven't yet got to the point that my Darlington associations provoke me into ecstatic celebration. It takes time for the love to penetrate.

For the second time this season, I watch top of the league Wycombe luck out and get a late draw ... *eight* minutes into injury time.

WYCOMBE WANDERERS 1-1 DARLINGTON
McGleish (pen) 90+8   Kennedy 58
Attendance 5,345

The day ends with an unreasonable number of beers with blokes called Sam and Dave – no, not the legendary soul singing combo of the 60s – both of these ones are in the forces. Dave's just got back from Afghanistan and has been waiting months for this game to see his mate. And then I gatecrash it ... and get him so drunk he won't remember wandering randomly into someone's back garden and doing archery or any of the bars that wouldn't let him in because of the dribbling. Sam was apparently found in the front garden the next morning covered in any sick he hadn't already emptied out onto Dave and I don't know why I kicked the side of a cab or why the cabbie wanted to fight me in the first place. Let's just leave it there.

But an away game is something you should do with people you see at home games, and I really feel the need for a game at the Arena to get a proper flavour of the Darlo regulars, to get me officially inducted, not just in a random afternoon with a pick 'n' mix of London-based or further afield fans like Sam and Dave who only get along once in a while if it's south enough.

* * * * *

MONDAY, 20 OCTOBER 2008. Back to today.
Darlo v Bradford

The Benson and Hedges-flavoured taxi tips me out at the Arena for a pooper-valve-shrinking 20 quid and promises to be back to get me at ten. *I bet you will, for that price.* Pitch black; spiteful wind-assisted rain cracks onto the side of my face like atomic rats' droppings. I usually love these midweek games, these inhospitable occasions that bring the best out in the fans and the worst out in the football. But I'm still not over Saturday. My blood doesn't feel right; I think it might have gone off. There isn't a transfusion service at the ground, so I head to the bar instead.

I'm not an enormous fan of the cavernous American-style sports bars with screens poking you in the eyes everywhere you go, but Darlington Arena has two of them that are uncomfortably straining to be hybrids between sports bar and the northern social club. But at least in these places you can get served quicker, as long as you pronounce the beer brand Coors as 'coo-errs' instead of 'corrrrs', because otherwise it might take some time for everyone to understand each other. People tend to huddle in corners of the bars here, maybe missing the tight squeeze of a town pub, the clamour that makes you feel as though you've earned your beer. The fans seem a little out of place; the matchday pub and the local pub are no longer the same place, leaving an uncomfortable and transient tension, stranded off a roundabout on a faceless A-road. To get here it's a bus or a car and gone now is the traditional walk from pub to terrace. The club's been moved out of the town's everyday life into the realm of an outskirts attraction, an occasional excursion.

In the bar I skim around the fans, meeting Darlo Pete, a hefty contributor to one of the forums and much vilified by some for allegedly being dull. He tells me how he's spent weeks nobly learning sign language so he can communicate with a deaf and dumb supporter who's always around but nobody seems to pay any attention to. I film his first attempt, which is met with relative indifference by the guy. Pete seems a little disappointed. I meet Cockney Pete, a fellow Spurs fan with a tash transplanted directly from *Easy Rider*, who moved up here and *needed* football, so now his loyalty straddles the two. In fact there are loads of strays around here – with Darlington on the way from the south to Newcastle, there are many who've stopped on the way up and never left. Then there's a guy called Chris, who really enjoys lifting his top and showing the camera some truly horrendous bodily scars, then unleashing a high-pitched laugh delivered directly from a snide hyena crawling in the pit of Hades. Other than that trip to the underworld, all is good.

I lean my 'coo-errrs' adapted head into the wind and pull my 'not enjoying this' grimace up to the main doors of the opulent club reception. The club crest is etched into anything that'll keep still long enough and there are escalators, *escalators* mind. Escalators in a football ground! An instinctive reflex inside me wants to jokingly try and check into a luxury penthouse suite, but I instead request my press pass. After worryingly not finding me on the list (and sneakily adding me), a couple of old boys brandish me with a press pass and physically escort me upstairs.

"Has the stadium ever been full?" I ask the doddery old boy with what appears to be war medals.

"Elton John nearly filled it recently," he replies proudly.

"Who was he playing for?" I joke.

"The other team I expect," he replies, deadpan.

We get to the press bit and I don't want to be here. I'm not proper press. I'm an idiot with a camera on a stick. Jeff Winter's here. I look out to the enormous Darlington Arena, the dome-shaped lavish new-fangly stadium that's hugely impressive but so broad and bland that it's hard to pick features out to describe. 25,000 people can fit in here; Darlington have an average attendance of nearly 3,000 and right now there are scant clumps of support, drowning in space and stewardship.

"What's *with* this stadium?" I ask Jeff, now tracksuit-less; standing in a suit and a shave.

"Well the previous chairman, as you might know, was a little bit of a character, let's say," Jeff starts, referring to local businessman George Reynolds. "He served time at Her Majesty's pleasure for safe-breaking and then he built this fantastic stadium that to anywhere else in the country would be amazing. 25,000 all-seater. They've not scrimped and saved. Inside, the décor, everything is top drawer." I should coco. "A town the size of Darlington probably needed a 10,000-seater stadium, so the sad thing is that at every home game there are usually 20,000-odd empty seats. I could think of many clubs in the Championship that would love to have this stadium. Far too big."

The stewards bumble around, directing me to the side of the pitch, to behind the goal where all the distant clattery noise of drum and a hundred fans trying to make themselves known in this endless metal tub sit. Floodlights credit the bleak night with brighter light than it deserves; some artificial cheer. Given my recent record with stewards, I decide to go and announce myself to one, just so I don't have to stand here being told off throughout the game by fat old men with bad breath, whistling corpuscle-ridden noses and axes to grind with humanity. He's a nice man though, this one, and radios through to the security bit up top, where all the people with superior swaggers and health-and-safety-shaped brains sit and watch us scum on screens. This goes on forever and by the look on his face, I just know what's coming. He looks so apologetic and I can't bring myself to have a go at him.

Put the camera away and get out, is the sentiment he's trying to politely convey.

They're throwing me out.

All my 'buts' and 'they saids' are falling on sympathetic ears that unfortunately can only do as mission control, the great Wizard of Spaz up there says. No explanations, I've just got to go.

*They're throwing me out. The b*****ds are throwing me out.*

I trudge, humiliated, back along the front of the crowd, passing the mascot – a terrible Dalmatian dressed in a football kit – furious they let *that* thing in and not me, and back out through one of the tunnels. I scramble out via whatever exit is available – camera still out and funny looks being blazed at me from the door staff.

"You won't be able to come back in, you know that?" says one of them with a school teacher tone. I don't reply.

Outside, I pace around aimlessly and manage to boil myself up to a broth of anger, furious that I've driven for five hours to this game having been told I could come in and film. I deserve an explanation, at least, don't I? I storm, well, trudge, again, sulkily back around to reception and ask for the media lady. She refuses to come down to see me, and just sends the receptionist to say,

"Sorry, you can't come in with the camera," which she doesn't enjoy saying because she can see my face is Hulking up for a biggun.

"What's changed since this afternoon then, since *before* I drove 250 miles?" I clasp my butt cheeks together, trying to maintain some sort of bodily control amid the rage.

"Sorry," she concludes, turning her attention to people who *are* allowed to be here.

250 miles and the media lady won't even show her face.

I call the rip-off smoky-cab man and ask him to come and smoke me out early. Right now please. As I stand outside the ground waiting, occasional muffled roars of the crowd carry out on the wind as fans kick the back of the rattly metal stand for a tempo to sing along to while their silhouettes in the plastic show them clapping, arms aloft. *This is a long, cold way away from home,* I think, hatefully. I flick through the programme and find a piece by club Chairman George Houghton, proudly welcoming The Gloryhunter to the club, telling everyone to look out for me and my camera. What on earth has happened here? A droplet of rain streaks down my long nose and plops messily onto the picture of Houghton's face, as the shivers start to set in.

And so here I am, at Scotch Corner motorway services, ten miles away, drinking minging coffee dredged from ditches. I try to work out where I go from here, seriously considering defaulting back to Luton, in protest – after all, the rules I've made myself are purely arbitrary. There's no International Federation of Gloryhunters that can fine me. I press refresh every five seconds on my mobile phone's internet page, to see if maybe I'm off to Bradford anyway.

But I'm not.

DARLINGTON 2-1 BRADFORD CITY
Austin 84   Daley 85
Burgmeier 90
Attendance 3,034

---

* * * * *

SATURDAY, 25 OCTOBER 2008.
Back at The Darlington Arena, with Dog Fing.

I decided to persevere with Darlo. After much arduous, tedious negotiation bouncing between myself, the PR company, the club and the Lord Jesus Christ himself, Darlington have finally agreed to allow me into the ground, with camera, for the home game against Dagenham & Redbridge. Hooray. The forums have been supportive. 'Heads must roll over this,' dramatically wrote DJ, and I think most agree that Monday night wasn't the club's finest moment in public relations. A howler, some might say. £100 in petrol, hotels and coffee brewed for dogs, I'd say. In reality, the club owe me nothing. But also in reality, here I am offering my spot on ITV as an advert for them to try and pull in a bigger crowd, which they *definitely*, desperately need. As all the clubs I've visited so far have agreed, it makes sense for them to co-operate.

Anyway, onwards and upwards.

Ah. Well, maybe not *upwards*. Upwards is where I *want* to go, sitting with the fans, because that's what this is all about. Instead, I get to the ground, go to the bar, carefully pronounce 'coo-errrs', carefully drink two of them, talk to Cockney Pete and Chris and Darlo Pete, collect press pass, announce myself at the reception which most hotels in Dubai have modelled their lobbies on, am taken to the correct stand and then…

…then I'm told that I have to stay down the very front, in the area with the ballboys and the gravel. For crissakes. I could punch a monkey. The rest of them are way up at the top of the stand – quite a way away – and here I am, wandering around infested with ballboys who've taken to calling me "grandad" or "cheeky chops", and no seat. Just *an area*. And the Darlo Dog.

Let me introduce you properly to the Darlo Dog, or 'Dog Fing' as I've branded it, because I'm starting to get a little bit fixated on it. Darlo Dog is without a doubt the limpest, most pathetically reluctant, token effort towards a mascot I have *ever* seen. It looks like it's been nicked off the skip round the back of a fancy dress shop that's clearing out its over-hired, moth-eaten old stock. It's not helped by whoever they put inside the bloody thing. Along it slowly slopes, shoulders rounded, flaccid tail dragging dirtily behind on the floor, paws like tumours and ears sagging like bits of steak dropped on the barber's floor. I bet it stinks inside there. Occasionally, it looks to the crowd and waves or tries to start a chant, but really, it's so far away and so lacking in credibility that literally nobody takes a blind bit of notice. Apart from me. Not even the kids want to shake its hand in case they get scabies. It's awful. But for some reason I can't stop watching it traipse along, depressed, occasionally imagining it writing a suicide note and putting a rope round its neck, but getting it caught on the flopping dirty old tongue in the head bit. Please, just cheer up, Dog Fing.

DARLINGTON 3-0 DAGENHAM & REDBRIDGE
Hatch 5, 55
Kennedy 51
Attendance 3,070

Darlo smash Dagenham, who apparently only travelled up this morning on the train. But I'm not getting any closer to understanding the Darlo fans; I need to experience it all – up there, with them. I'm close to declaring war. Which apparently is what the club are worried about – the only explanation I've had is from the mouth of a steward, who said it's in case my camera is used as an "object of violence". As David Gray once said ... "for crying out loud" ... Gray then went on to say "Babylon", but that wouldn't make any sense in this context. Health and safety bonkers. Risk assessment doolally.

'How did he die, doctor?'

'Ma'am, I'm afraid he was filmed to death.'

In the bar afterwards I decide to take action and start a campaign:

Free the Gloryhunter 1

The fans are all happy to come on camera and shout the words and I amass quite a collection of voices for the show. One guy even strips off and sings *I'm Too Sexy* in its honour. That wasn't requested by the way, and I'm not sure it'll be especially pervasive in getting the point across. But all contributions welcome.

* * * * *

TUESDAY, 28 OCTOBER 2008.
Rotherham v Darlington.

Three days later, at the Don Valley Stadium. The coldest night of the season so far. My spinal fluids have iced up and I do believe someone just mistook my frozen snapped off nipples for Cadbury's Buttons. Good luck with those. This stadium, with its five floodlights and pitch half a mile away, was made for athletics, and they should have left it to the weird pole-vaulters and peculiar triple-jumpers, because for football, it's a horror. Home and away fans sit on the same side and the other is left empty, leaving the view like watching a mid-table end of season college match in Norway. Rotherham have no problem letting me in though, and I further my campaign, enlisting Darlo fan Woody, a young round-headed chap whose mouth runs way quicker than his brain, leading to all sorts of verbal silliness. He endorses my efforts to camera, and also admits he hasn't seen any of the game because his eyes are too drunk. And then he puts out his own appeal: for females, specifically 'MILFS' to come forward and get in touch. They don't.

My fourth game as a Darlo fan, and I'm still at an impasse with the club. Where is this leading? Will I have to get Arthur Scargill in?

ROTHERHAM UNITED 0-1 DARLINGTON
Ravenhill 61
Attendance 3,322

---

* * * * *

WEDNESDAY, 28 NOVEMBER 2008.
Midnight, Darlington Civic Theatre.
The lights are off and apparently the ghosts are out.

Nothing. Nothing at all. Just utter pitch black darkness. I suppose it's better than watching Letitia Dean in *Puss in Boots*, but in this beautiful old theatre that dates back to 1907, you'd expect at least a friendly 'boo' from Signor Pepi, the dead old flamboyant Italian owner of the place. As part of my getting-to-know-the-area routine I randomly asked Claire and the gang at Northern Ghost Investigations to take me on a typical Darlington ghost hunt, if there's such a thing, with all the gadgets and crystals and Yvette Fielding type moments of chilly crisis. So they kindly brought me to the old theatre at midnight and turned all the lights off to make it all nice and haunty for the ghosties. Brilliant fun; but apart from Jacqui having a funny turn by a ladder and me feeling a slight draught in the stalls, there are no spectres the size of Mumm-Ra from *Thundercats* bursting through the safety curtains at us. But in between my fits of wheezy whimpering (once again playing the Shaggy role in the *Scooby Doo* version of this ghost hunt), I start thinking about ghosts in a less literal sense...

If Darlington FC really don't want me to be a part of their present, maybe I should go digging up some of their past instead.

Perhaps I should invoke the spirits of bygone Darlo...

(Insert mysterious laugh.)

* * * * *

"Georgie boy? Well he was good when he first came and we all loved him. Then he turned into the biggest arsehole the club's ever had," said one Darlo fan at half-time away at Rotherham.

"He took us out of our old stadium to a new stadium and we're in debt because of it," said Woody with his fast-talking teeth.

"Sad old man, I wish he hadn't done what he did," said Ted ruefully.

"The man is an absolute lunatic. He's built us a bloody stadium no-one wants to go to. Why? There's only 3,000 of us and there only ever was. Can he not count?" ranted another Darlo fan.

I'm not sure that with the plethora of things I could feasibly cover surrounding the club (apart from the club itself, of course), how happy the Darlo fans might be that I seek out controversial, and from what I can gather relatively unpopular, former owner George Reynolds. They've probably heard enough of that particular chapter. But the curiosity has got the better of me.

I'm always wary of people who carry the 'colourful character' tag; they're so often egotists who've conceitedly create the description for themselves. True eccentrics, I believe, don't know they're eccentrics, and anyone else is just trying too hard. But George's tenure of Darlington was colourful beyond purely his personality. The supersized stadium, the time in prison and the stories I've heard from fans of him turning up in the middle of the night asking for a punch up ... I just couldn't resist seeking a séance with this particular Darlington ghost and getting his side of the story.

I'm staying at a travel tavern in a town up in County Durham, genuinely called 'Pity Me'. And I do; there's nothing in this arid landscape other than roads and a shopping centre, but George's industrial unit is nearby and as I sit awaiting his call, I look up his past on the web. George is 71 now, I find, and renowned for his earlier years on the wrong side of the law as a safe-cracker. He later went on to make a packet in making kitchen worktops, perhaps becoming the biggest manufacturer of them in the world. In 1999 he bought Darlington Football Club, hoisted them out of home ground Feethams and into the 20 million quid's worth of newly built and selflessly named 'George Reynolds Arena'. Amid concerns about the size of the stadium for the size of the town and club, *and* the fact that they're penned in by Premiership clubs in the area, he claimed the 25,000-seater wasn't simply 'George's Folly' – as they took to calling it locally – but that he always planned to have big concerts once a month (such as the Elton John show) along with trade fairs and car boot sales, but that the council were stopping him from doing so. Subsequently, Darlo went into administration in 2004 and after being found with half a million pounds of cash in his car boot, George was sent back to jail for cheating the tax man.

What am I to expect?

I arrive at George's industrial estate unit after way too much time negotiating directions with him on the phone, and eventually him having to lean out a window and wave me down. It's one of those new types of units; nondescript metal and plastic and not necessarily built to last. George comes to the door, gut-first, a big towering lump of a man, and I'm surprised how old he looks. The photos I've seen include his locally infamous comb-over that was apparently coaxed into position by any number of hairclips; but now there's a bald unkempt head with sprouts of hair freely flourishing, running wild on tops of ears, nose and eyebrows. He looks tired. Great pendulous bags drag his eyelids almost closed. He looks defeated in all but words, particularly the ones on giant signs he's had put up everywhere; the sort of mantras you'd find in American 'How to be Brilliant and Handsome' type self-help books.

The offices are immaculate, totally organised and sparsely arranged. As a dyslexic, I guess paperwork isn't George's bag; maybe Stu deals with that. I don't know what George would call Stu's job title – he's like a timid right hand man, perhaps in his 40s, who stands to attention at George's slightest whim, makes tea and talks when spoken to. I can't quite get a grip on the relationship, but they each seem to be comfortable with the set-up.

George must have been out of prison for a year or so and has clearly been busy. So I ease in by asking about his latest enterprise, 'Enigma'.

"Oh, I'm doing tremendous," he coos, gloatingly. "I've never been so well off in me life. I've got no worries, no overheads; in fact I've got no bank borrowings. I've never been so well off. I'm flying. I'm on the crest of a wave to be honest." It's a gloating so inflated that it feels defensive, as though he assumes what I really wanted was to come in and see him on the floor, penniless and sobbing.

I should say now that my approach to this meeting is purely one of curiosity; what happened between George and Darlo and the fans is between them. Interested to hear about it? Yes. Out to accuse, settle scores or make a judgment either way? No. I've not been around here long enough to deserve such privilege; it's none of my beeswax, I'm an alien, just honoured to be involved. I certainly have a loyalty to Darlo fans when it comes to football, they're becoming my friends, but I also have an obligation to approach George – a man who's invited me into his place – with an open mind.

"I supply 'airspray, mouthspray," George continues, regarding the business of 'Enigma'. "I put them into vending machines. I'm looking to put them into long flights with things like the nicotine spray." His accent is strong and I occasionally have difficulty Londonating it. "See, I like recession, 'cos it sorts the men out among the boys doesn't it?" he adds playfully. It's all very dramatic with George. It reminds me of a slightly more sedate version of when American wrestlers do their pre-bout interviews. He keeps his overacting solely to the eyes though, leaning forward for his serious piercing stare and then leaning back with wry smiles and wise looks for words of victory. He's leaning back now, exacting a long, long pause. "You look for niches in the market and with the cigarette ban going on, what we do is take the cigarette machines out, make them into commodity machines and put them back in. So that way the general public's happy and then so's the government." It's doubtlessly a clever idea. And he knows it.

George settles down in a seat next to his desk, strangely arranging himself so that a prosthetic sort of rubber pig thing is in the back of shot with its tongue hanging out. George doesn't say anything about it and I forget to ask, though I assume he knows he's got a big rubber pig behind him. And so the whole interview goes on with the pair of them in shot.

"So before starting Enigma, you were in nick weren't you?" I prompt.

"Oh yeah, that were alright, nothing wrong with that. The staff were very good, the cons were good, I was treated very well. It didn't bother me. I can't say I relished it, but I can't say I disliked it either."

"It would scare the life out of me," I say, offering a weakness, implicitly suggesting willingness to bargain truths, hoping to break past the bombastic showboating with honesty.

"I was done for what they call cheating. Now let me tell you about cheating. There's people fetching stuff through the tunnel. Cigarettes, whisky ... *that* is cheating. I reckon if they did everyone for cheating there'd be nobody left. I were never done for tax evasion or money laundering or anything like that. I were done for *cheating*. But, the other side to that is that the case will get reopened 'cos I didn't owe any tax. I've got a letter to prove it." He goes on to discuss his theories on police vendettas against him. And then onto the half a million in notes they found in the boot of his car when he was arrested.

"You see that money was my own personal money and people were saying well, what were you doing with that in the boot of a car? But if you've got a tramp with a hundred pound, a hundred pound's a lot of money for a tramp. But half a million pound's not a lot to someone with forty one million."

I don't really want to get into the intricate details of his tax case or finances, so I decide now's the time to bring in the football club. I tell George that of the people I've spoken to, the mention of his name doesn't bring a positive response. It's simply a statement that's true of my experience thus far, but one I know could inflame.

"Well let me tell you about that. You see, it's not *all* the fans. We get a tremendous response from the fans in Darlington, don't we, Stuart?" – a grunt comes from the kitchen area – "Giving photographs, autographs. But I'll tell you something. Feethams would 'ave 'ad to be closed. It was finished, it'd 'ad its day. So if it 'adn't been for me ... there'd be no Darlington Football Club." He leans forward, holds a wide eyed, high eyebrowed expression, a bit like Alfred Hitchcock. "Realistically, it wasn't *all* the fans; it was a small minority of fans. And empty cylinders make the most noise ... " He sits back and grins broadly, the wise old man look smugly written all over his face.

"Now let's take a look at Darlington. When I was there, we were bottom of the league. In the new stadium. We were gettin' just under 7,000. And we were third off the bottom. And now, even when they're third off the top ... " he leans forward again and whispers, " ... they're getting 2,800. So tell me how you work that one out? In fact they sometimes get 2,500." He pulls a face of disgust, like he's just eaten a rancid fish. "So what does that tell you?"

Now this is where the interview goes a bit wonky.

George wants me to answer the question as to why attendances are lower now than when he was there. I tell him I don't know the answer. I'm here to get his side of the story, not posit my own notions. He goes through the same attendance figures time and time again, asking me constantly to answer the question. Each time, I still don't know, and he gets more insistent and more aggressive. George seems to have decided that I'm trying to prove and argue a point on the fans' behalf, and has begun a war in which I'm not a willing fighter. I simply want to hear his side. But George wants to make a fight of it and this goes on for some time because I won't retaliate. But it does give me a bit of a sense of how he operates. He's like a boxer forced into a corner at all times, punching his way in and out of situations, perhaps needing conflict to get the best out of himself. He said earlier off camera that he doesn't work for the money, he just likes the aggravation, and right now he's proving that.

"Put it this way, I've got newspaper clippings I can show you where the *Northern Echo* and the fans said 'when Reynolds leaves, the crowd will treble'. Not double, *treble*. So three sevens are what?" He looks at me for an answer, but I'm getting a bit fed up and I'm not going to do his calculations for him. There's a silence. "Three sevens, Stuart?" He demands without looking over.

"31," Stu shouts from the kitchen. Ten thousand out.

"There should be 31,000 according to the newspapers. But it's not. Nobody can answer it. I'll ask you for the fifth time now…" Off he goes with the same figures again. At one point, my mind wanders off so far that I find myself internally debating as to whether lizards get malaria.

"So what you're saying is that they're missing you?" I eventually crack and try to put words into his mouth. Anything other than this bloody attendance conundrum.

"I'm not saying anything, you're saying that. Can *you* tell *me* why they don't get the crowds in now?" He leans further forward, arms crossed, scowling.

"Are you in any way bitter about the whole thing?" I try to edge away again.

"Nooooo," he dismisses quickly. "No I'm not bitter. I'm quite enjoying it to be honest. I sit and I get the paper and the first thing I look at is the attendance. And I go 'tut tut tut, what's gone wrong 'ere?'" He smiles slyly, glowing with hubris. Not bitter?

"You see, I gave them 37 million pound. Me own personal money. Hard earned. So it's like somebody knocking on your door and they go 'there you go

Mr Spencely [sic], it's nice to see you, there's ten million pound', and you saying 'I'm not having that', and hitting him over the head with a hammer. So really, the ones who dislike me ... what reason do they have for disliking me?" He adopts a sarcastically soft, forlorn manner. "Do they dislike me 'cos I saved the club from going bankrupt? Do they dislike me cos I built a new stadium? Whhhyyy do they dislike me? Could it be jealousy? 'Cos remember, in America if you do something, you're praised. In Britain, it's an offence. So could it be jealousy?" He goes back to normal mode very quickly. "I'm not bothered what they think really. Doesn't interest me. I don't worry, I'm doing quite well. What have I got to be worried about? I'm on the crest of a wave, I'm flying again." But I suspect that what people say and think *does* bother George a bit, maybe more than he realises himself, and I decide to throw something out which someone said to me at the ground the other day.

"They said that the crests everywhere, and the stadium itself, was a bit of an ego trip on your part." He sits up, an incensed air wafts over and his collected demeanor drifts into less controlled rant territory.

"Do you want me to show you what an ego trip is? I had a seven million pound yacht. That's a bigger ego trip than a stadium. I had helicopters. If you wanted an ego trip, you wouldn't have a football club. No. You see ... that's rubbish. That is complete rubbish. I didn't have to have an ego trip. I had Direct Worktops, I was supplying to France, Germany, Belgium," – he goes on to list the countries, exhaustively – "that's a bigger ego trip than any stadium, I'd already done that, so where's the ego trip? They're completely wrong and they're talking rubbish. And by the way, whoever said it, I don't want to know their name, what have they ever achieved? Are they working at the stadium? Probably one of the girls, maybe some jumped up little manageress or summat like that ... what have they achieved?"

"Do you still love the club?" I wonder, knowing that deep down, apparently he's a Sunderland supporter.

"Oh yeah, it's a nice club. There's some good fans of Darlington. But my there's some bloody rubbish. But the things is, Spencely [sic], you still haven't answered me question. Surely there's an answer? I'm so bad, and I was third off the bottom, getting seven thousand ... " And off we go again with the attendance figures. He points out that he's asked me 11 times. He needn't, I'm well aware.

"But I want to hear *your* answer to that question, George."

"I know the answer; I've got a general idea."

"Go on then." Please, for the love of Christ. He pauses, smiling.

"Because Iiiiiii'm loved." The grin bananas further, sitting back in his chair, the final scene, the final act. The show is over bar the epilogue. "Wherever I go, I'm loved. Believe it or not, it doesn't matter where I go. I get offered to speak and I get standing ovations, I am loooved in the north-east 'cos people love a character. And there's very few of us left. I am loved. And the proof of it is, how come when Sunderland were playing away there used to be a load come down to support *me*. Middlesbrough, Newcastle … but they don't come to support them now, so *there's* your answer." The missing attendances are because fans of other local clubs were there purely for George, that's his claim.

Subsequently, I've checked out the facts about Darlo's attendances. This season, the average attendance is 2,931. In the last season at Feethams, 2002/03, when George was in charge, the average attendance was 3,312. He then took them through their first season at the Arena, where the average was 5,023. I guess it's up to you whether you believe the missing 2,000 are, as George puts it, "voting with their feet" and not going because they support him, or whether other variables have been in play, such as one a fan pointed out to me, that in the first season at the Arena, George had a buy-one-get-one-free offer on season tickets. Who knows?

But with George feeling as though he may have won his imaginary war with me, he asks me to stay for some food and leaves little room for negotiation. Off goes Stu, down the local Chinese place and George relaxes a bit. Any semantic link sets him off on a pre-recorded after dinner speech story, but he's not an unpleasant man to be around. I quite enjoyed sitting chatting with him, as long as we didn't get talking about attendances. He's had an interesting life, that's for sure.

He tells me of some of the ways he got back at Darlo fans, by personally turning up at their houses in the middle of the night asking for a one-on-one fight, because a group of them had waited outside his house to try and do him in one night. These are wildly different to the versions the fans told me the other day I might add, but in truth, the whole thing seems so ridiculous that whoever's right … how does a game of football turn into that?

I emerge at ten o'clock, five hours later, and I've no idea whether George's hospitality has been generosity or mind-games to curry favour for when it comes to editing the video and writing the book. It's hard to tell with George, everything seems to be a game, a battle of wills, and I suspect the whole Darlington saga is just another one of those wars that are part of life to him. I can't feel sorry for what's happened to him, he's made his bed and he's lying in it. He's won some and lost some and I suspect he's loved every minute of the battle along the way.

But there's something about George that suggests to me he'll *never* be totally satisfied or at peace; whatever he achieves, he'll always want to fight for more.

9.

MY SLIDING DOORS

The gooey romantic dream-snatching of statistical glimpses down the paths which may have lain ahead of me ... the wondrous musing of things that *could* have turned out just that little bit differently ... it consumes some of the lonelier moments in the Glorywagon and hotels up and down the country. *What if* drives me crazy; it's those split-second moments on the football pitch, totally out of my control (barring a barbaric dash onto the pitch and getting my ass banned forever, which could happen if Arsenal enter the equation); they dictate my course and leave me peering curiously down the other fork of this crazy road, asking ... *Where would I be now?*

During those blurry-edged schismatic episodes, I've been using the first match of the season as my *Sliding Doors* moment. Grimsby v Rochdale wasn't exactly a romantic occasion, but it was the first time I had just two distinct paths and a whole season in front of me. So where would I be now if Rochdale had sneaked a winner in that first game?

Well ... (takes a deep breath)...

Rochdale went on to lose to Bradford City, who lost to Aldershot, who lost to Swindon in the Cup – hooray, League One – who lost to Leeds, hmmm, who lost to Peterborough, who lost to Dagenham and Redbridge (I'd have been relegated to League Two by the Cup, booo...) who lost to Rotherham ... and after Ricky Ravenhill scored that second half winner as Darlo beat the Millers at the freezing Don Valley athletics venue the other night, my alternate reality would have had me traipsing from the home end to join the Darlo fans and continue my journey on exactly the same tangent as I am now.

How odd, that with all the possibilities available, all those multitudes of variant courses, that I would have ended up in the same place albeit via a detour to another division and various different places all over the country.

With those sliding doors now slammed shut and their paths synchronised, I have to look for another moment to use as my day-dreamy *what if*. So, I consider the next available true split second of destiny – Brentford's home match in the JPT against Yeovil. If you'll remember, amid boardroom floaters, it went to penalties and without the heroics of goalkeeper Sebastien Brown, I would have been packed off west with the Glovers. But if I had, where next?

Well … Yeovil lost in League One to MK Dons, who lost to Oldham, who lost to Stockport, who lost in the LDV Vans Trophy to Bury – seemingly a tour of the outskirts of Manchester – and then back west to Exeter, who lost to Chesterfield. And that's where I'd be now, back in League Two, cheering Jack Lester from the home end of fortress Saltergate. I'd have had an excursion to League One and would have met a whole different set of people; I might be dead in a solid gold coffin or married to a millionaire fisherwoman with one lung or sitting in a hot tub with Burt Reynolds. Who knows?

10.

†HE KinG OF rOSEBErr4 †OPPinG

THURSDAY, 30 OCTOBER 2008.
Bishops Hotel, York.

Just 60 minutes ago I was congealed like a weeping sore glued to a bandage, to the covers of my draught-infested, damp, dank travel tavern bed that smells like cats in a pond, surfing the internet, looking for different ways to continue exploring Darlington's past. There's still no word from the club on letting me into the stand with my camera, the cold war is-a-raging and I'm still an outsider. So back in time I continue.

"Is that Marco?" I asked on the phone diffidently, having spotted a number for the Bishops Hotel in York and deciding to chance my arm and call it. You wouldn't expect him to, but he actually answered the phone. I nearly pooped, swallowed my tongue and then stuttered my way into asking for an interview, accidentally calling him 'Marky' along the way. He wasn't wildly keen about doing an interview or being called Marky, but went along with it anyway. After having a shower and actually coming out drier than the air in the room, for the following 60 minutes Emma directed me smoothly to beautifully ornate York. Things between me and Emma, by the way, are pretty good at the moment (apart from the roundabout incident at Wetherby Services the other day, but I won't go into that).

Before I know it, I'm in Marco Gabbiadini's wicker-dominated Habitat-showroom conservatory – looking out across an immaculately manicured lawn garden you could stage a flower show and/or a play-off final on ... although play-offs are a touchy subject in this household. I'm drinking Gabbiacoffee, sitting on the Gabbiasofa and waiting for Gabbiadini to finish off his Gabbiapaperwork in a little office/cupboard under the Gabbiastairs. The turnaround for this visit has been so fast that I feel as though I've been Gabbiabeamed here directly from my bed-swamp.

For Nottingham-born Marky Marco, it's come sort of full circle. He started his career at York City, before scoring himself into becoming a Sunderland great – netting 74 times in a 157 games and winning all sorts of promotions along the way. He then journeyed around like a football gypsy, parking his metaphorical caravan in Darlo for two years between 1998 and 2000 – scoring 47 in 82 games and eventually being voted the club's greatest ever player. He hung up his boots while at rivals Hartlepool in 2004, and now here he is, back in York, where he owns the Bishops Hotel.

"It's just a little venture my wife and I started before I finished playing, four or five years ago now," he says humbly. They've done pretty well though for a little venture; set in a posh street of great, looming and austere Victorian houses that you daren't pass wind or say swears in, this place won 'Guest House of the Year' in 1999.

'Try our Venetian suite…' seduces Marco on the hotel's website, '…luxurious and spacious four poster suite decorated with sumptuous fabrics and crystal chandeliers, comfy sofas and lots of extra touches for that special romantic break.' Phwoaar. By 'extra touches' for romance, does he mean free condoms stuffed down the back of everything? I bet his footballing team-mates would have crucified him for the 'Sumptuous fabrics' bit. Sumptuous fabrics? Do me a favour.

"What's your favourite customer complaint?" I wonder; perhaps occasionally people explode with ire if the fabric isn't quite as sumptuous as they'd been promised.

"We don't get any, Spencer. That's the idea," he chides mock-defensively.

Maybe crow's feet have taken grip, but he's still got a jaw line and keeps himself in shape. In fact, Marco doesn't really look any different to when I remember him playing for Sunderland; still the same floppy side-parting and bulked out barnet over the ears that's he's been donning since the 80s. Although he's not so similar to my memories that he's still wearing a Sunderland shirt. That'd be a bit strange; like a football version of Miss Havisham. But I do imagine him in the shirt, celebrating a goal and spewing words of frustration at the referee. It seems weird to think of this very collected man behaving, as footballers do, at the furthermost parameters of emotion. Especially in a hotel lobby.

Marco's got a very straight, down-the-line business-like way about him, the sort of manner I've oft seen in footballers and sports people who compose themselves as winners; always conveying a positive and confident manner, playing out the constant competitive mental strategies required to win. It's that sort of seriousness that I have an innate compulsion to subvert with tourettes-esque oddities; like suddenly reaching over and honking his nose, putting a pair of pants on his head or covering his face with hummus and bits of marinated red pepper. I don't do any of those though, obviously.

"Have you got a room or what?" I ask cheekily.

"I don't know; you don't really come up to our standards Spencer." He smiles more cheekily, trumping my cheekiness; the cheek of it. Thank God he hasn't got a room for me though. I don't think I could have handled such an extreme concentration of orgasmic pleasure that the fabrics would send me into, I'd just end up congealed in damp again; different damp.

"What are your memories of Darlo then, Marco?" I ask, as he stands behind the reception counter looking all proprietor-like.

"Good ones actually, I had a good couple of years. A little bit soured by the play-off defeat at Wembley, which was one of the worst nights of my career." He's referring to the final loss against Peterborough in 2000. "I got beat five times in the play-offs so it was to be expected. I probably shouldn't have played; I was probably a bit of a jinx. But I thoroughly enjoyed playing there; great fans, very passionate." I get the feeling that although I'm sure he enjoyed his time at Darlo, in truth it didn't compare to his heydays at Sunderland or Derby and he feels obliged to wax lyrical about all his subsequent clubs out of politeness.

We chat for a while about how Marco wants to get into television punditry and what he thinks of Stan Collymore ... ahem ... and I end up pretending I can pull a few strings – mainly because he's done the interview for nothing at short notice and I feel as though I should bring my bottle of wine to the party. But in reality my wine is Blue Nun; I don't know anyone at ITV Sport because I've only been in there once to get some money in a brown envelope.

"What do you remember of the old ground, Feethams?" I ask as I'm leaving, a loaded question in relation to the rest of my day.

"I remember we had terrible trouble with the pitch up there and some guy decided that it needed special worms. They were digging little holes to plant the worms in. It was just surreal really, it had come to this." Ohhhkaaaayyy.

* * * * *

"Can't cry on camera, can we? But it is a bit disappointing that they've not done any-thing with it," says Deano, the gangly dreadlocked Sideshow Bob-alike Darlo fan, clamping a stiff upper lip on the trembly bottom one and making his accent even more jagged. As I look around at what's left of Feethams – a plot close to Darlington city centre – and the adjoining cricket pitch that's still in use, I find myself uncon-sciously humming Fairport Convention's *Who Knows Where The Time Goes* – a haunting wail of languishing homesick sobs for what's no more – and I get a prickly surge of nostalgia clambering up my spine, which is strange, because I've never been here before. There's something funereal about the place; the carcass of the old tin shed, once the home terrace behind the goal, packed with hundreds of black and white shirts … now just a dilapidated skeleton with faded advertising hoardings for businesses probably no longer trading and rusty, time-blistered corrugated metal. It's hard to imagine this wasteland hosting a football match, that this long grass with straw-brown reedy patches, clumps of thorny weed and camouflage-green wind-wobbled fledgling bushes was once a plush-green clipped turf with holes for the special worms. There's no sign of the other stands. Just nothing. No stray seats poking like badly buried murder-victims out of the earth, no concrete foundations, not a metal post jutting out to let us know it'd been here. Just a desolate scrub, ruth-lessly raped of its historical allure.

Deano works for the club's Football in the Community scheme and he and his colleague Anthony have popped down to have one last look at the old place with me before leaving it to continue the sad demise alone.

"I remember it like it was yesterday," says Anthony, wistfully glancing around the place. Deano tells me about an alleyway that used to be behind the stand on the other side of the ground, and how a dead body was once found in a carrier bag there. He's not sure which supermarket the bag was from but reckons the alley stunk for ages after. This doesn't help my romantic mind's-eye conjurings, but still somehow I submerge into a frivolous mental wander; the entire stadium colours itself back in as if monochrome before; the chaotic grass grows back down to a wormy carpet and the Tannoy rattles out team changes. The stand re-forms itself to my right, proudly erect with its black and white seats spelling out 'Darlington', the tin shed wins back its barriers and the fans bang on the back of it, a roar erupting … howay the lads … and swoooosh, I snap back and Deano and Anthony are still in the stand while I've wandered out unconsciously to where the halfway line was, feeling the aura of yesterday but now seeing only space; wondering if this soil has memory, spiritual remnants of its days as a dumping ground for pent energy and desirous frustration. *Who knows where the time goes*, I hum again. If this was White Hart Lane, I'd be a sobbing wreck, collapsing into a pathetic pile of bloke, blabbering random Perrymans and Galvins and Archibalds. But the first thing I'd ask is how White Hart Lane got to be in Darlington in the first place.

Anthony and Deano are clapping out a Darlo song in the very positions they would have stood five years ago, Deano climbing up onto the ledge they'd be forever told to get down from, banging the metal sidings one last time – that recognisable clanging pitch, resounding around the structure for the first time in five years. I feel for the fans; from this once-cosy, quirkily run-down, unpretentious ground, just the right size, to being thrown into that mostly-empty chasm on the edge of town.

"The last game at Feethams we drew two-all. Neil Wainwright, Darlington's longest-serving player, scored the last goal to equalise," says Anthony with a distance in his eyes. He shouldn't have told me that. I can't leave things alone, can I? We work out where the goal would have been, put down jumpers for goalposts and I feebly hammer at a tin can until it goes past Deano, to where once was a net … I scored the last ever goal at Feethams. Ever.

Then the phone rings.

It's the PR company representing the club. It seems my 'Free The Glory-thunder 1' campaign has put the wind up them. Actually, I doubt it. They've just decided that I can come into the stand to film. But on the condition that the camera doesn't go on its plastic stick. It seems the plastic stick is specifically the potential object of violence. They're right; sometimes I walk down the street and before I know it I've clubbed 30 people senseless with it, most of them to death, some just critical but stable. Honestly. Anyway, I'm in. It's over.

I haul myself out of the good old days and back into the present.

* * * * *

Like George Reynolds – well, not quite like George Reynolds, but you know what I mean – over the next few weeks I'm flying, I'm on the crest of a wave. I have a tryst with County Durham and it feels as though this dalliance might just be reciprocal. I live the Gloryhunter experience in exactly the way I envisioned it all those months ago; a mixture of football glory and embracing the country that birthed me. All my festering concerns and paranoia feel dealt with and put away in a memory box in the loft, along with Uncle Ken's revolting watercolour painting from the 70s of Auntie Sandra in the nude with fruit. Despite the grey days and dark nights of winter huffing and puffing me up the far end of the year, and the temperatures passing me on their way down, I get out there and take lungfuls of the place.

Darlington centre, a historical market town, works surprisingly well with the backdrop of moping nimbi buckling under its own sogginess; it pulls the disquietude out of the old Victorian buildings and into a striking stern rock-grey that refuses to be noticed from merely the corner of an eye. I perambulate laps around that town centre like an aardvark snuffling ants; through the 'Pedestrian Heart', as they've called it since cars were replaced by expansive walkways topped off with a postcard-intended staircase water-feature. Despite their bases being amputated by the pandemic of chain stores, if you scoop your eyes off the frenetic carb-addicted scenes of the McDonald's doorway, you can see heritage maintained; the old Quaker house, the clock tower still chiming as if conducting a collective rally to keep us together in the face of time's ticky-tocky piss-take. I change travel tavern brand to the purple coloured one, a much happier experience, dry off and hide out in cosy pubs, deliberating how else to explore an area that otherwise I would rarely find myself parked up in for more than a day. Things get better and better as I wade thigh deep into Darlington and all its nooks. The only thing I rue is that with the club's epicentre being outside town occupying theme-park territory, the fans don't seem to have a day-to-day life together as they do at Brentford, whose four corner pubs facilitate such.

In extending my glorybeak beyond the town centre, I find myself winding the glorywagon up the curly-wurly hills of the Durham Dales in the North Pennines, a patchwork frenzy of rugged craggy slopes with an exposed wildness only just kept in order by dry stone walls. And then poking out of the horizon, there's a huge wooden wheel. Beneath the wheel I drag my waterlogged heels through a sloshy black travesty in the old lead mine-turned-museum at Killhope (pronounced 'killup', so yes, it rhymes nicely with 'trollup', should you wish to do so), banging my outsized yellow-helmeted canister 17 times on the slimy stone walls as the guide chuckles like broken bicycle chains. It's a slimy nightmare down there; I'd sooner work for the BBC than have to do that.

The reason for this adventure underground is so that when later on I visit the first ever World Cup – yes, I did say the *first ever World Cup* – at the local football club, Northern League side West Auckland, I have a sense of what the players at the time did for a day job. And that's where they went to work: an underground hell of sludge and damp. No wonder they wanted an adventure elsewhere...

The story goes that long before the Uruguayans pretended to be the winners of the supposed first World Cup in 1930, Sir Thomas Lipton, owner of the famous Lipton teas we've all enjoyed, decided to create a competition to find the world's best team. It was 1909, 21 years before that other World Cup was won, and when the stuffy old FA decided not to enter a team, somehow or other the pit-mining lads of West Auckland pawned their own possessions to get over to Italy and take part in Lipton's grand folly. They ended up running out winners without conceding a goal.

West Auckland were the first ever winners of the World Cup – not Uraguay.

Then, the buggers went back two years later and had the cheek to win it again, and took the cup outright, beating some team called Juventus along the way. Despite their best efforts to lose the enormous Lipton Trophy at the train station on the way back, it was kept proudly at the small village's club ever after. Until, that is, some greedy twonk nicked it. What a selfish tit. But my visit to the club is to cop a grab of the like-for-like remake of the cup, a huge grandiose silver monument featuring a footballer holding a ball aloft.

It somehow seems incongruous, sitting on its box in the scruffy car park of this threadbare Northern League ground, but proud they are of their amazing lesser-known history. The coveted cup is about the size of a five-year-old boy, and it gleams in the winter sun. I touch it all over, just like I did on a Wembley tour that had exhibited *that* crossbar from the 1966 World Cup final. Touching history makes you a part of it, is my bizarre rationale.

And the adventures continue. With my visiting mate, Cockney Dave, we travel 20 miles to the North Yorkshire border to conquer Roseberry Topping, a cone-shaped mount from which I imagine hearing the echoed grumbles of the Grinch (that stole Christmas). The cloud-scuffing peak looks a bit like my mid-90s quiff, but upon reaching it, you could compare the flat top to that Macho Pictionary thing in Peru, albeit more English, with Teeside in the distance on one side and the Yorkshire Moors on the other. *God bless England* I think, as I take a lungful of our air, and my brain takes a smack-like hit of uber-nourishment from the abundance of oxygen while the gusts blow a recreation of my aforementioned quiff out of the receded mop that time's been kind enough to leave dwindling on the top of my head. This is on the route of Wainwright's coast-to-coast walk, and my God, old Wainwright must have been of his face on oxygen.

Eddying in the wind and the spirit of England, we cockney our way to the top, where Dave offers three sheep out for a fight. The mugs run off.

Over these weeks I have the sort of time that a montage-compiler would have a field day with, probably using *Flying Without Wings* by Westlife as the cheesy underscore and lots of shots of me, drunk, in slow motion. It's almost too much to list: I fall over, sober, at the Angel of the North and send it off to *It'll Be Alright on the Night*; I pretend to be the world's northern-most cockney, with a tomato ketchup nosebleed at Hadrian's Wall; I do all the things up here that you promise yourself to do 'one day', although with a little more stupidity. I even go to Newcastle University for a one-on-one lesson in speaking the Darlington accent. I fail. I sound like I'm eating scorpions. But still, I'm having the time of my life.

I also take on the challenge of finding 'Mr Poopoo'. No, not a euphemism for a gay love affair. Darlo have these red away shirts that fans have paid a tenner to have all their names printed onto. A great idea. There are hundreds of tiny names listed all over, in the weave of the shirt and thus into the history of the club … and one of those names is a certain 'Mr Poopoo'. Debate on the forums suggests a Hartlepool fan may have done it in an act of bitter sabotage, but I find out through the now helpful club that the guy whodunit is a Walsall fan. When they played at Darlo, he happened to be in the bar and was approached by the promotion girls selling shirt-space. Mr Poopoo, it turns out, was the handle of someone who's been banned from their club forum, 'upthesaddlers.com', for his controversial opinions. And so the guy did it, relatively innocently, as a tribute to him.

Finally, the truth is out, no Monkey Hangers in sight. Mr Poopoo is unmasked; you can breathe out now, the mystery is solved. I am The GloryMarple.

On the football side, Darlo have embarked on an amazing run that's keeping my Facebook status update firmly in a north-east dialect. The fans are more than buoyant; they're having to tie themselves to their seats. And just after the news that I'm allowed full Gloryhunting access to the ground, Darlo play away at Grimsby, from whence I began…

* * * * *

SATURDAY, 1 NOVEMBER 2008.
The Imperial Pub, Grimsby.
So, here we are again.

It feels like longer than 88 days since I was here; like a blooming lifetime ago. Maybe it's because my life at the moment is moving much quicker than anyone else's; so much has happened – I've probably met more new people and moved home more times in the last few months than most people do in five years, and subsequently, my brain has artificially convinced itself to age my mate 'Ghandi', who I befriended earlier in the season. Or maybe it's the mood around the place that's wrinkling poor Ghandi up; things haven't been going well for Town. The atmosphere is sour now; doom and hopelessness hang in the air like guilty farts, and Ghandi's face is deflated like a slab of sun-dried plum.

"Since you've gone, you've jinxed us," says plum-faced Ghandi, morosely, shaking his head in time with the other shaking heads of people having similarly defeatist conversations around The Imp. The whole half-empty pub is like a synchronised head-shaking event. The energy is flat and heavy, a mid-season malaise with little hope for the rest of it. I feel like I've gone on holiday to a crematorium.

"Are you scared about dropping out of the league?" I ask him, lowering my tone to funereal to fit in with the prevailing morbidity. It's not out of the question; they're properly in the mire.

"Not one bit," Ghandi rallies, almost believably. "If it happens, I'll run on the pitch at full-time, naked." Oh Christ. I think about clearing the room of anyone who's already had their fish and chips in case the head-shaking and the prospect of naked Ghandi combine to turn the whole place bilious. But he sparks a trend of others who make the same pledge – Josh from the Trust and an old fella with an ill-fitting bobble hat that goes to a strange tepee point and covers only one lughole; even he promises he'll run on the pitch naked if they go down. What sort of outrage have I potentially organised?

"What's gone wrong?" I ask a dead ringer for Russ Abbot, outside.

"The fish has gone off," he replies, deadpan.

Conversely, what happens inside the ground probably constitutes my best matchday experience of the season so far. Despite the bitterly cold penis-shrinking coastal wind screaming 'be cold you slags' across the ground, it's sizzling in the away end. Cold? What cold? We're wrapped in a glowing warm Ready Brek forcefield of glory; invincible, untouchable.

"He's Darlo 'til we lose, he's Darlo 'til we lose," they sing, but it feels as though they're never going to lose, those players are becoming immortal deities. When Ricky Ravenhill detonates an atomic long-range bender that almost destroys half of Humberside, the away end revolts into a riotous public disorder of fist-waving and faces that mean it.

At last, my Darlo hymen is well and truly penetrated; the great throbbing rush picks me up and spurts joy through my bloodstream. "He's one of our own, Gloryhunter…" they sing at me. I didn't think it'd happen; not here, not today, not against my old mates; but that's just the way it goes. You win some and, well, if you're me, you win some.

"Ee eye ee eye ee eye oh, up the Football League we go…" resonates, unchallenged across the rattly, tinny old away end as the final whistle confirms that Darlo are top of the league … and I can wave to old Georgie boy on his adjacent wave crest. For the first time this season I'm with a bunch of fans who truly believe this is it; this is their year. What an experience; from Luton's battle to Darlo's rampage, the full spectrum of football emotion truncated into a few weeks. The laughing policeman has thrown his flat cap spinning into the air and Simon's eyeballs are bulging so poppingly that his glasses nearly shoot off. Woody can hardly see the game because his eyes are drunk again, although he finds the words to make another heat-of-the-moment plea to the MILF community, while a guy called Lucas tells me that he used to live next door to Rubens Barrichello. It all happens in a football crowd, among us mismatched brood of disparate football-addicts, dragged together to form this bizarre, overexcited, mashed-up mass of madness.

We emerge from Blundell Park in that gorgeous football-coloured dusk; winter headlights glowing through rain-spits. And the flickering pub lights creating cinematic silhouettes holding pint glasses.

Phone goes off.

> ⊠ TEXT MESSAGE
> FROM: PERRY BRENTFORD
> Smiffy's getting off with Fraulein
> in the corner of the Griffin!

Not so much speed dating as snail-pace dating.

Serendipity, my friends, serendipity.

GRIMSBY TOWN 1-2 DARLINGTON
Kalala 71 Clarke 7
Ravenhill 15
Attendance 3,509

DARLINGTON 1-0 BURY
White 53
Attendance 1,651
JPT Trophy Northern Area Quarter-Final

DARLINGTON 0-0 DROYLSDEN
Attendance 2,479
FA Cup First Round

DARLINGTON 2-0 LINCOLN CITY
Hatch 47
Foran 90
Attendance 3,534

11.

dro4Lsden-Gate

FRIDAY, 21 NOVEMBER 2008.
Channel Five News Studio, Isleworth.
Live to the nation.

Why now, so far into the season, in November? Why do they suddenly want to cram me into this little studio, on a blustery Friday night, to be interviewed on their primetime news bulletin? Could it be that despite promises not to mention it, they're going to Paxman-ate me? Are they planning to grill me flat like a George Foreman Lean Mean Grilling Machine over the sordid Droylsden-gate affair, until my guilty fat drips into the cleverly designed scandal-tray? I'm caked in bloody make-up; a painted chamois leather. Sweat is starting to permeate the powder like a crusted clown. She's not looking me in the eye, this news anchor, I'm sure she's going to spring Droylsden on me: the shame of it ... pressured into a clammy stammering heap of twat on live television. Does anyone watch Channel Five? I'm hot, paranoid. Lights shine in my eyes, cameras stare at me. This sofa's not meant for sitting on; it's breaking my arse-bone. Here we go, coming back from the break. I'm used to being *behind* the camera in these scenarios, not sweating myself raisin in front of it; five, four, three ... *Don't mention Droylsden, don't mention Droylsden ... make a plan Spencer ... if she mentions Droylsden, suddenly leap up and start singing* Copacabana *... no, no, no, too camp ... maybe pretend you think you're Lembit Opik and twist your face round into a weird moon ... or how about*

pretending to have a fit, a wild seizure with frothy spit and mental eyes ... yup, that'll do it ...
   "And now, a man who likes winning a bit too much ..."

* * * * *

Three days earlier
TUESDAY, 18 NOVEMBER 2008.
Butcher's Arms Ground.
Droylsden v Darlington, FA Cup Round One reply.
15 minutes played.

Allegedly, the ones making cut-throat signs are mostly Manchester City fans, hijacking Droylsden's big day to have a frivolous midweek pop at the Darlo lot. This is after all the 'Butcher's Arms Ground', ominously but affectionately nicknamed *'The Slaughterhouse'*, or *'The Abattoir'*. Gulp. Big Gulp, as 7-Eleven would have it. I've counted two policemen. *Two.* Apparently a Darlo fan has already been clumped senseless by a baseball bat-wielding Manc just outside the ground and pint glasses have been flying through the air at the nearby pub. Droylsden can smell it. The fear; the blood and guts and the money. The FA Cup: probably one of my last chances to break out of the lower divisions, if that's necessarily a desirable thing, and here I am in a brooding boiling pot, bubbling with rancid tension that threatens to throw me inescapably into the Blue Square North amid bits of rock being hurled across the corner of the bulging ground with the full force of non-league inverted snobbery at the supposed prima donna League Two fans. It's a chaotic ram of some dedicated, and many occasional fans; Mancunians gathering as one, baying for north-east blood and scalp. Dare I be the pot and call the kettle black: a ground full of gloryhunters.

* * * * *

Channel Five News Studio
"So Spencer, what's made you go on such a bizarre journey?"
   I can tell by the tone in her voice, she means 'why have you turned your back on non-league?' doesn't she? Does she? Or am I stewing in my own paranoid delu-

'One Gloryhunter' song at various grounds.

A local at The Imp, Grimsby.

First goal of the season at Grimsby.

...ndi is accosted by fellow Grimsby fan.

My home, for ten months.

The Brentford to Wycombe walkers.

Stan Bowles, down the pub.

Sven of The Swebees.

Brentford's 91/92 Promotion winning side.

Greg Dyke lurks over my shoulder.

Brentford fans do anything to get on the show.

Jonesy and Stu make me over, away at Chesterfield.

Brentford physio tries to mend me.

Smiffy and Fraulein, the first kiss.

Tidy wins the bet. Unbelievable.

on's Nick Owen.

'Shoes off, if you love Luton!'

Darlo fans remember Feethams.

I score the last ever goal at Darlington's Feethams ground.

Darlo go top away at Grimsby.

Jeff Winter, found asleep at the Darlington Arena.

Hotelier and legend, Marco Gabbiadini.

Away at Wycombe with Darlo. Photo thanks to Ted Blair.

Darlo Dog, most depressed mascot in the world.

Darren Anderton mugs me off at Bournemouth.

Former Darlo owner George Reynolds, in full flight.

John Garard's 'Reeeeedddddd Arrrrmmmmmyy!'

Bournemouth fans suffer the world's hottest chilli pepper.

Bournemouth beach, in December. *scream!*

Bournemouth fan Steve celebrates a goal

Blyth Spartans fans … giant killers.

Brentford boss Andy Scott admits it's down to me.

Hamer versus Hunter.

rentford's late equaliser v Notts County.

View from Brentford's home end.

Me doing a piece to camera…missing a goal, as usual.

Smiffy and Fraulein away at Exeter.

Smiffy celebrates away at Lincoln.

Tidy being thrown out at Lincoln.

Smiffy and Fraulein, the Posh and Becks of Brentfor

Big Jim, Macclesfield Town steward.

Macclesfield PA legend Andy Worth.

Andy Worth IS Barry White.

Rotherham's Reaction Dave, well, reacting.

Rotherham's greatest ever XI

The mysterious bum at Swindon v Scunny.

Me doing a spell for Hartlepool at Stonehenge.

Big Bob's big celebration.

Mayor of Hartlepool and cheeky monkey, Stuart Drummond.

Jeff Stelling's cousin at Hartlepool.

Peterborough fan Adi Mowles.

Adi Mowles sings the blues.

I make Mr Posh eat biscuits.

I accuse Fabio Capello of eating the last Poppet.

My one and only go on a speedway bike.

Rain at The New Den, Millwall.

Paragliding over Brighton.

The goal that kept Brighton in League One.

Brighton fans claim their glory.

I'm home, White Hart Lane. Thanks for the lend, Harry.

Brighton manager Russell Slade held aloft.

sion? God this studio is hot. Armpits drenched, brow sopping, itchy balls. Face looks fat on the monitor, like a bloated Robin Williams. Make this ordeal end, please. Why did she blink like that? Was it a secret signal to the producer in the gallery that she's about to go in for the kill? I'm on alert you cow ... I'm ready to go for the fake seizure, they'll have to go to a break ... first sign that she's going to bark on about Droylsden and I'm going to start flinching and seemingly unconsciously shouting the names of biscuit types. Bourbon. Garibaldi. That'll throw her off the scent.

* * * * *

26 minutes played.

The press had their headlines ready a week ago, the neutrals raised collective eyebrows over the draw at the Arena and I think even the Darlington players know that the will of FA Cup folklore stipulates that this inhospitable replay is supposed to be Droylsden's night. The players have that uncomfortable mid-poo face that says they just don't fancy this muddy old gaff. The air is thick with the stench of uprising underdog and all are preparing to see the natural order thrown into disarray.

And then it happens. Of course it does. *Ker-thwack.*

Matthew Tipton welts both the Droylsden faithful and its occasionals into an insane stupour, a war-mongering delirium, a double-jointed game of Twister, leaving Darlo fans edging towards the exit like an over-heckled magic act, keen to forget the FA Cup and its illusions and get to the station before their heads get kicked harder than their collective dignity.

But this isn't going to be an easy *thank you – goodbye.* Liam Hatch goes down with what appears to be a broken neck (but which turns out to be just a yanked click), and the half an hour it takes to get an ambulance on and him off the pitch serves only to prolong Darlo's agony.

"Something wicked this way comes, and unfortunately its name is Droylsden," says Chris, like a deer about to be pancaked by a lorry, pupils the size of snooker balls, sweating the essence of pure fear juice.

"What can I say? Terrible. Atrocious. Like watching Sunday morning football. *But ...* if any ladies out there want a piece of me, come and see me," says Woody, suffering and over-sexed.

"Absolutely poo. I wanna cry, I've got a lump in me throat, look," says Deano, stroking his bumper adam's apple. They're not enjoying this.

Final whistle. Onto the pitch they stream; emotions exploding uncontrollably like a marauding tribe of incensed savages; some bothering to race over to the Darlo end, gesticulating and jeering incoherent mockery, others just charging over to jump on the players and lick their faces, with puffs of steam rising from the jubilant scrabble. Hysteria and dejection; heaven and bedlam; separated only by different sides of the ground.

"What do I do now?" I ask Mr ITV on the phone, frantically trying to work out what'll become of me. It's not as simple as it seems, the implications are huge. But ITV aren't really fussed what I do, it's my decision. They're committed to following the project wherever it goes and are happy to leave it to me. In a way, I'd rather they tell me what to do, absolve me of the decision. But it's *all* on me. Do I continue this journey in non-league?

"Maybe you could get kidnapped?" says Mr ITV, offering a way to crow-bar destiny into shape. It's not even Christmas; can I afford to go into non-league so early? It's not as if it's likely I'd get back into the league, what with other fixtures lined up before Droylsden's next FA Cup game. Beyond the initial ironic hysteria, will people maintain their interest if I go so low down? Will I be able to keep my own enthusiasm if I'm confined to one of two leagues with no way out for the rest of the season?

What should I do?

* * * * *

"Good luck with the rest of the season, Mr Gloryhunter," finishes the Five News anchor, with the smile that always follows a 'crazy bonkers' *and finally*, before moving seamlessly onto the dreary doldrums of the weather report. *Oh. It's over. No mention of Droylsden. Shall I have a seizure anyway? Nahhh.*

My paranoia was misplaced. It's clearly a scandal swollen in my brain beyond the extent of anyone else's interest. As I walk out into the pitch-black Isleworth industrial estate, the rain smears make-up into my eyes and I wait in the moist West London freeze for a cab. I start thinking about the kidnapping I staged after the Droylsden game; a bunch of Darlo fans in a punk band called Misled Icons bundled me into their car and drove me away, back to the familiarity of

League Two. My on-screen explanation was simply that "I'm a gloryhunter, what do you expect?" But there's more to it than that. Words from the emails I've received rattle around in my headache like blunderbuss pellets; 'cop-out', 'fraud', 'good decision' … a confusing mixed-bag of reactions. It wasn't an easy decision, or even necessarily correct. I like the people I've met from Droylsden but this is my personal once-in-a-lifetime journey and not just a job for ITV. I needed to take a tiny bit of control of my own destiny.

Had this been April or May, I would gladly have plunged myself into non-league. No qualms whatsoever. That's why I didn't employ the non-league rule to match the 'no Europe' rule from the start. In retrospect, I could have imposed it with a date curfew attached, but I didn't think that far ahead. I'm not at all scared of not getting to a final or top of the league, I'm not hell-bent on the Premier League; I actually think it'd be just if this quest for glory 'fails'; it is after all merely providing a juxtaposition to, and highlighting, exactly the opposite of what I'm doing: the admirable loyalty through thick and thin. But it's not even Christmas yet. The fact is that if I go to Droylsden, because of the way the fixtures go, there's a good chance that the number of games before the next FA Cup tie will mean I won't find my way back into the league at all, let alone out of the Blue Square North. And the format of getting as high as possible will be blown at not even half way through the season. It's too early for that. Plus there are the weeks on end of postponed weather-beaten matches at this level that would have me rattling around without matches and struggling to fill content for the show.

So, I make my decision to stay at Darlo.

By Jove, I've had a *lot* of emails about this. It's a bloody minefield. I don't consider myself blameless, but I do consider myself a little misunderstood. I feel both guilty that I'm not doing the non-league thing and innocent in the sense that my reasons aren't as cynical as people suggest. The explanation above is simply all there is to it; to be trapped so early would render the thing stale.

Some of the criticism I can't really disagree with. As a football fan who enjoys, delights in and wants to protect the lower leagues, I agree that I could have done some good, brought some light to the non-league scene. I'm not sure that's my charge though. And I don't see those people who are criticising me getting out there and doing what they want *me* to do either. But most of the criticism surrounds a) money and my alleged hunger for making it at all costs; b) that I've apparently 'bottled it', and c) the integrity of the project has been smashed.

So for the record, here are my answers to those specific accusations...

I think the biggest misnomer is that they see this whole thing as a money-making exercise that will now conjure cash for my wallet at the expense of exposure for the non-leagues. I wish it *was* about money, because that would mean I had some. I've had to get external funding to be able to do this, yes, but I'm doing it more or less for cost and there's no difference in monetary gain for me between the Premier League and the non-league. You see, even if I do end up at Manchester United, or the likes of, this book may have an even lesser chance of selling because it'd be among hundreds of other books about the club/global brand; it'd be drowning in a vast ocean of sycophantic hardbacks and I suspect the ones with big pictures of Rooney's vacuous grin would sell substantially more. In fact, I think I'm probably getting more local press and attention with the lower league clubs than I would with the bigger ones because there's less media competition. But money isn't it at all. In fact whatever happens, I'll most likely come out of this pretty much penniless, unless this book takes on Jade Goody proportions...which for a story about a beer drinking twonk sitting in Darlington pubs, is unlikely. Personally, I'm just not especially bothered about money, much to the chagrin of my accountant; I'm more interested in spending my mobile years on this planet doing things that interest me. If those things earn me a bit of money – fine. If not – fine. I'm not driven by it one bit.

Then there are the accusations based on machismo, that I bottled the non-league. That doesn't really hold weight with me either. Bottled what? I've played a fair bit of lower non-league football and watched a fair bit. Just because my local team is in the Premier League, I'm no stranger to non-league football. What's there to bottle? Is it that I'd somehow be more of a real man by standing in torrential rain on a Monday night with 15 others? How long would it be before viewers would get fed up with the 'Gloryhunter in the non-league' irony? Does it not take more bottle – if bottle really *has* to be an issue – to go into another club's home end with 2,000 people, a few of whom have threatened to set light to you? Personally, I know what I'm more scared of, because I've stared it in the face already.

"Integrity? Look at what you're doing anyway!" says Councillor Kirton on the phone, when I ask him about the other accusations that the project has 'lost its integrity'. I thought if there's anyone whose opinion would strike a chord with me, it's his. And he's right. This project is all about the bloody minded cheek of cheating the football experience, just for one season, just to see. It's all about the gall of *forgetting* integrity, allegiance and loyalty and chasing glory. It's a random bit of silliness designed to have a laugh, travelling around, watching football. So by tweaking the rules, am I not just going with the character of The Gloryhunter, villainously cheating the football experience to my own gain once more? The rules were made by me, arbitrarily, in the first place anyway; does it matter? Does anyone really care what I do? I agree that the integrity of the format will suffer if I make a habit of it, but I've made clear amid derision that this will be the *only* time. I enjoy the whim of fate too much to tinker it to death; although people don't seem to believe me – once again using the money argument to suggest I'll just make it up as I go along to maximise those imaginary profits.

So there it is, I've made my decision, and an addendum to the rules of Gloryhunting is **no non-league**. For now it's about keeping the dream of reaching the summit of football alive, although in truth I think I'd be happier in the lower leagues anyway. But while there's a chance of 'going all the way', it keeps alive my wonderment and fascination with the globes of difference that are possible and *what might be* if I make this decision to stay in League Two.

Shakily, and with acceptance that some of the arguments against me have validity ... I make my toughest decision, but one which I think will be best in the long-term for the project, and move on in League Two with Darlington.

"Turn around when possible," says Emma on the way back up to the north-east. And I do.

DROYLSDEN 1-0 DARLINGTON
Tipton 26
Attendance 1,672

---

* * * * *

SATURDAY, 22 NOVEMBER 2008.
The Griffin Pub, Brentford.

"I like MILFs."

"I like grannies." A bizarre, calamitous collision of two of my football worlds has just impacted on the raucous pre-match saloon of The Griffin. Tidy and

Woody. Uh-oh. Lock up your, erm, over-40s. They're virtually the same person these two; morally mirrored, mere accents dividing them. It's been a while since I last saw granny-groping Tidy. At a time like this, when I'm getting bombastic pelters from all angles over the Droylsden affair, this is just what I need; the two clubs I've spent the longest time with coming together for a glory-off. It's exactly the bosom for a pillow I need right now.

London Pride ale seeps warmly into the stomach lining and my concrete shoulders relax doughy amid the familiar clattering of bottles and fairylights around the room that leave neon streaks in the eyes as beer clouds up a fuzzy filter. Landlord Ralph faux-complains that takings are down since I left and took my trade to the substantially cheaper bars up north while those two wrinkle-chasing deviants discuss preferable age ranges – both edging on the upper borders of dubious and each trying to talk louder than the other until it feels like we've wandered into a hearing aid convention.

"Oi, where's my score? Pay up you c***," says Tidy with usual decorum, upon remembering the £20 I owe him after his bit of work for Age Concern in Luton. I think I'll string him along a bit longer on that one.

My homely return to Brentford ends in a fair enough draw. Darlo stayed one-up for ages and should really have won it, but a late equaliser makes no difference to my path and allowed Tidy to show up on my uber camera-zoom, offering single finger salutes towards the away end. On the way out, familiar faces nod and wave, jibing, ribbing and I notice that three o'clock kick offs are getting darker and duskier by the end; dominated now by the lofty luminescence of stark floodlights trumping the soured sun that's now just a fading puce blush, smudged onto a horizon scored by puffy trails from planes, we who remain plunder further yet into winter's clutches and deeper into mid-season.

BRENTFORD 1-1 DARLINGTON
Osborne 90+2   Foran 60
Attendance 4,837

"Why didn't you turn up for the date with Smiffy?" I accuse Fraulein ironically.

"'Cos I wasn't interested in seeing anyone, but it's OK, it's early days," she replies, coyly, before having an atrociously productive but unrelated coughing fit.

This is my first chance at getting to the hairy bottom of what's going on between my two speed-date victims, having only received the odd text suggesting it's all kicked off between them with public combinations of kissing and touching. Ages ago, Fraulein stood Smiffy up and left him in the pub talking about a dying octopus … but it's all changed now.

"What's happened then, Smiffy?" *Come on you quirky little sod, spill it.*

"I made some moves and things worked out," he replies, with a Ron Jeremy tinge. He may as well don a dressing gown and puff a cigarette in a long holder, such is his suave self-satisfaction. They're both being ever so cagey. I can't imagine Smiffy 'making moves' at all; I wonder if these moves involved sumptuous fabrics, perhaps Gabbiafabrics, because we all know the power of them.

"We just started talking to each other," says Fraulein. Yup, talking definitely helps … although in my case, not always. "It was awkward talking to him after last time." She flashes me an accusing look.

"Did you force her into it?" I ask Smiffy, trying to provoke *something* juicy out of them, even if it must be a bit of vehement denial.

"No, no drugs were involved," he confirms, almost as though it was considered a possibility.

Well, that's all I can get out of the Brentford Posh and Becks. But definitely confirmed: *it's on.*

(Insert hackneyed joke about buying a hat like Cilla Black here.)

As the night blurs itself rowdily into the bottom of a glass, Smiffy and Fraulein hold hands in the corner and Christmas starts to introduce itself to the jukebox. They look happy, excited; those first clingy tingles of imagining a life with someone new … and I start to wonder when, or *if,* it'll happen for me. The life I lead, constantly chasing something that isn't now, forever breathing tomorrow's oxygen, it's not exactly conducive. The thought of stopping in one place confuses me; it's scary yet intriguing. Trapped yet secure, or free and alone? While I'm thundering my way around England and the world, living out whimsical fantasies others dream of, my own dreams begin to morph back to exactly what I've run away from. That life of sharing love seems somehow beyond me now; it's a distant idyll that occupies other people's lives, not mine. I am indeed the dog that wants to be on the other side of the door; I am the man who chases greener grass. The penalty I pay for my frivolous adventures is that I live them alone. Despite being here among people I like, I'm still just a visitor, a bystander who flits from one existence to another without ever really becoming truly a part of any of them. At some point between Chris de Burgh and Bing Crosby, I decide I really do need to stop my folly and try to find a life with someone, although I promise myself – and womankind – not to draw someone's name out of a hat containing all 30 million of them and marry one until…

At this moment, with that jingle jangle of festive togetherness in another group of people's 'now', it seems a world away, another adventure.

During Whigfield's disturbingly bad rendition of Wham's *Last Christmas*, my phone goes off. A text message, and I don't recognise the number.

> ✉ TEXT MESSAGE
> FROM: ??????????
> Love to lick and suck you hun all over and then let you play do you want hun

Lick? Suck? What? Who? As Shakin' Stevens gives way to Slade, I try to refocus my glassy old eyeballs through the hopsy film of London Pride to make sure I'm seeing this right. I start to wonder whether my musings over the last hour – about me maybe finding someone – have sent some sort of desirous love-energy out into the cosmos and delivered me an immediate and mysterious prospect. I'm not sure that licking and sucking strangers over a text message is the usual way to find a partner, nor would someone who does such be necessarily the right one for me, but I don't often get attention like this so decide to allow intrigue to enter the fray. My brain extrapolates it to something much more exciting. Is it Charlize Theron at last?

'Who are you?' I reply cautiously, deciding against 'Well hello Charlize'.

'Well who are you then? You sound lovely hun', she replies. Well isn't this ever so confusing? Text messages fly back and forth as I try to get her to tell me who she is, but the replies just seem to feature more and more offers, promises and variations on the theme of licking and sucking. So much licking and sucking, in fact, that if reality bears the fruit of what's on offer, someone's going to end up with cramp in the jaw and tongue-ache. 'Send me a photo then', I text, trying to coax her out of anonymity, looking around the pub in case it's someone sitting in the corner with a cheeky grin and a cleavage made in heaven.

'Ok hun love it. No what, your lush and sexy love to lick and suck you all over, send a photo babe ok'. *Alright, alright, stop licking and sucking for five minutes and show your face woman,* I think, never one for a drawn out courting process, especially with the amount of saliva it seems it's going to cost.

Around ten minutes later, at last, an MMS arrives. I excitedly open the text and a photo appears.

She's not quite what I'd allowed myself to imagine. Not at all.

"It's gonna be lonely this Christmas," sing Mud.

For a moment, my eyes won't let me believe it, thinking it's just a girl with either a very long nose or a weirdly thin face. But it's not. She's not a *she* at all. And *that's* not a face.

It's a penis.

Yup. A man's penis. A great thronging, erect, solidly engorged shaft pointing to the sky and ready for, well, probably licking and sucking. I immediately want a shower of hot bleach and scouring pads. I want to change skins. Needless to say, I don't reply. But licky sucky does. A lot. Long into the night and over the course of the next morning, I get message after message; each becoming less coherent and more repugnant to read.

'Well you not text hun why?'

'Well you send me one sexy love it do you'

'Well are you send me then sexy love it'

'Me me me ok hun love to suck bite and lick you hun love it come and join send your photo then why not ok'

'Well are you not talking then hun well up to you then your lose'.

Oh. My. Days. Yes, my lose, indeed. I try to imagine exactly which toilets and where, that some football fan has scribbled my phone number and offered licking and sucking as a service. I suspect that's what's happened, and whoever it was, you know who you are. Droylsden maybe? Or maybe it's an honest mistake; maybe the guy got to my webpage and misread it as 'Gloryholer'.

I conclude that my romantic situation probably isn't going to be miraculously saved by a random text message. I order another pint and sing along to Mud with a very brave face and my phone off.

12.

it's gone a bit wonky on there

SUNDAY, 30 NOVEMBER 2008.
A travel tavern, wedged like a pile of mouldy old tit into the outskirts of Chester, Cheshire.

RE: ITV GLORYHUNTER

Shane
Is it legal for me to wish to pour lighter fluid over this Glory Hunter t**T and set him alight if he dares come near our Club?
LEAVE US IN OUR MISERY GLORY*UNTER, IT'S OURS SO p**s OFF.
Burner
Can we burn his car out if we lose?
Shane
Yes burning stuff is good Burner. Is he in the car or not?
TheGloryhunter
Nice.

Here we go again.

Welcome to the Chester City internet fans' forum. Oddly though, being told I'm going to become the guest star of a belated bonfire night on a council estate somewhere in Blacon (on the outskirts of Chester), doesn't really give me that rats' nest in the rectum feeling anymore. Not, of course, that if it did happen I'd politely help them douse me in lighter fluid with smiles all round like a family in an advert for MB Games; no, it's more that I can now rationalise this sort of reaction into something less sinister. They're lashing out, and that's just how some people express the passion and frustration that comes with supporting their team. And with Chester limping along like a tramp's dog in League Two, to them I'm just that annoying ITV bloke poking his pointed beak into their family's business at a difficult time.

However, in a sleepless, early-hours session of gazing at the flashing LED on the smoke alarm (which is just about hitting rhythm nicely with my internal rendition of the theme tune to *Casualty*), such things amplify themselves mentally into gruesome films that kids can't watch.

What do they look like, these internet creatures? Were they born or did they just manifest? Vast gargoyles in jeans and vests, I reckon, permanently stained in saveloy fat and pickled onion juice. Tattoos, yes, definitely tattoos, of pornographic dogs fighting over a whore. And the whore looks a bit like the late Terry Scott. Are they outside the hotel? Holding medieval tools with bits of other people's gums still clinging to rusty edges? Are they waiting – chomping on more saveloys – until I emerge, when they'll forcibly fold me the wrong way up into the Nissan-Almera-of-flames, then lock the doors with assorted gunfire and chant Chester City songs as I slowly cook into the sort of Turkey Twizzler that Jamie Oliver does his nut at?

No.

But that's what a lonely sleepless night does to my ridiculous brain box. They're probably nice blokes called Steve and Gary who I'd most likely get on all right with if they'd let me. But the odds are I won't even meet them; the odds are I'll meet some other nice blokes and get on all right with them instead. I've finally got to grips with being talked about by strangers as though I'm a tumoured-up slab of old bollock; I've stopped dissolving the diatribe into crises that will destroy all of humanity. I've taken the pinch of salt required. Look at me daddy, I'm all grown up, and salty.

DARLINGTON 1-2 CHESTER CITY
Purdie 7   Lowe 37
              Kelly 53
Attendance 2,416

Given current form, nobody expected Chester to turn Darlo over at the Arena. But Chester are unpredictable and Droylsden seem to have punched the Darlo players further up the collective trachea than we thought. It had, after all, been eleven matches and one FA Cup drama; nearly a quarter of a season since I got up to the north-east. It had to come to an end at some point, and the north-west seems as good a destination as any to start spreading my tour fairly across the nation.

"Glory is dead but he'll never be forgotten," whimpered one of the kids nostalgically as he got to the front of the hand-shaking mini-queue at final whistle, as though I'd already perished in, for example, a Cestrian car fire. While I'll miss the people up there – Woody and Cockney Pete et al – I feel satisfied that the adventure has been a full and complete one. Had it been a bra, it would have been a well-worn double D-cup filled with an excellent pair of plumptious bangers.

I walked out of the Arena that night content; that my work there was done, that my D-cup was full. I did, however, acknowledge to myself in the cab back to the hotel, that my metaphors need some work.

WELCOME tO CHESTEr

OK, so, Chester started as a Roman fort called *Deva Victrix* (hence the name of the football club's ground, Deva) and eventually, quite a few years later, Russ Abbot was born here. The fans on the message boards find my mentioning of him in the show a little tedious. And now I've just done it again.

The city straddles the river Dee, has an oceanic climate and is right on the cusp of Wales, hence the football team's rivalry with Wrexham, or 'Wrexscum' as they're known to Chester fans. Famously, the football ground actually straddles the border between England and Wales.

"Oh yea, oh yea, oh yea…" bellows the town crier from somewhere cavernous at the very bottom of his bellyguts, right down the lens, thoroughly clumping my ear drums slap bang at The Cross, in the heart of the shopping area of Chester City … before he's stopped in his tracks by a couple of really quite insistent old ladies. They look like off-the-peg stereotype old ladies; wigs, winceyette and probably a pound of mints in each respective handbag.

"Which way is the car park? We're not from here you see," they ask him. The town crier is astounded that of all the people they could have stopped and asked, the silly moos felt the need to curtail him, in the middle of being filmed doing the only thing he's on this planet to do – cry, in the middle of town. He bemusedly points them in the right direction and they waddle off like a couple of constipated penguins in fur coats.

"Oh yea, oh yea…" he continues, exceeding Brian Blessed decibel level and further blanching my inner ear, "Ohhhhh yeaaaaa … At last … he has come to Chester's fair city. God bless Chester, God bless our team. God bless The Gloryhunter, God save the Queen!" and off he thrusts an oddly triangular hat with a grinning, triumphant salute. I'm not sure if he's calling *me* a queen, or whether he's referring to *the* Queen … so I decide not to take issue and thank him for taking time to come and see me with his glory-tailored cry. What a job, dressing up like a Les Dennis pantomime nightmare every day for city ceremonies, weddings and Bar Mitzvahs; all that gold-trimmed baggy velvet and a white curly wig you'd definitely shout 'syrup' at in the street. I wish they'd mentioned this at careers day in school.

Along with the well-kept tradition of the town crier, Chester's history is irresistible. Even to the historically numb, it's like stumbling through the very past the books depict, albeit implanted with McDonalds and the rest. Its past is more complicated than the black and white cake-icing display in the centre of the city suggests, with all its medieval, Jacobean-style Victorian mishmash being penned in by the Roman walls you often see as the focal point of a falling down the stairs storyline in *Hollyoaks*. (Note to self, no more *Hollyoaks* references … it's starting to look pervy.) Walking along Eastgate, roasting chestnut smoke plumes out of blackened pans filled with hot glowing coals, up my nostrils, implanting in me the very essence of a Dickensian Christmas.

The old Eastgate clock snobbishly overlooks proceedings – apparently the most photographed clock in England (after that Big Ben one somewhere in London). Ornately perched in spindly gold detail above the swathes of shoppers (all lugging bags full of pre-unwanted presents they can't really afford) – the clock reminds us with austerity that we will *always* be time's bitchslag. The half-timber buildings crouch as though they might just trip over and drag the rows of twinkly Christmas lights stretching out way down the cross-sectioning roads with them, into a big drunk pile of black and white quaintness and Yule. I slide around the stupidly icy Roman walls, falling over on average most of the time and once just like

Todd Carty on that ITV ice dancing show. I trek all over the city, mentally going through the ages like a *Blackadder* retrospective; romancing myself into all of them as Edmund. I love Chester; this is just the sort of place to inject England back into my soul. But conversely, my football experience here is drawing a gloomy blank, I haven't managed to pull any of the fans into my silly flight of fantasy.

* * * * *

WEDNESDAY, 3 DECEMBER 2008.
Ye Olde Boot Inn.
On the first floor of one of Chester's two-tier medieval shopping galleries that occasionally waft scents of assorted urine.

Just as the weekend away game down in Bournemouth draws closer, I eventually get a bit of semi-friendly purchase from a Chester fan, who reluctantly agrees to show me around the pubs and explain the club's predicaments, of which there seem to have been way too many in recent years...

Mike begins just as suspiciously as his emails suggest; eyeing me up and down as though I've committed terrible sins, as he goes through a well-rehearsed potted history of the place and its football team. He performs it with almost the theatre of a tour guide; a pint of ale at his side instead of a wacky umbrella. This suspicion goes on for a while, which makes me suspicious, so here we are, drinking far too quickly and jousting with our terse suspicious faces on. It's like Middle East peace talks (and I don't know which of us would be Hamas). It's a curious encounter, and after seven beers it's revealed that Mike's reluctance and stoic diplomat-like behaviour has been because he came thinking I might be wearing a wire.

A wire. Me? Do me a favour. It's here that I realise how sensitive football fans can be. We can be such a suspicious, sensitive lot. I explain that this isn't called 'Gloryfellas' or 'The Gloryfather' and that I have no desire to unearth scandals or force anyone into a position from which they may need to plea bargain, all because they said a full back can't head the ball. Mike finally accepts that I am not recording our conversation, and the frosty relations become a flourishingly diplomatic part-nership. If we were countries, we'd definitely be trading arms. A tremendous drink-up transpires that stops short only at holding hands or exchanging plutonium. But he does lead me around the stunning Roman-walled city by night – romantic whoever you're with, even Mike – visiting pubs with hearths that masturbate the winter idyll perfectly.

Chester itself glimmers, but in contrast, Mike tells me all about the troubles and strife the football club has been slung through in recent times; the fractious relationship between fans and owner Stephen Vaughan, the obvious titters over the fact that both his sons are in the first team and the current bizarre wrangling over Vaughan wanting to sell the club – with a certain John Batchelor in the frame to buy.

Batchelor. Oh my days, what a surreal scenario ... Batchelor is an ex-racing driver who once had his drive funded by Blackburn Rovers, which seems strange enough in itself. After retiring from racing personally, he went on to run a racing team, and then nudged his way into football by becoming owner of York City – changing the club's name to 'York City Soccer Club' in 2002, to increase its appeal to the American market. Well that worked. In Los Angeles you can't walk five minutes without hearing someone mention the Minstermen; they're York City mental out there. He even added a chequered flag into their club crest to reflect his own penchant for racing, the poor sods. Instead of becoming the new New York Yankees though, the club went into administration and Batchelor, surprise surprise, received death threats.

In 2008, Bachelor re-emerged and decided he wanted to take over little Mansfield Town. He wanted to ... wait for it ... change the name of the club ... to ... wait for it ... Harchester United.

The name is of course borrowed from the fictional club of the same name in the now passed-on, plastic-acted Sky One drama *Dream Team*. Needless to say, any self-respecting fan of any club with any sort of history would *not* want this; dag-nammit I wouldn't want my Sunday side called that, not even as a joke, not even in a training match. Obviously, the proud people of Mansfield didn't want this either and shooed him out like a scruffy urchin trying to nick an apple. You couldn't make it up (unless it's already a fictional football team, which it is).

And now it seems *he's back* – again, trying exactly the same thing on with Chester City – or perhaps in a few weeks time, the new Harchester United. In fact this week there's an open meeting for fans to question Vaughan about the whole ownership scenario, and rumour has it that Mr Dream Team is coming along too.

A couple of fans on forums have sneaky suspicions that the whole thing may have been designed to show the fans that with this joker standing on the sidelines,

Stephen Vaughan is perhaps not as bad as some think after all. Who knows? But it makes me wonder what it is about the ownership of these lower league clubs that sees them so often slide off into the farcical arena of businessmen with egos larger than their business sense. It happens time and again; I've already seen the like in the recent histories of Luton, Darlington and Brentford. It's no wonder some of these clubs are facing financial ruin, they're being run by the most absurd men you could imagine. If I ever start spouting on about buying a football club and re-naming it 'Keith' or something, please, someone, be aware that this means I've gone the wrong side of eccentric and unless it's Arsenal, *stop me*.

I decide not to go to the meeting; not only to preserve my car from the flames, but also because I feel my light-hearted five minutes wouldn't be appropriate for the clear turmoil the fans are experiencing, and the sensitivity it's causing among them. This thing isn't about forcing my way into others' misery and I know when I'm not welcome.

By the time Mike and I leave the fifth equally cosy pub, he loosens up amid the pintage and instead of trading international weapons, I buy him a curry, the international language of bloke. However, near the end he mysteriously disappears in a cab, staring at me blankly as it pulls away. *How odd*, I think. He looks like an unmanned puppet; utterly vacant and without an ounce of recognition in his eyes. I suspect he's just hit that point where the body has been so ravished by booze and chillies that it steadfastly refuses to co-operate. As he drives off expressionless in the back seat of the cab, I wonder if that's about as close as I will get to the Chester faithful: a man who believes me to be an undercover agent wearing a wire.

My Chester is one of contrasts; falling in love with a city of English perfection … yet mostly unrequited and untrusted by its football fans.

* * * * *

BOURNEMOUTH 1-0 CHESTER CITY
Anderton 88
Attendance 4,154

"There are lots of Spurs fans here for you Darren, have you got a message for them?" He laughs sarcastically and just walks past, offering just three words: "Keep it up."

That's the in-depth interview the press guy promised me with Darren Anderton after the game. I conclude that I am not Louis Theroux. I'm not even Russell Harty. If Mike from the other night was watching this, he'd finally realise for sure that I'm entirely incapable of wearing a wire for journalistic gain.

And so off he walks, former Spurs, Portsmouth and England international Darren Anderton – out of football forever, without even looking me in the eye on the way through. The floppy-fringed ponce. He didn't even stop to say those words, "*keep it up*", he just breezed past smelling of Lynx and retirement, hardly even bothering to open his mouth wider than a fag paper to say them, and with so little vocal effort invested that my microphone could barely detect his feeble audio output. He's made me feel like a complete floppy breast. Dazzling Darren Anderton has mugged me off. And so brutally, that upon such a blow one can only consider an immediate suicide reflex, without even thinking about it, just an instantaneous gun to the head as quick as a knee jerks on being hit by a hammer.

But I do still loves him. Sicknote might have cost Spurs a fortune in medical expenses, but he was with the club for a long time, like a cardigan you can't bring yourself to throw away. Tonight is *his* night and definitely a *Sliding Doors* moment, for both of us, with Anderton this time as Paltrow, if that's even vaguely imaginable. It had to happen; it was written. A thumping volley, 88 minutes gone, his swansong lash that sent Bournemouth fans into a dizzying frenzy. As the sky turned cherry amid silhouettes of people leaping up and down on the other side of the ground, so did I. And aside from making me look a proper Gaffney – let's forget about that now – Dazzling's dipping swipe, his last ever contribution to our professional game, has sent me down south to live with the Dean Court faithful. It's an honour for this momentous split-second to have such a significant bearing on my direction, as well as Dazzling's.

I did, in the end, meet Chester fans who I'd have liked to have spent more time with. Nice, genuine supporters who may well have embraced what I'm doing. And some good look-alikes among them; a little Alan Carr who goes on the drum, and a Michael Owen. Perhaps the Owen look is the indigenous facial composition of a Cestrian (something that clearly leaped over Russ Abbot). They were gutted, but most of them couldn't begrudge Anderton his last bit of glory.

"Hung like an Arab stallion, apparently," one offers as a soundbite to accompany my coverage of this little moment in history. Maybe Dazzling would have paid more attention if I'd quizzed him on his allegedly enormous penis.

Me and Chester, it seems, was never meant to be.

WELCOME tO BOUrNEmOUtH

A survey in 2007 showed Bournemouth, 105 miles from London on the south coast, to be the happiest place in Britain. Despite that, it was the first town to introduce CCTV cameras for street-surveillance. Happy but watched.

Novelist Mary Shelley (who wrote that *Frankenstein*) is buried in nearby Boscombe, and her son Sir Percy (whose name is taken up by the local Wetherspoons pub) came to settle here. *Lord of the Rings* writer J.R.R. Tolkien holidayed here for 30 years and eventually retired and died here.

You'll probably already know this, but Bournemouth is, of course, twinned with Netanya, in Israel.

---

* * * * *

TUESDAY, 16 DECEMBER 2008.
The Masons Arms, Blyth, Northumberland.
A sea of green and white, with a little bit of red.

"I am a Trojan of the Spartan territories of Northumbria. I want to welcome yous all. Don't shag wor women, enjoy wor beer and never forget you've been here because half your friends won't even know where Blyth is."

He's right, this big likeable oaf, puffing an enormous accent through five per cent proof condensed air into the Christmassy night outside The Masons Arms pub, in this place called Blyth. I've never even considered where Blyth is before. Do I know tiny villages in Africa? Yes. Do I have a clue about Blyth? Not the foggiest. I feel stupid and guilty; *this* is my country and all these years I've been guilty of ignorance and treason; *treason I say!* The long drive to reduce my ignorance of Blyth almost crumpled me into a drooling wreck who may have off'd someone's head if

I'd had to listen to another second of Andy Goldstein flexing his substantial ego on TalkSPORT. It's virtually Scotland, this place, and *that* many hours of radio 'chat' is clinically dangerous. I am proof.

"You do naa that Blyth is the drug capital of the north-east don't you?" said the taxi driver after picking me up from the sterile, geographically neutral travel pit on a non-descript A-road out of town. Funny how people enjoy and feel the need to warn you about their town and its dangers, with a kind of cocksure pride. I've noticed the same of so many places – pub names mentioned with a wince that comes packed with a proud gleam, as though I'm a sensitive, naïve journalist experiencing everything for the very first time, as though they're in the real world and I'm not. If I took half of these people into the Walthamstow pubs I was alcoholically schooled at in my teens, they'd come away sunken, gaunt and would instantly take up clicking rosary beads in thanks that they came away with a workable smile. And now I've just typed that with the same inverted pride that these people do.

What I actually find is that Blyth is as ordinary as any other town, and just like everywhere else right now, its Woolworths is being gutted by bargain hunters who are even buying its shelving for pennies. Blyth is another example of a town whose main industries have either moved or faded into history – in this case it's ship building and coal mining – although its port still offers a route to Scandinavia. But one proud aspect of the town is its football team, Blyth Spartans, famous for an FA Cup giant-killing run in 1978 that saw them barge their way through to round five. And as I walk around town with a bag of stodgy fat holding together the odd vinegar-logged chip, the sun sinks into an FA Cup night sky, with a bite in the air and the atmosphere; a little edge that suggests this town wants more cup stories to carry through the years.

For me, this match would appear to be a freebie, because after the addendum rule I added last time, Blyth's Blue Square North status can't drag me up here. But not quite. For both me and my new south coast friends, there's enormous consequence at stake because Bournemouth's furthest ever competitive match could lead to a next-round tie against Premier League Blackburn. Is this it? My carriage towards the glory that the face of this project is pointed at? Surely Blyth can't assassinate Bournemouth? There's plenty at stake…

For a group of the fans who've made the journey, it's a pigging midweek nightmare. Their plane from Bournemouth was cancelled, so through gritted teeth and blind dedication, they hired a car at the airport and have driven all the way up here.

For a weekday evening, that's impressive; literally from bottom to top of the country, up and down in one night, and moreover, this game is live on the telly tonight! Absolute head-cases. Even before the game starts, their faces have the drawn look of knowing they've got a journey long into the night ahead of them that could break the resolve of most rally drivers. I've plumped for a travel tavern nearby. Oh no, you won't find me sobbing in tatters in the toilets of Wetherby services at two in the morning, covered in my own snot and with bleeding, overbitten finger-nails. Not again. But for this lot; where does it come from, this devotion? Because in my experience, not all of them necessarily *watch* all of the game – they're often late because the pub was warm and beer-flavoured, and then they natter over half the action anyway. Is it an obsessive box-ticking thing, a new ground to add to the list like a trophy? Or is it just to be with their friends? I love my football, really I do, but it's never dominated every aspect of my life as it does some of these people. I'm halfway between admiration and amazement; and occasionally a bit disturbed at the extent of their endeavours.

This particular foray into the non-league is a much friendlier experience than the cage fighting, blood-drenched astmosphere at Drolysden in the last round. It's like a carnival; fancy dress, painted faces, beer up the walls and the live TV cameras in the pub having to cut back to the studio because of the incessant jeering everyone's decided to interrupt the Alan Partridge-esque presenter with. There are men in green Santa costumes and enormous green afro wigs dancing around the place and it's virtually impossible to get to the bar to even attempt to drink *wor beer*.

Croft Park is as full as it can be. Cold? Cold, yes. Confirmed. It's as bitter as a childless spinster with chlamydia. My nose has turned into an icy shard; fingers like fleshy straws full of pink Slush Puppy. The Blyth fans are bouncing up and down, almost sweaty; one of them inexplicably wearing an enormous Frank Sidebottom style papier-mâché head; many of them equally as foxingly wearing Roman centu-rion outfits. Just like the Droylsden fans, albeit dressed by surrealism itself, Blyth fans can smell the fear. For Bournemouth the night has the tension of an aptitude test that you really shouldn't fail; like the fear I have of taking an IQ test, lest I discover that I am actually a complete spastic. Half of the Bournemouth fans have faces like they're trying to swallow a ping pong ball. It's the sort of night that can turn underdogs into firm favourites.

For a couple of north-east based Bournemouth fans, their rare chance to see the Cherries live is all a bit much. They look a little bit like the Mitchell brothers from *Eastenders*, but angrier, drunker and again, angrier. I really don't want a glass of what they've been drinking because it's turned them into portents of seething shoutface. Of course, I get lumbered with sitting next to them, and as the first half progresses with typical FA Cup brutality, they get more irate and spitty – actually with fellow Bournemouth fans, because they don't consider the singing output to be of a high enough standard or volume. It gets so naughty that I have to move, because elbows are starting to dig into my riblets and a smattering of Christ-knows-what laced saliva has gone in my eye and been blinked in. I don't know how to deal with the idea that I've just ingested one of these men.

"They were having a go at us because we weren't singing," a part-traumatised, part-giggly teen Cherry tells me, "then they said they'd lump me one if I didn't start singing. And then they did a wee wee on my friend's flag." It's half-time and the Mitchell-brothers-on-acid have been chucked out … because they *had a wee* on someone's flag. I stand confused as to how there can be any reason why anyone can end up urinating on a flag in the stand at a Blyth Spartans match.

At the break it's looking shaky for Bournemouth. The stench of upset gets stronger and the rabidly rabbiting press box behind me is a babble of conspiratorial rhetoric leaning heavily on the side of the underdog. The home fans continue to bounce and the bracing night air seems starched stiff with tension. The Bournemouth fans' ping pong balls are swelling to tennis balls, and you try swallowing one of those … ah, that takes me back … God bless uncle Kevin, we told him the tennis ball was just *too big*.

"I don't know what he's doing … it's gone a bit wonky on there," says John, or 'Nonny' as they call him. Now let me tell you all about John, because with him may well be the answer to the question I asked about where the dedication comes from. John is adored, cherished by the Bournemouth fans. He's known by many because he can be heard from any part of any ground, and quite feasibly by inhabitants of far away galaxies, leading a 'reeeedddddd aaaarrrrrmmmmmmyyyy' chant that often continues for throat shredding durations. John's a big bloke – he likes his food – and is hearing and vision impaired. He lives in an assisted community and within the extended Bournemouth family of fans is at the centre of the tight-knit nucleus of supporters who take responsibility for getting him to and from games. They aren't related, but this is about as close-knit a family as you can imagine. There's Steve, a Matt Lucas look-alike with hair, a man for whom Magners is all five of his five-a-day; the unofficial matriarch of the group, Serena, who works at the club and straddles the fan/employee horse; Dave, who goes out with Serena (therefore is also straddled) and is persistently on the other end of Steve's jibes about his prominent lugholes ... They're all part of a cluster of Cherries who regularly wedge into the booths of the local Wetherspoons, The Sir Percy Florence Shelly in Boscombe – not far from Dean Court – from breakfast until sunset with a bit of matchday in between. They have the sort of set-up I wanted and expected to experience when I started this expedition. With most Spurs fans I know just congregating on match days and then getting a long train journey back to wherever it is they've moved out to, I wanted to see how football genuinely centres in people's lives. And here it's as good an example as any.

Most of their social focus is on John's peculiar turns of phrase and the verbal slips he makes. Although they laugh at him, it's with a fondness and affection that they know he appreciates. The 'Non-isms' never end and their impact is accentuated by his delivery, which is affected by his deafness, and the innocent simplicity of his view of the world. "It's gone a bit wonky" is my favourite, and one I've decided to use at the end of every episode of my show from now on in. It's like a motto, because despite its clumsiness, he's right; eventually, everything will go a bit wonky.

"The general appeal of Non is that he's fanatically loyal to AFC Bournemouth," Steve tells me, through gargles of Magners, "and through that, he's made tons of mates and had much more of a life than he would have done normally. He lives in an assisted place, but enjoys a fantastic social life and revels in his local 'fame'. He's one of the most caring blokes I've ever met; he'll do virtually anything for his mates. The sad side though, is that he's desperate to find love and become a dad. He gets quite emotional about it at times and it's really hard to see him get upset about it when you know there's a chance he might not ever realise that particular ambition. He sees things very simply and when he comments on them, it seems funny, because he doesn't get confused by the detail like other people do."

There are even Facebook groups where people can go and list their stories about John; like when a fan called Vinny asked him if he's worried about getting mad cow disease from a burger, John replied, "No, it alright, I have cheeseburger." Or when he was asked what the time was, he said, "Errrr, it a bit cloudy." And that's why these fans travel all this way. Their little group is a family that's pinned together by the thrills and spills of following the club no matter the distance, the cancelled planes, the gloryhunters jumping on the bandwagon, the result, or even if your flag gets covered in piss. For John, the football and Steve and the rest are at the very heart of his existence, and he theirs.

So, when clubs like these find themselves in financial difficulties, the ructions and reviling among the family becomes something of an almost unbelievable soap opera. And tonight, I begin to get an idea of the bizarrely complicated political picture that surrounds the club. As Blyth run time down, the squawking journos prepare their shockety shock shouty headlines and one of the floodlights gives up the ghost amid half-hearted protestations around the theme of abandoning the game ... Steve and the gang are preparing to mob the Bournemouth directors and angrily demand explanations. Spartans win 1-0, an 89th minute winner from substitute Ged Dalton, and the associated pitch invasion ensues. There are handshakes between fans and bouncing drunk green santas dancing with Roman centurions. It's a bit weird, like a north-east version of *Moulin Rouge*. Thankfully though, it's the Blyth fans singing an incoherent muddle rather than Ewan McGregor.

Everybody seems to love everybody and it only just stops short of free love as per the 60s because of the cold. Apart from between Steve and the directors; that certainly isn't a love-in.

45 minutes after the game, the last few fancy dress oddities drag their various cloaks and plastic swords out of the ground, while I'm still outside with Steve, Dave and Serena; dreaming of the warmth of the pub and the freezing cold *wor beer* ... But Steve *really* needs to speak to the directors. I try to get to the bottom of what he's going to say, but I'm not sure he really knows himself. It's Paul Baker – a confessed Chester City fan – he's after. He's the Bournemouth chairman, but I've heard that he still goes on the Chester forum under a pseudonym and I suspect I know which one, and he wasn't kind to me (although I can't be sure it's true). Steve also wants a segment of Alistair Saverimutto – or Savvy – the Chief Executive.

And so eventually they emerge, looking harassed, stressed, tired and absolutely *thrilled* to see Steve. Maybe not. But in Steve goes, angry-faced, his jowls juddering ruddily with the rage; beginning heated and turning boiling, and not saying especially much other than an approximate *"what on earth was that?"*. And then he's at the players, offering friendlier advice on their game. No-one wants this, 500 miles from home and the local press probably already whirring up to print off the witch hunt. Serena, meanwhile, is caught up in the middle; partly as Steve's friend and partly as an employee of the club who sees these guys every day. It's the fact that the club is so small that this can happen; the fans have a much more tangible sense of ownership, of closeness to the club in a way we as Spurs fans can't. I can't imagine me waiting outside Bill Nicholson Way for Daniel Levy to emerge. Maybe some do, but I just don't feel the need for that sort of connection to the club. Does that make me less of a fan, that I just want to go along and cheer them on, then go back to the pub? Would it be different if I still lived in the area and considered it an emblem of my manor rather than just a football team? Maybe I really am a gloryhunter; perhaps I hadn't considered that real fans do that bit more than me. I feel half embarrassed for Steve, because this whole exercise whiffs of geekery; and half embarrassed for myself, to think I may after all be more of this gloryhunter twat on the internet than I thought.

When the last coach departs and Steve's run out of people to confront, we watch it head off into the now gloomy after-the-party Blyth midnight, taking with it my carriage to Blackburn in the next round, and maybe the Premier League too. If I don't get with a club that's still in the cup soon, this will be it, League Two or round abouts. But possibly I'm starting to turn to the geekside, because I really don't care about all that; for once, I'm happy where I am.

ROCHDALE 1-1 BOURNEMOUTH
Le Fondre 67   Bradbury (pen) 45
Attendance 2,285

BLYTH SPARTANS 1-0 BOURNEMOUTH
Dalton 89
Attendance 4,040
FA Cup second round replay

---

* * * * *

"Steve, if you undermine me again, I'll cut your f*****g legs off."

Not the words of a rampaging lunatic full of crack and bitter Freudian resentment – although it would fit someone of that ilk. And no, it's not Paul Danan in a reality show rant either. Not even Prescott. Nope, those are the words of a senior official of AFC Bournemouth, who'll remain nameless because I can't actually verify or prove it.

Cut. Your. Legs. Off.

I mean it's not an easily carried out threat, you can't just lash out in one swipe and lop the things off; Steve's big old thighs would take some coaxing to actually *come off*. It's not massively surprising that the intense bouts of badgering and whining from Steve would provoke such a response, although the extreme and gruesome nature of it is a little surprising; it would probably make Fred West baulk. 'That's a bit much,' Fred would say.

Steve claims this sensational outburst was hissed at him after the home game against Bury, just outside the players' and officials' entrance, where all of the fan-player-official 'debates' take place directly after games. I've already had my own bit of bother at that entrance; there must be a rancid portent of energy occupying it, maybe the aura of still-alive Luther Blissett has saturated the cosmic make-up of the place. The door to the main offices is watched over by a bouncer called Bob, who hates me, and I hate him back. In short, I had a press pass *and* a ticket, but when presenting him with both to gain entry to the offices bit, big Bob decided that only the ticket, to the stand on the other side, was valid. Apparently it trumped the press pass. *Oh you tedious-nosed egg-arsed lump of potato leg, just let me in*, I thought, randomly. Half a season in and a bit hacked off now with stewardship and the like, I made sure he overheard me on the phone saying:

"Yeah, this bloke who really fancies himself won't let me in," to which he replied, just as audibly, "I wouldn't if I were you sir." *Oooohh, Bobby big voice*. And then he watched me with great big angry sockets wherever I went. So I made his eyeballs work for it … I walked up and down outside the entrance around 23 times, back and forth like a walking tennis match, each time smiling over at him gaily as I returned. Some people think I'm a little passive-aggressive, I don't know why, but if they say it again, I'll imply something.

Anyway … Steve reckons the leg-cutting-off exchange was overheard by a copper, who asked if he wanted to make a complaint. But instead, Steve says he sought a little clarification from the guy, who then claimed … I love this … that it's just a phrase that means 'I'm going to stop communicating with you'. I have to admit that I'm quite good on colloquial English, but this one I've never witnessed in practice. Have you ever got irate on the phone to a utility company over a bill or a repair man not turning up and had the person on the other end saying:

'Sir, if you don't calm down I'm going to have to cut your legs off? Or have you ever broken up with someone by saying, 'listen (insert name of former romantic partner), things aren't going great, I think it's time we cut each other's legs off?

In terms of the ownership and running of the wild west League Two, Bournemouth are up there with Harchester. From what I can make out, the players and officials make the mistake of reading what's said on the forums – a familiar mistake for me – and that seems to have been the case here (even though Steve doesn't go on the forums).

But the stories don't end here...

I meet Chris, a nice, quiet man who wears his Bournemouth hat so that his ears really stick out. I don't know if he realises it. But then I've been wearing jeans with a massive hole in the arse for three weeks, so his ears, compared to my potential cross-section view of ballbag, are nothing. Before the Bury game, before any legs have been hacked off, we walk calmly to the ground after a thorough beer-clobbering at the Percy. When we get to the entrance, before my incident with staring Bob, the lady at the counter tells Chris that there's a letter for him, and hands over a piece of folded A4 that's got bits of felt pen bleeding through like a drawing a child's brought home from nursery.

I'll keep the identity of the sender hidden, because, well, it seems only fair. The handwritten letter reads:

FAO CHRIS
If you ever make reference to me taking drugs or any of my team-mates you won't be so lucky to get away with a phone call next time.

XXXXXX XXXXX

(The X's aren't kisses, by the way, they're just where the player's name was written on the letter, and the number of X's in no way indicate the number of letters in the name, so don't try that one, buster.)

Astonishing. The club passes on a letter from a player to a fan that is essentially a very thinly cloaked threat. *Astonishing.* Maybe the sender would argue that 'you'll be lucky to get away with just a phone call' is just another rare colloquial phrase that again I've never heard which means he'd bloody well bring a bottle of wine to his house and toast to world peace. But I doubt it.

Personally, I'd have been thrilled off of my gob if David Ginola had sent me a handwritten stream of flounce (probably inked in a beautiful Gallic-scented calligraphy) for comments I may have made about him being caked in a forcefield of too much hairspray, but it just seems unfeasible that this sort of stuff goes on ... and Chris, poor little pokey lugholes here, is standing outside the ground holding this letter, really quite shell-shocked. And while the letter is open, people who hadn't previously heard the rumours are queuing up to have a look. (Maybe the letter wasn't such a brilliant idea, Mr Player?)

I had no idea that anywhere in the league, players had such personal associations with fans. But in these lower leagues, they're all friends on Facebook. I'm friends with Ben Hamer, the Brentford goalkeeper, and forever get his sweary unrestrained intercourse with team-mates popping up on my page. Is this a good thing? Are we taking the shine off these 'idols', or are we all starting to realise they're just people like us? Maybe this closeness to those previously seen as untouchable will show those loose-mouthed detractors that their words *do* have consequences and they ought to be responsible for what they sling around about another person, whoever they are. Bloody hell, I sound like flipping Fern Britton. Someone, please, de-sanitise me before I get offered daytime TV.

The whole letter thing once again boils down to cyber-bravery and unrestrained jibber jabber on the internet forums, where Chris was apparently part of a thread that discussed some current rumours about what the players get up to in their time off. I of course do not support nor seek to assert these claims; they've clearly quite upset one of the Bournemouth players and if they are untrue I can't really blame him for wanting to make it known. But what an odd way to go about it.

After a resounding victory against high-flying Bury, and just as importantly, maybe, John breaking his record for the number of consecutive 'red army' chants (13), the night passes off down the Percy – where the screams and howls of a cowboy saloon bar match the mood at the club – someone nicks my phone and Chris's bizarre day finishes with two girls previously unknown to him snogging each other on his lap.

My immersion into the world of the Bournemouth fans has been a splashy one of heart-grabbing closeness and political incidents more akin to something you'd see in Zimbabwe.

It's never dull at Dean Court.

```
BOURNEMOUTH 2-0 BURY
Igoe 39
Partington 44
Attendance 3,479
```

* * * * *

My resolve is cracking. There's something inside me making a fundamental shift, and for once it's not my guts. I came on this journey with nothing but resentment and bitterness towards the country which sprouted me; its ignorance, its anger, its pessimism. But Chester city centre and Bournemouth's beach – ah, Bournemouth's expansive, horizon-clinging beach and its blazing winter sun splatted in the middle of perfect blue skies ... it's making me realise that England is here to be loved, and that maybe all those things I despise about it are actually inside me. If I suspend my anger and frustration and my own ignorance for five minutes ... here it is, England, in all its glory. But as I stand atop the heather-smothered cliff-ette overlooking the gawp-inducing breadth of the beach that I was having a Christmas paddle in just five minutes ago (which was so cold I emitted rat-noises), I realise that beyond any of the backdrops, whether it's this soul-restoring beach or a drug addict's kitchen sink full of sick ... it's the people you surround yourself with that make the real difference to your life, not necessarily the place you're at. For years now I haven't surrounded myself with anyone in particular; a social drifter, a fly-by-night, constantly chasing something or other. But what? It's slowly sinking in that it's not where you are, it's who you are and who you're with, in this very moment. As the seagulls screech out their own personal melodramas in the Bournemouth December haze, it clicks inside me that while my adventures curing nostalgia in my last book helped me look to now and the future, this adventure is helping me rule out over-consideration of future and the relentless chasing of an impossible one. I've already worked out that yesterday doesn't exist, and now I'm discovering that chasing a tomorrow that will never actually arrive is futile too. Now is all that counts. Just now.

I grab hold of Dorset like a million dollars; I get out into the New Forest on a Ruud van Nistlerooy-alike horse; canter along through thick woods, unruly plains and wild horses staring at me as though I've just walked into their living room (which is probably true). Then I drive an hour down this awesome coast to visit a couple who grow the Dorset Naga – possibly the hottest chilli pepper in the world. This is 160 times hotter than the jalapeno and could blow your head clean off. I gather some and, of course, feed them to the Bournemouth fans in order to gain footage of gratuitous chilli-pain faces.

Cherries fan Danie looks like she's pooped herself, with virtually urine passing from her eyes, while Nonny actually thought he was popping a cherry in his gob ... oops.

"It got me very sick," he says with blood-red eyes, "it all came out in the loo, it all went out. I thought it cherry." Bless him.

Just as Bournemouth starts to become my home and I consider the idea that actually, I could see myself living this life, a bombshell strikes to upset the cherrycart ... I'm struck down with the scourge of menkind. MAN-FLU.

Now ladies, let me tell you all about man-flu. It exists. And while you've got it, *Paint it Black* by the Rolling Stones plays itself over and over in your head, backwards, sung by Slade on helium. And then there's the body pain. It's like being put through a garlic crusher and then pan-fried and slung into a hot curry dish. Maybe this is my burning penance for shoving one of those scud-missile chillis down poor old Nonny's throat. Without a doubt, it is the worst illness known to hu-men-ity.

Christmas is cancelled. My family are entirely wiped out by it. No presents, no turkey, not even a pickled onion. No crackers exploding out cheap tat everyone throws away, no tables being turned upside down amid a row over a game of rummy, no liqueurs that taste of off-perfume and no after-dinner charades that nobody can get because nan's trying to do *One Flew Over the Cuckoo's Nest* and we all think she's doing *Rambo*. And along with my family Christmas, down the swanny goes my traditional Boxing Day football game; yet another trip down to Griffin Park, and yet another Glory-off.

The texts fly in all afternoon, and eventually confirm what I'm squinting at on teletext ... Bournemouth have handed me back to Brentford. I feel like I'm The Ashes, and I may as well be, as my flu makes me start whining on deliriously about *maybe it's Multiple Sclerosis with a touch of plague and that they should just cremate me now because it would be cooler than my temperature.*

Me and Bournemouth are over, and there's no soppy goodbyes. Just a few text messages and a pint of Night Nurse to get me off.

There's no place like home ... there's no place like home ... there's no place like home...

BRENTFORD 2-0 BOURNEMOUTH
Bean 22, 45+1
Attendance 6,450

13.

†HE MaCC daddy

SATURDAY, 17 JANUARY 2009.
The Albany Pub, Brentford.
Crapping myself. I mean really, very very scared indeed.

"No, no, no … you know what you meant," booms six feet of muscle and fight-face, with a maniacal but controlled, pre-combustive, tone. The calm before the storm. *He's going to batter me.*

"So then tell me what you meant." His eyes are stabbing my face and the raucous sounds of the pub have faded into underwater murmurs. *Oh deary me. What a pickle.*

By now I don't even remember what I've said or what we were talking about or how it came to this most awkward of confrontations, but I'm definitely fearing for the immediate future of my face. This enormous eye-bulged hillock of a man called Piers has suddenly turned on me – *suddenly*, and he's gripping my puny bicep like an orangutan grabbing irritably at an off banana. I search my brain and find various keywords such as 'idiot', 'my', 'big' and 'mouth', but still can't recall what, amid the overflowing bubbles of silly beer, I've gone and done with my stupid fat gob now. Whatever it is, Piers doesn't like it much; his reddened head is right on top of mine – we're almost a Venn Diagram of overlapping faces – and his breathe is condensing on my eyebrows. My bicep, my poor little cluster of nearly muscle is being pressed into a funsize turkey nugget and I'm starting to perhaps regret my outing with this bunch of Brentford fans who have that slightly edgier reputation.

I've already seen a man turn up to the pub absolutely drenched in blood, with that added gruesome bonus of claret dripping down between his teeth to complete a comprehensive horror smile. He really was quite pleased with himself and I suspect he hadn't hilariously hit himself with a hammer doing DIY; no, no, no, that was definitely fighting blood, and I didn't personally like the look of it. I just don't get all of that. And I met another bloke who it turns out was the first person to be CS-gassed by the Hounslow police.

"Sweeeeeet," he says of his claim to fame. I'm not sure I've got the stomach for all this. I might be from Walthamstow, but I'm about as hard as Angel Delight.

It was away at Exeter on December 28 that I first met some of those naughties. I say 'naughties', because it was at the game at St James Park that I first heard of their 'naughty bus', which they were all aboard on the way down.

That Exeter game was my first return to the warm embrace of the Brentford faithful...

I arrived at the ground three hours before kick-off to negotiate my press pass. I expected the full-on Darlington-style treatment of having to explain myself and apologise for everything I've ever done (perhaps including the time I trapped the dog in a phone box). But they just half-heartedly asked me if I've got press accreditation, I said *no*, they said *never mind*, bunged a photographers' pass on my coat and lead me through the tunnel out by the side of the pitch and into the away end. The man who led me around seemed to be the king steward, but had no real interest or idea as to what I was doing. I had my camera-on-a-stick extended and was talking into it profusely like a whopping lunatic, but he didn't raise an eyebrow. Even when I stopped and said: "Sorry, just a second, I eat grass, you see..." in reference to my continued but largely momentum-less quest to eat grass at all grounds in the Football League, he just accepted it matter-of-factly.

"Oh right. Well you have a bit of grass then," he replied, still nonplussed and totally unmoved by the notion. And so I ate some grass, and I continued, unquestioned. Maybe he thought I was a little bit special. It tasted vaguely of sick.

There was that sluggish post-Christmas malaise on the terraces; bellies still stacked up to the windpipe with roast and cake and sherry – seemingly inhibiting voice boxes from singing anything other than a marinated pickled onion gurgle. The packed Brentford end remained silent, hungover and absolutely frozen raw. I slotted back into the Brentford I know; stood with Smiffy and Fraulein and had my first public exposure to their pairing, which has got to the stage where they like to kiss on the lips in regular reassuring intervals; the 'public displays of affection' stage that makes the rest of the population want to bring up bile. It still seems bizarre, those two, together. And it's all my fault.

"The toes are the worst," says Smiffy of the cold, standing behind Fraulein with his arms around her. "What about the fingers?" I ask, looking at my frosty digits of blood-slush and bone.

"No, I've got them warmed up," he retorts, with the obvious inference that they were lodged in a warm place we'd rather not consider thank you. Fraulein justifiably clumps him one.

"As I said last night, don't take it the wrong way." Smiffy digs himself deeper. *Look at them, they're a proper couple.* Then they kiss. Again.

"Does she let you suck her toes?" asks Perry out of nowhere. I take this opportunity to seek out a cup of tea.

Among all those almost comfortable old faces, I get talking to the naughties. One of them told me they'd secretly left the 'naughty bus' in a village somewhere, having been tracked by the police (which I think they really enjoyed as a validation of their hardness) and then got the train ... only to be greeted at the other end by the police again. *'Ello,'ello,'ello.* They were then shepherded to a pub that was prepped and waiting for them. They were then shepherded again into the ground without even half a chance of a punch up. Of course, I express my disgust and act as though I'm gutted for them, *what a choker,* even though I just can't get my head around wanting to be involved in all that.

Brentford scored. Twice. The first half hangover suddenly cleared and everyone went loopy mad-face, as though a mental-switch had been turned on, and amid the bananas, I ended up finally giving Tidy the £20 I owed him for snogging the old Loch Ness Monster all those months ago.

* * * * *

"Come on, *tell me what you meant,*" insists Piers intensely, in the most drawn out act of bullying I've ever been party to.

And the day started so well. Bees scrambled a last minute equaliser in the hugely frustrating home game against Notts County; the Ealing Road end turned into a Baghdad-revolution-alike, missing only people hitting statues with their removed shoes for it to really resemble a significant moment in world history. Men leapt on me, screeching undefined, unrefined terms of ecstasy. One man embraced me like a tearful reunion with a lost child.

"Yes, yes, yes, f*****g yes Gloryhunter, f*****g yes!" he shouted – half voice, half the breathy screech of a blocked Hoover – as he drew me so far into his bosom that my head almost became a third nipple. I wish it had, because right now I'd be in that man's vest, somewhere else, instead of having my arm withered into a blackened scab for clearly saying something heinous to a man who's wider than I am tall. His neck alone is bigger than stuff I've seen being sliced in the butchers. *Run away Spencer, sprint like you've never sprinted before, run like a complete nutter, into the night, long into the night ... oh, and gets some chips on the way* I think ... but then realise if I do that, I'll have to leave the arm at the pub, in his fist, and I like my arm, it especially helps with eating chips. "Leave it, Piers, what's the matter with you?" one of the others says, looking a bit worried himself when he notices the discomfort in the way I'm trying to swallow. "No, he knows what he said." What is this? Bloody *Goodfellas*? This bloke's like a hulked up Joe Pesci pumped full of Stella. A pause. A fairly pregnant one. And I'm just waiting for the first blow. I arrange my face in a pre-emptive wince. How best can you prepare a face that's about to be punched? If I just leave my mouth open, will the teeth provide a spiky defence? *Go on then, do it, if you're gonna do it. Smash me up like* Rocky 4; *just get on with it.*

"Ha ha ha ha ha! You mug!" bursts out of his face. Piers's head lights up into virtually another bloke; like Hannibal Lecter morphing into Des Lynam. He got me. He got me good. Fair play ... he kept to the Joe Pesci script and played the psychotic nutter perfectly. Relief floods through my bloodstream like a tsunami of alrightness, and with all that fear draining away, I feel three stone lighter and have an arm back ... although it's so numb that I have to leave it dangling limp for a while as the pins and needles herald signs of life.

"You f*****g c*****g f*****g b*****d you scared the c*****g f***k out of me you c**k," I rant, which is probably way worse than whatever it was I said that started this whole gangster movie charade in the first place.

Piers, it turns out, is a gentle giant; a lovely, funny bloke who after all seems unlikely to cause the sort of atrocities his face suggests it could. In fact, all of this 'edgy' lot, including CS-gas man and another called Mark, who really should be performing stand-up comedy, are top notch. Just another branch of characters you'll find in any cross-section of 5,000 people who go to a football match. I don't really talk to them about where the 'naughty' tag comes from – I don't really want to imagine this lot taking part in pointless punch ups with northern strangers in car parks, and I've no idea if they ever do that anyway – mainly because I've never really put a friendly face on people who do that sort of thing, I just don't want to know.

I have a great night getting messed up on beer with kindred football folk, and my Brentford landscape has spread even wider. I'm glad to be back here, and that old Orient resentment I considered the first time around seems a very distant figment.

EXETER CITY 0-2 BRENTFORD
              MacDonald (pen) 75
              Wood 79
Attendance 6,791

LINCOLN CITY 2-2 BRENTFORD
N'Guessan 6   Bean 12
Elding 66   Bowditch 23
Attendance 3,932

BRENTFORD 1-1 NOTTS COUNTY
Phillips 90   Facey 12
Attendance 5,465

---

* * * * *

"What do you do with your time after training then?" I ask Brentford goalkeeper Ben Hamer, a lanky Westcountry lad with cheekbones sharper than a hoodie's blade. He's here on a season-long loan from Reading and I'm back at the Brentford training ground to film myself having a penalty shoot-out against him as part of an episode I devised on a bored evening in the travel tavern, whereby the fictitious story goes that myself and Hamer have been at war ever since he stole my wife, my grandmother and my Walnut Whip over the course of the last 50 years. Utter drivel. Spare time during the week does strange things to me, I don't know where this non-sense comes from. Maybe it's too much *Deal or No Deal*. And I'm surprised that the club have given me access to act out my peculiar notions at their training ground, with their first-team goalie. But that's what they're like at Brentford, a very embracing bunch.

And seeing as midweek spare time turns my brain left at Dali and Magritte Street and straight up Noel Edmunds Boulevard, I wonder whether the spare time during a footballer's week sends them to strangetown in the same way it does me. Ben Hamer is young. 21 years old. When I see these blokes out on the pitch, I don't consider that some of them are a good 15 years younger than me ... blimey ... I'm probably just about old enough to be his dad ... *oh Christ, I'm probably just about old enough to be his bloody dad.* As I stand talking to him before our shoot-out, that very idea crushes me. It absolutely kicks my heart in the mouth and then rubs salt, vinegar and lemon juice in it. It's the same sort of belly-punch that comes when you finally realise that you will *never* play for England. No matter how rubbish you are at football, the moment you realise that the dream of being a professional player and celebrating a goal at Wembley is over, it comes as a brutal hammer blow. And similarly, realising for the first time that a fully grown bloke standing in front of you is so much younger that you could technically parent him, hits just as hard as any blow to the knackers.

"I go on Facebook and meet birds," Ben replies about his daytimes with astonishing honesty, especially to someone who might just write it in a book. I suppose it's better than getting larruped on WKD or playing weekly wage-sized hands of poker in some strip joint or chucking talc up your hooter. Compared to some of the antics footballers have been known to get up to in their spare time down the years, flirting on Facebook is a relatively mild confession to make.

With my made up history of *Gloryhunter versus Hamer*, I line the ball up for my first penalty against this gangly professional goalie, who despite being slight and science-lab-skeleton bony, pretty much fills the area. And off goes my ticker, racing around my ribcage like a great thumping evil canary. My head starts spinning like a fairground waltzer. *Concentrate Austin, come on, you can bury this young punk ... Old enough to be his dad, my arse, I'll show him there's still led in my pencil...*

When I thought of doing this penalty thing, I didn't imagine that I'd actually be bothered about winning; it was just supposed to be a bit of silliness to fill airspace. But with the revelation flapping around in my mind that I'm old enough to father this six-foot stick, suddenly it's become a test of virility and ridiculous male pride. I can feel it rear up inside me, uncontrollably. I know it's stupid, but I now have it in my head that winning this penalty shoot-out against the Brentford first-team goalkeeper will somehow show the world that I'm *not* past it. While poor Hamer just wants to take part in a bit of fun, I'm getting ready like a great prancing phallus: wanting, *needing* to win at all costs. Hamer's on his line, jumping up and down, waiting for the first strike ... while off in the distance, Brentford manager Andy Scott watches from the pavilion. Suddenly I feel like I'm also having a trial, which is ridiculous, because I'm 34, wheeze on stairs and have legs made entirely of beer.

Smack! *Have some of that.* Hamer was nowhere. Right into the corner. I let out a testosterone-fired scream and celebrate in a way that I know I'll regret when I look back at the tape later. It's a real Dean Gaffney of a celebration ... Smack. 2-0. *Oh, yes. Gloryhunter strokes it like Hoddle in his pomp, an effortless sweep into the corner again. I. Am. Back. Get a load of me, Andy Scott.* Hamer didn't get near it and this time he lets out a girly hoinky squeal, as the ball squeezes cheekily into that bottom corner. But now the doubt sets in; one more to win ... *Can I really do a professional keeper over? Of course I can. I might be 34, but the magic's still there. I know, sod it: showboat, Austin. Go on, really show him up. Go for something nifty, hook a trick shot down his throat.* Poomph. 2-1. I go for an unfeasible hook stab that involves my legs wrapping around each other and the ball not even reaching the goal line. How did I manage to kick myself in the leg while taking a penalty? Maybe if I'd gone down I might have got another one. My confidence crashes and burns, smashes and smoulders. I look a complete muppet (Fozzie the Bear).

"Come on then you cockney weasel," sledges Hamer in his tractor accent, almost as though Enid Blyton has supplied his script. *Just make sure Austin, keep it simple...*

Kersmack! Hamer beaten, the ball flying into the top corner ... but *crack*, it twats the post and flies across the face of the goal ... *crack*, again, hits the other post ... and out. I've thrown the lead away; is this symbolic of my youth fading away? Oh get on with it you big tart. What a wally, putting so much pride on a silly game of penalties. But whatever, because right now, this last penalty means much more than it should.

Ker-twat! Low. Hard. It's tight. Hamer guesses right; the bugger's gone the right way. *Oh Christ. Don't get to it Hamer, you streaky shard of piss, you.* He's at full stretch. But ... fingers ... can't ... nudge it. The ball looks like it's in slow motion, Hamer in the air forever ... it clips the inside of the post and ripples the net like a beautiful shimmering curtain of gold. *Get in there my son!* Hamer with head in hands, me jigging around like a Flump ... *oh the glory, get some of me sunbeam, I'm the daddy, I'm bloody superman, I'm King flipping Kong.*

3-2 ... I win. I bloody *win*. I did it. I'm not some washed up has-been. Hamer might have been one of the few to win the *Soccer Am* Crossbar Challenge, but he's not got what it takes to destroy The Hunter. I've still got it....

...although, I felt my hip go on that last one. Best lay up with a Horlicks and cod liver oil tonight.

* * * * *

"How much of your current success do you put down to The Gloryhunter being at the club?" I ask Brentford manager Andy Scott in his little office that's decorated with the typical whiteboard with football pitch and coloured magnetic pieces that never seem to be arranged in any sort of order. He's just finished his bowl of soup and is still getting the bits from the extremities of his mouth. I think he likes a soup. "Well, it's obviously a massive part of what we've been doing, you know." Andy's got a serious look about him; he's only 37 and maybe needs it to convey the authority required to be a Football League manager at such a young age. But it cracks into a silly grin when he can't bring himself to continue with the pretence that Brentford's success so far this season has been down to me being there.

His story is an interesting one. At the age of 32, he found himself being forced to retire from playing after doctors told him a rare heart condition meant that any form of physical exercise could see him drop down dead on the pitch at any moment. Hypertrophic Cardiomyopathy is a condition that involves the thickening of a heart muscle that restricts blood flow, and it famously and tragically claimed the lives of Cameroonian international Marc Vivien-Foe and York City's David Longhurst on the field of play. Despite the fact the condition can be detected with a cheap ECG, many aren't diagnosed until an autopsy after they've collapsed during a game. Luckily, Scott noticed early signs: heavy legs, shooting pains and headaches (sounds like a regular hangover to me), and managed to cut his playing career short before his name was added to the list. Since then, he's risen quickly up the ladder after taking a coaching role at Orient, then migrating across London to assist Terry Butcher here at Brentford and then converting a caretaker role into the real deal when Butcher left.

I can't believe that he's actually heard of me. I didn't imagine that anyone in the serious business of football would be bothered with whimsical parasites such as myself. "Your name's chanted at every ground we've been to so far. It's great that you've come back and hopefully you'll be here for a long, long time, because it means that we're doing well."

"Do you hear the fans singing your Andy Scott song?" I ask. I often wonder, when in the middle of an important game and while their attention is sucked deep into the battle, whether managers or players ever really notice what the fans are singing. "I only manage to hear just as they're about to finish, so I manage to give them a wave. Otherwise they'll think I'm blanking them."

"Ben Hamer, what are your thoughts on him?"

"Well he can't save penalties, can he? Not from you."

Even though I make it clear I'll do it on a pay-as-you-play basis, Andy doesn't offer me a deal (something about my moobs not fitting into the shirt). So I save face by claiming that I've decided to retire anyway. I think I get away with it.

Later, I receive Facebook message from Ben Hamer. Thankfully he's not trying to pull me, but apparently the other players have ripped him to shreds over his shock defeat.

I gloat to myself over a cup of Horlicks, and settle down to *Antiques Roadshow* and a Rich Tea.

* * * * *

This second spell at Brentford moves out of the territory of adventure and simply into a way of life. I feel as though I've transplanted my existence, just simply moved across London and pressed refresh on my friend list. Except in East London I doubt I would get away with forcing my friends into taking part in ridiculous pie-eating competitions that distort their faces into horror films about obese zombies; but here I am, commandeering the back yard of The Griffin to stuff meat pies down Tidy's throat as his opponent Boy Bradley almost chunders up the vegetable slices he's been stuffing down his boat like it's the last time he'll ever see diced potato and carrot in a suspicious sauce. But then that's the power a tiny of a camcorder that shoots stuff for ITV; as soon as people see the little black camera on its stick they want to come and stand in front of it, often drunk as lords and utterly unintelligible, but keen to up their status with an appearance.

At the Lincoln game, two people full-on kissed the lens and one bloke did a sort of weird jig and said in a drunk, surreal sort of way: "Eyyyyy, geeeezer geeeezer, oi, oi, oi, Beeeees, Beeees, Beeees, 'ave some of it, 'ave some of it," and then fell back into a perfectly ordinary demeanour and thanked me politely for filming him. I feel like I've become the bizarre sideshow, the *It's A Knockout* of the lower divisions, with me as a giggly Stuart Hall as the fans go through my obstacles like the bumbling Belgians dressed in Tweedle Dee costumes that Hall enjoyed so much. In fact, at one point I get a guy called Nick Bruzon to accept a surprise challenge of slipping into the enormous Buzzy Bee Brentford mascot costume and taking on a mission to get the Ealing Road to do a Mexican Wave. It turned out it was his lifetime ambition to wear that sweat-marinated outfit and he let a little moist-eyed quiver pass through his hugely shocked Muppet-puppet looking face when I revealed it to him. Quite literally, he was buzzing.

While Brentford are rampaging their way towards the top of the league, the fans start to get those whiffs of impending glory and I too go on a rampage: of silliness; even getting likely candidates Smiffy and Fraulein to go with me to a local photographer's to have a sort of 'glamour shot' (no, not that type of 'glamour', you pervert. Honestly, your mind). This helped me try to build a story around them becoming the Posh and Becks of Brentford. But it turned out more grubby than glam.

The little studio, somewhere in Hounslow, was a heating-free, Asda Value-type budget affair. The toilets ... oh my days ... the khazi pans were stained so brown they could have been made of teak, and while I tried to get my baulking bladder to allow wee into it, I could hear the photographer inside, requesting Fraulein to take that extra layer off. But once we'd imposed our regal Posh and Becks standards, he got the idea and we Photoshopped a proud, stately shot of them into a photo of a Buckingham Palace room ... and our campaign to establish brand Smiffy and Fraulein was on track. At the draw at Lincoln's Sincil Bank, I revealed the photo to them. They immediately burst into whooping cough laughter, Fraulein almost bringing up what sounded like a lung slug. "It's upside down, you no-mark," said Smiffy. I turned it the right way up. They sort of cheered, with that hint of bewildered bemusement. *Why did we actually do that?* we said with our eye contact.

"What next for brand Smiffy and Fraulein?"

"Hopefully, some kind of *Hello!* spread," said Smiffy, optimistically.

"Oh f**k off," bucked up Fraulein, with a sneering screwed up face like a rotten peach. "More like *Take A Break.*"

* * * * *

SATURDAY, 24 JANUARY 2009.
Oxfam Shop, Mill Street, Macclesfield.

Brentford fan Top Cat (or Tim) has worn that poxy jumper almost every time I've seen him. It's a humdinger. After we went to Stockholm, I actually tried to ban it. Of course, I know I have no jurisdiction over his wardrobe, in fact I have very little control over my own minging hotchpotch of mismatched rags, I'm about as fashionable as Terry Nutkins; but this thing, well, this monstrosity is an absolute rotter. It's a woolly black and white flecked effort that from a distance looks like droopy chain-mail that clings onto him like a depressed cat; bearing stains of over 30 years of wear and tear and the vague scent of medieval. Tim should know better; he's only 49, he shouldn't be having trouble dressing himself respectably *just* yet.

"It's been all around the world with me. It's been to New York, Red Square – somebody tried to set fire to it once but I rescued it; I paid four shillings for this!" … shillings. The man paid for this morbid bit of dishcloth in *shillings*. Decimalisation in the UK happened in 1971, three years before I was even belly-barged out by my mum. He's been wearing this homeless fodder for 38 years. Man alive, that's disgusting.

Nope, I can't have this, if he's going to be in front of my camera, we're going to have to do something about this outrageous insult to sheep. So before Brentford play away at Macclesfield, we're going shopping. Just two blokes, clothes shopping; probably a bit suspect, but I don't care; this is for the sake of Brentford's reputation in the Football League and while I can do something about it, I simply must. It's mercy shopping.

Macclesfield feels like it's in the bottom of a landscape bowl, with lumpy hills surrounding the centre and atop one of them, a cigar shaped funny industrial stork thing that keeps my eye wherever I am. The main shopping street is the same as all the others, and I'm getting a bit bored of reporting that yet another city centre is very similar. It's a cultural tragedy. It twists around the same old brands and up towards the grand looking town hall at the top, where you get a view of the cigar thing again. It's watching me. I start to feel like *Close Encounters*: drawn to it, infatuated with it. Everywhere I go; there it is. It's sending messages to me. Or possibly that's just a text from Tim, telling me he's gone into Oxfam as part of my 'Top Cat's New Clothes' episode, trying to donate the jumper back to the charity that sold it to him in the first place. My God, to think even before Tim got his nipples under this blanket of filth, it had a history with someone else who deemed it acceptable for a while. The thing could well be Victorian.

Tim exits Oxfam with the jumper still on. Even *they've* turned their noses up at it.

So while we decide how to dispose of it in a humane and hygienic way, we head into Next, the home of fashion for mid-30s who still reckon they can carry off a humorous t-shirt or two … the sort of mid-30s like me. In Tim goes, all confused and tripping up a little bit on things he should have seen. I feel as though I'm putting something back into the community each time I send him back into the changing booth, each time getting closer to banishing his rancid jumper forever. Although what he's coming out in doesn't necessarily fit or suit him, he parades around in clothes that hug his sinewy frame in a way heterosexual men at 49 years old perhaps shouldn't. For example, the skintight Dangermouse t-shirt. *No Top Cat, no.* The nipple-revealing v-neck. *No,* even I know that's a wrongun. At one point he even emerges in just a bare chest and a tie, with a clueless look on his face that suggests he really doesn't know what he's doing. *Really Top Cat, no.*

Down the road, with the cigar winking away at me, we stop with the backdrop of hills and a quaint old church, wedged slanted in the distance, and hold a ceremony. Scissors in hand, Tim gets stuck into his old friend with the snippety blades. *How did I go from a pub in Covent Garden to watching a man cut his jumper up in Macclesfield?* Maybe Tim's thinking the same, but with each rip goes a memory, a moment; every time those scissors glide through a hole, the hole's cause evaporates into a distant past no longer physically represented and therefore, finally, gone. It's about as emotional as cutting up a putrid old sweater can be, and I get the feeling that there's something cathartic in this for Tim, as his face sinks a little, his eyes glisten, his favourite jumper that travelled the world with him lies in a pathetic heap of retired shreds on the pavement, somewhere up north.

Tim bids farewell to his old friend in a random bin near Macclesfield Town's Moss Rose stadium, and while he flashes his new self around the terrace like he's been done up by a snide Gok Wan with a stigmatism, he definitely Travoltas his gait up a bit, amid mixed reaction from the other travelling fans.

"I'm not altogether sure," says Chris from the Wycombe walk, eyeing Tim up and down like a piece of meat.

"Are we here for a football match or what?" protests Anthony, a bloke who looks like a mutated Macaulay Culkin, outraged that I have turned half-time into a fashion parade.

Standing in the exposed away terrace, the bright winter sun makes it feel like we're atop an arctic iceberg, and we're dazzled into submission. The Silkmen of Macclesfield sail to an unexpected victory in the backdrop of rare Cheshire blue skies. Like Tim said goodbye to his old jumper, I too say goodbye to what feels like a bunch of old friends (although I don't go at them with a pair of scissors). A couple of Brentford fans sing *We'll Meet Again*, utterly out of tune, and most of the rest file back to the train station and a journey back to their lives, to what's been my life, down south.

Sitting in the pub with a few of them before they head back down, I feel like I'm at my own wake, except there are no free sandwiches, and I'm actually alive, as mild warnings from the barmaid tell me that some people around here don't like Londoners.

Off Tim swaggers like his piles have ridden up to his tits, still not used to wearing shoes less than 20 years old and clearly wondering quite where this change leaves his personality. I wander in the opposite direction, back through the dark, dank streets, now with a fine drizzle upon me, sprinkling my face like a spraymist dispenser…wondering where this change in location will leave me. A couple of drunks waddle past, a horrendously Chardonnayed woman tries to have a fight with a passing car, until the accompanying horrendously beered bloke, with a Paul Calf tash, drags her by the arm and shouts "Get here now you." The chippies' lights glow through the rain and I walk right under people's front windows, gaudy ornaments in place and everything settled as they like it, them inside doing their nightly family thing – plates of chip-based meals on trays on the lap, gawping at oversized flat-screen tellies and probably moaning that there's nothing on *again*. I walk on by, up past the terraced cluster, out past a field and settle down in my new A-road travel tavern. Chilly. Alone again.

I am a Silkman, of Macclesfield.

MACCLESFIELD TOWN 2-0 BRENTFORD
Sinclair 45+1
Evans (pen) 58
Attendance 1,942

---

* * * * *

TUESDAY, 27 JANUARY 2009.
Moss Rose Stadium, Macclesfield.
Cold, damp, perfect.

Just two days after being dumped in Macc by Brentford, I'm hunched like a depressed heron on a terrace, shivering my breasty flabicles into juddering masses of wobbly cockney, as the driving rain cuts through lingering *Sleepy Hollow* mist and floodlight beams over the sparse smattering of umbrellas in the harshly exposed Moss Rose stadium. Macclesfield have never been in the big time; the ground has the feel of a former non-league outfit – some of the seats are even salvaged, magpie-like, from when clubs like Stoke City moved ground. It's a small, community-oriented affair and I'm not sure how much the fans aspire to climbing the leagues, in relation to the sometimes unrealistic expectations of others. I get the feeling they're happy to have a club here at all. Nights like these don't attract a massive crowd. The smells of wet concrete and dirty cloud welcome me drearily into the stadium, but there's still that footballish buzz; behind the goal, the Star Lane End is compacted under a low roof, a mid-season huddle of bobble hats and scarves for the game against league leaders Wycombe. Burgers and freshly pierced pastry pie casings puff steam into the ether combined with the slow comely moisture curl of hot Styrofoam tea cups. I'm going to get chapped to the bone here, perhaps it'll be a hospital visit for 95 per cent chapping, but I wouldn't have it any other way; this is exactly how I imagine a midweek, mid-season fixture of not a great deal of consequence, in Macclesfield, should look. One for the hardy perennials ... and here I am, probably a marigold.

ШELCOΠE †O ΠȝCCLESfiELd

Somehow, 'St Michael's Field' may have mutated to become 'Macclesfield'; a place from which 'Maxonians' hail. Situated in East Cheshire, the club has the nickname of The Silkmen, not because they enjoy wearing silk, although they might, but because at one point Macclesfield was a world-famous silk weaving hub – with many producers supplying London's Spitalfields Market.

Nowadays, it's not silky anymore – that finished years ago – and many consider Macclesfield a pleasant commuter-belt town, outside of Manchester.

As I stand here shiver-gyrating with complete strangers – some of whom know what the camera on a stick is about, most of whom are more concerned with the survival of their extremities – a lone figure out in the middle of the pitch, exposed to all the biting elements driving themselves into his long trench coat and across his face, projects his disproportionately deep voice down a microphone to a relatively un-roused 1,306 of us rattling around in this 6,335-seater stadium. It would be pitiful if he wasn't putting every single piece of his soul into it; going to each side of the ground in turn with half a Pete Townsend-style roundhouse guitar strum and half a Mick Shannon goal celebration, trying to whip up a cheer from them respec- tively – mostly ending up with a vague day-care centre murmur. Unperturbed, each time he demands more, and gets perhaps three extra people joining in. *That's a football fan*, I think.

When Andy Worth talks I can feel my kidneys vibrate. He looks like an older version of Mark Owen from Take That, I guess it must be a bred-in Manchester sort of look. He's immaculately presented and well-versed in media speak: a typical foot- ball PA announcer, I suppose.

"In the lower leagues, these, to me, are the true fans of football. You're part of a community here, everybody matters. We love football just as much as your Premier League giants. And this guy here is one of the legends." Andy points over to a huge hairy dumpling of a man with a riot of a tash, called Jim, who's wearing the fluorescent jacket of a steward and a look on his face that says he's just had a pie – and life doesn't get much better than the post-pie high. He's not quite the sort of steward I'm used to; usually it's the skinny wretch type with nostril hairs reaching out and bi-focals forcing their eyes even closer when they're demanding my credentials and hoping I haven't got any so they can chuck me out. No, he's a big grinning lump, this one, despite the rain tracking its way down his face as he guards a lesser used gate. Jolly, but bloody huge.

"I'm a little bit scared of you, Jim, I won't lie. You would destroy me if it got tasty."

"I would if you were a tasty pie," replies Jim, still with a Buddha-like contentedness glowing through and beyond his DayGlo coat. I'm slightly disturbed that he could even begin to imagine me as a pie, and so turn back to Andy.

"I'm a born and bred Macc lad, I've followed them for 40 years and I still love them as much as when I was a little boy. I always try to make the away fans really welcome, I think it's really important here." Touched by his sentiment, Andy then leads me to the back of Star Lane with the noisy boys and immediately starts chanting a round of "You're support is f*****g s**t!" while pointing with a grin over to the poor weather exposed Wycombe fans who are trying to thump their soggy snare drums through the cold, trying not to accidentally slip into the beat of the Death March. The irony of Andy's previous statement and his immediate actions really makes me laugh, but all it goes to show is how Andy covers all bases, from leader of tormentors on the terraces to the chief official host.

The Macc Lads grind and splash out a waterlogged nil-nil draw with Wycombe; a good result, but it's an absolute stench of a game. Andy leads me from pitchside across to the bar in the main stand, and it's like a cheesy 80s movie where a popular office worker arrives at work and walks through the place high-fiving and dishing out cheeky comments to older secretaries who clearly want to shag him. It's exactly like that; except these are older stewards and the high fives are slightly reserved northern style 'how-dos'. I see people come up to Andy asking for help; little whispers in his ear here and there. He's the man. He's the Macc Daddy.

> MACCLESFIELD TOWN 0-0 WYCOMBE WANDERERS
> *Attendance 1,306*

* * * * *

The next day I discover that maybe my comments about the irony of Andy welcoming away fans, followed shortly by a foul-mouthed chant conveying the opposite, may have been overheard and taken a little seriously by one fan, who on a forum has claimed that Andy's actions were 'a disgrace', and that he should be stripped of his PA role, and 50-odd similar complaints had been made to the club about him. I speak to him on the phone and although he makes a good show of not being bothered about it, I can tell by the fact that his voice sounds slightly further down-the-bottom-of-a-well that it has rattled him a little.

But what happens then is like the day Diana died. I don't mean that people started laying miles of flowers outside his front door, but that is jars many of the other people to post in Andy's defence, and the whole thread ceomes a tribute to him, the kind that's usually posthumous, when the person can't hear it and get all bigheaded. I go on there, breaking my self-imposed forum ban, and sing his praises also. The bloke who wrote the initial post doesn't emerge again. I think he's on the Macclesfield Town fans' Most Wanted list.

But it's still left me thinking that I'd like to do something to thank him for making a cold Tuesday night much warmer than it might have been…

* * * * *

"But I *can't* sing, Spence," he doth protest unknowingly loudly as he stands there with gigantic headphones wrapped around his head – properly looking the part in a professional recording studio that I've hired for the day. I couldn't resist it. When a man has a voice as low as that; when his growl rumbles from below the ground somewhere near crude oil and Hades, you simply have no option but to put him in front of a microphone and induce a Barry White out of him. And tonight Matthew, Andy Worth is being well and truly Barry White. His half-hearted struggle ("Oh, don't you dare, oh no, I couldn't possibly…") was never quite believable; there's a tentative excitement written all over that moosh. Roger, the man out of sight in the control room who's produced music with the likes of Michael Jackson, gives him directions as we run up to record. Andy's a little nervous (and I think he might have just let one go), but he's up for it; really up for it. I think about how quickly these days I seem to be worming myself into these people's lives and getting them to do things that are perhaps outside their comfort zone but hopefully still within the realms of enjoyment.

So go on then, Andy, Barry White me up.

Well well well. Cover me in chocolate and honey and call me Mr Gooey; because that's what Andy's voice makes you feel like. Actually, don't do those things please. Andy rumbles out a pure molten schmaltz, he booms the opening lines of *You're the First, the Last, My Everything* with the resounding cacophonous knicker-moistening smoothness of the very White himself. Roger and me gawp in shock at this otherwise normal-looking white man making such noises. I worry that he might possibly end up making the microphone pregnant, but Roger assures me it's on the pill. By the time he's finished his wildly ambitious spoken-word adlibs (incongruously about coming down to the cold old Moss Rose) the room utterly honks of sex.

Within half an hour, Andy's back in the control room, beaming. He has a CD in his hand to take home for the missus, and I've got a camera-full of Mancunian Barry White.

"Will you be playing that in the bedroom?" I ask. He recoils in coyness and flushes puce, but eventually says "Yeah", and changes the subject.

* * * * *

Thankfully, the drive across the peaks from Macclesfield to Sheffield – from Moss Rose to Don Valley – is so spectacular that any residual thoughts of Andy playing his new track in the bedroom, perhaps dancing along to his own voice in a thong and maybe even blacked-up, are totally Tippexed out of my brain.

This is the England I want to love. Emma SatNav is loving it; I never take her on a day out like this. Great undulating blunt peaked beauties, the most serene rollercoaster landscape you can imagine, with the freshest of air, that icy hit that scorches the lungs and seems instantly to detox the blood. I dribble and twist the car along the Cat and Fiddle Road, through Buxton and the White Peaks in the south: a limestone oasis plopped in the middle of the country, a thousand feet above see level (for the most part) and surrounded by chimneyfied industrial cities like Sheffield on to the east and Manchester to the west. The skies are arctic blue; the sun shines a blinder. This is sensational. It's amazing. I stop and gasp massive lungfuls of the air, stretching the old chest sacks wider than they're used to. You wouldn't want to put quite as much of that London air inside you. I feel alive, so alive ...

* * * * *

... Which is more than I can say for the Don Valley.

"What's your bra size?" I ask a man they call 'The Moose'.

"What?" he replies, very confused. But when a game's this drab, you have to make your own entertainment.

"34 C," he eventually retorts, modestly.

The pitch is somewhere way off in the distance, seemingly with a blur of players on it, and the Macc fans do their best to rouse themselves in the cold. One of them is wearing an old lady's skirt and fur coat, despite being a 30-year-old man. It's his stag do. Big Jim's having a pie, hopefully not imagining it's me. He likes them upside down with a dollop of ketchup on. It's so dreary that I actually interview Jim about his pie eating techniques.

And it turns out that this is my first, my last, my only away game with Macclesfield. Rotherham ease to a humdrum but comfortable 2-0 win, and I become a Miller. I don't get to drive across the Peaks again; my north-west adventure is over. I leave early and get one last look at the loyal clump of Macc fans with Andy in the middle of them, standing next to a man dressed up like an old lady.

ROTHERHAM UNITED   2-0   MACCLESFIELD TOWN

Hudson 12

Reid 76

Attendance 2,945

14.

EE ƎꓕE EE ƎꓕE EE ƎꓕE OH...
UP ꓕHE FOOꓕBƎLL LEƎGUE i GO

SATURDAY, 14 FEBRUARY 2009.
St. Valentine's Day.
A hot date.

"Oh, *wow*. You look wonderful tonight, really. Just wonderful."

"Thanks, that's lovely of you, but honestly, I feel like such a mess, I just couldn't find anything to wear apart from this curry-stained Rotherham United shirt, and..."

"No, no; *really*, I mean it, you look fabulous. Perfect. And it's just great to be here with you. Would you like another Ferrero Rocher?"

"Oh, ambassador, you're spoiling me. Don't mind if I do. I'm so glad to be here with you tonight, too; everything really is perfect ... it's just, so, perfect..." I close my eyes and lean forward, with semi-puckered lips that must look like a cat's arsehole. They bump with a squeak against the cold glass surface.

It's amazing how Valentine's Day can turn a single person into a single person talking to, and snogging, himself in the mirror of a hotel room in Rotherham. It doesn't get much more single than that. The only hot thing about this date is the Pot Noodle that's going through its compulsory soaking period over in the corner.

As if this commercially created day of pretend romantic evil, designed to bait the lonely into clinical depression, isn't bad enough, a futile trip down to London to watch Rotherham *not* play at Barnet – because of the torrential snow that's blanketed the country over the last few days – saw me drop by to visit Smiffy and Fraulein in Brentford, at their request. *What's this all about?* I thought. *I fancy a scone*, I also thought, but that's not relevant to the story. I probably knew what it was about, it had the stench of obviousness, but I didn't want to think too hard about what they were planning to tell me – especially as the abject horror of being lonely enough to try and get off with my own mirror image was still sinking in.

"Fraulein…" Smiffy starts, eyes darting around nervously in a dark corner of the travel tavern bar that smells a little bit of marzipan and rain. The camera rolls away, recording this little bit of history, trying to pick grainy detail out of their pubby silhouttes…

"Will you marry me?" he continues, with a little gulp.

I knew it. I knew it was going to be that. *Oh. My. God.* It was only a few months ago that I was hawking the poor little sod around the Griffin Park forecourt like a second-hand terrapin at a reptile convention, and now … now they're getting *married?* What have I done?

What are they doing?

Taking her time to reply, that's what *she's* doing.

"Of course I will." Eventually, whispery – a proper bird moment, with moistened eyes grabbing a sparkle and sending flares across the lens. A grapefruit-shaped swell suddenly bulges my throat shut.

Pleased for them? Of course I bloody am, I'm ecstatic. But also *jealous* – of what they've got; this lottery they've won. And while I'm stuck in the hotel room back in Rotherham, having already been bored enough to try and iron my tongue twice and beat my personal best in the amount of hairdryer air I can swallow … I just seem to have got stuck on pause, transfixed on a nothing out of the window, beyond the snowman that has a carrot for a penis and into an over-exposed bright white middle distance that the snow flakes streak across as fleetingly as life itself.

The football matches are being called off all over the place, and I'm trapped in a wintry netherworld, a whiteout ether; everywhere is shut down and the only traffic is that of toboggans.

* * * *

I manage to skid down to the town centre, a slush-filled square where the helpful ladies at the tourist bureau tell me they can't think of anything that might be interesting for me to do. It's just across from the controversial 'Jamie's Ministry of Food' drop-in shop – the Jamie Oliver project to get people eating vegetables instead of chemicals with dripping – which ironically sits next door to a chocolate shop. There are Greggs and Cooplands bakers *everywhere*; this place is a pastry colony, a lard out-post, and subsequently there's a town full of people squelching around in filth-coloured snow-sludge, carrying white paper bags that have gone translucent from the seeping oil of fat-drenched bakery items.

A bunch of teenagers throw a snowball at me next to Boots. It misses. They call me a c**t.

Where some of the other northern towns I've been to have had a touch of Victorian market town elegance about them, Rotherham doesn't. This is indus-trial, baby, and I don't think you're meant to come on holiday to Rotherham. Even the hotel staff looked at me incredulously when I appeared through the door with a suitcase, almost about to give me a standing ovation. The town centre does have a nice bit; in the centre of All Saints Square there's Rotherham Minster, with its immense steeple angrily slicing the sky, tearing open the cloud for a direct link to the Heavens, but the place has an awkward edge to it that maybe only visitors can sense. I'm somewhere *really* real now; tourists can stick to Sheffield; Rotherham's for the people.

WELCOME to rotherham

Iron and steel. And I don't just mean the women; those industries have been in the area since Roman times, and with the River Don passing through this South Yorkshire town between Sheffield and Doncaster there's always been industry using it to keep the place going.

Famous Rotherham inhabitants include former Conservative leader William Hague and England keeper David Seaman.

In the insomnious midnight gloom, I allow myself a peep at the 'Millers Mad' internet forum. *I know, I know*. I'm getting a thorough mauling. Apparently, I said something derogatory about Rotherham, months ago, when I was at Brentford and was helping with the commentary on the club website. I've no idea what I said, I was half-cut on lager cups, but I try to make it clear on the forum that if I *did* say something, anything, it would have been faux-partisan, playful banter within the remit of my charge. I neither know nor care enough about Rotherham to bother slagging it or them off. But I don't think the objectors quite get that this project is about the pretence of hating everyone until I become one of them; that it's a pantomime folly and I'm a mutated Widow Twankey. And now they've gone silly-abusive – some idiot has even created a profile and is pretending to be me. It really is enormously clever stuff. I decide not to look anymore; Rotherham fans deserve more than to be represented by this bunch of tit-ends.

Instead, I decide to come up with a way to do some good for the club and perhaps make their abuse look as unnecessary as it is. And with that snow stuff brutally cancelling everything else, including even a Partridge-style walk down the side of the A-road to the service station for a tin of Lynx Africa, I come up with a plan to save me from a snowy insanity that will also hit back at the fans with deadly kindness.

After some Googlising, I find on their fan site that they've recently had a vote for their greatest ever 11. Ever. So, I decide to get out there and bloody well track them all down, get them to sign my Rotherham shirt, and then donate it to the club to auction off. A nice gesture, no? (Albeit spitefully nice.) The autographs of the greatest ever side should surely bring in a bit of cash, even if the legends do have trouble finding a section of my shirt that isn't already claimed by a curry stain.

On initial enquiries (i.e. more Googlising), I discover that these players/giants among men are now scattered all over the country and smeared all over various divisions, careers and existences. But of course they are; people move on, they move around, disperse. So, with the bit well and truly clamped between my gob bones, I drive like an escaped prisoner to get to the training grounds, offices, homes, bars and alleyways that they're all hiding in. And without the good-will of the fans or the weather behind me, this task is a whopper. A big whopper – like the popular burger, but less tasty.

* * * * *

One by one, I stalk them into a signature.

Tony Towner
I embark on a mammoth journey down to Brighton, overnight, along motorways

with no streetlights and just my own dismal Nissan headlights torching dimly, which after a while becomes so samey that it mixes into a meaningless blur. But at the other end is one of the Rotherham favourites, Tony Towner. A Sussex boy, Tony played at Brighton and Millwall early doors, before being shipped up north in 1980 and becoming a wing-jigging legend. Unlike many, little Tony escaped the game years ago, and got into removals. I manage to excavate him from the back of a van as he manhandles a wardrobe outside his plain looking home in a plain looking area somewhere near Brighton. He looks like a jockey; a little man with Grand Canyon wrinkles carved from under his eyes across to his ears. He looks a bit like he's been left out in the rain, for years. But he's chirpy, with a quick brain that flits in starts and jitters, and maybe that's what made him a jinking winger.

"Yeah brilliant, yep, loved it, yep, enjoyed my time up there, it was fantastic, yep," he says speedily, with a little lisp snaking out between his angled front teeth. "Oh, winning the championship under Ian Porterfield. And Emlyn Hughes, great manager, yup," he says of his memories. Tony went on to Wolves after Rotherham, and years later after retiring in the late 80s, he's got his removal business.

"The weirdest thing?" he responds to my request for a removals-based anec-dote. Not being especially interested in removals, I had to get *some* value out of his post-football life.

"We was doing a job for a guy, he was only a small guy, little dwarf guy. We was trying to move his wardrobe and we picked it up and moved it and didn't realise he was in there, trying to put a shelf back in. That was quite amusing. Honest truth. That was funny," he giggles, producing more wrinkles all over his face. I keep myself amused on that story for much of the day; Tony Towner carting a dwarf around in a wardrobe. You don't get that sort of coverage on Setanta, I tell my ITV camera. I'm easily pleased when it comes to dwarves in wardrobes.

Lee Williamson & Alan Lee
Darn sarf I head to Watford's training ground, a place I used to play at during uni-versity days, out at London Colney in Hertfordshire, amid fields and the loom of the M25. This time, rather than dealing with hungover students, my visit sees me inches away from mowing down Frank Lampard Senior and Mark Bright in the car park. That never ever happened back in the uni days, not even once. It's a double manslaughter that would have caused quite a stir, but luckily I swerve in time and avoid a Lampard-Bright bloodbath. I doubt, however, that the double killing would

have raised the eyebrows of Lee Williamson, who seems pretty nonplussed generally, and especially at having made the Rotherham greatest 11. The 27-year-old was only at Millmoor for two years and I get the feeling those days are miles away, a distant stepping stone that lead to better things, including a pair of blinged-up earrings that Dame Edna would be proud of. But Lee's polite enough in accepting the accolade, as he stands with the backdrop of the training ground, the two massive diamond earrings swinging off his lobes when he speaks. If Williamson had trouble appearing bothered, down in South London at Crystal Palace's training ground, Alan Lee goes in the opposite direction and hams up his response like an excited extra in *Eastenders*. After committing the cardinal sin of parking in Neil Warnock's parking space and being breathily shooed out by the groundsman (my training ground etiquette seems to be distinctly unpolished; apparently you don't park in Warnock's space, you just *don't*), Irishman Lee pretends on camera that it's the first time he's heard about it.

"Oh excellent, I had no idea actually, that's fantastic," he says, lying, because I told him a minute ago. What a pro – he's done the media equivalent of taking a dive in the penalty area, and I salute him. It was nice of him to ham it up for me, and his 37 goals in 111 appearances do genuinely seem to evoke fond memories and a cheeky monkey goalscorer's grin. "Everything just went right. The goal that got us promotion was my best," he says of the last game of the season in 2001. "In the last moment, a very tense game, Reading were losing and we were drawing at home to Brentford. Watson played it in to me and I just swivelled and shot, it just crept in the far corner and the feeling afterwards was fantastic. I've got goosebumps thinking about it."

Mike Pollitt

"No, he won't have time for that, but I'll ask him and get back to you…" said the Wigan Athletic Press Officer. Hmmm, of course you will mate. Press Officers. Apart from a notable few, it seems most of them are merely installed to stop things happening and yet talk in streams of promises that they *will* make them happen. Even the Rotherham bloke, with the carrot of a free signed shirt for the club to auction, is being a little flaky with helping me track down the players. "I'll let you know", "I'll get back to you", "I'll leave a ticket on the door" they say … and as soon as I put the phone down, I know that if I don't chase them up, that'll be the last I ever hear from them and their promises. This Wigan bloke is no different, so when he doesn't get back to me, surprise surprise, I use 'other means' to get hold of goalkeeper Mike Pollitt – the only one of the greatest 11 to be playing in the top flight – with Wigan these days. I get to exchanging texts with Pollitt, which is a bit weird, to receive text-speak from a Premier League footballer, and it turns out that he *does* have five minutes for my folly and has no problem with me driving over his shrubs to visit him at his home. Well, he doesn't know about the shrubs, and I don't mention them. Sorry, Mike.

He welcomes me into his electric-gated Habitat showroom up north; a gleaming, chrome-ridden flat-screen haven with kids running about and a beautiful wife swanning around in the definition of suburban family perfection that even contributors to Wikipedia wouldn't argue over. *Oh, the jealousy, it aches.*

"It's quite a privilege; Rotherham United goes back a long, long time. I started there in 1998," (achieving the highest number of clean sheets – 77 – in the club's history), "and left for a year, quite an infamous move to Chesterfield, and then I came back under Ronnie Moore in the Championship years. I'm at Wigan now, but Rotherham's the first result I look for every week. I wish them all the best."

Mike Pollitt is two years older than me. Aside from my bitter jealousy about his home, wife, kids and career, as I interview him, for absolutely no reason whatsoever, I can't stop looking at a teapot that's behind his shoulder in my camera viewfinder. Just a little black and chrome teapot. So, I leave Pollitt's house having had an experience dominated randomly by an innocuous teapot, sitting politely in the background. And this isn't even a story thread that'll make sense later on, a plot that'll marry up with something else like in a clever murder mystery book. Nope. Just a teapot, round Mike Pollitt's house. Am I losing it? *Is this challenge sending me chicken oriental?*

Ronnie Moore

Across the Peaks again, I land up on the Wirral, in the reception at Prenton Park, Tranmere ... waiting to see Rotherham's greatest ever manager, who's also credited with being the club's other greatest centre-forward. So much greatness packed into one silver-haired man. I'll always remember Moore for that time when he thought he was being sought by Ipswich, to become their manager, and came out with an emotional farewell to the fans ... and then it emerged that the talk of Ipswich chasing him was just rumour and that they weren't interested after all. How embarrassing. And as I enter his office, it's only the framed picture of Ronnie with the

Chuckle Brothers (the kids' telly comedy brothers) that stops me from chuckling myself. Why does Ronnie covet a picture of him with the sinister Chuckles so?

"They're mad mad keen supporters of Rotherham. But there's something a bit scary about the tashes and hair that they've got." He grins a Bruce Forsyth chin poking out like an elbow and his hair spiked up like a man substantially younger. This man's one of football's success stories, having fashioned a managerial career out of a decent playing career and taking Rotherham up to Championship level and keeping them there. Although he's at Tranmere, a division above the Millers now (and has already taken a Gloryhunter whipping from Grimsby this season), I get the feeling his soul rests at Millmoor.

"We had seven wonderful years at Rotherham," he waxes.

"Would you go back?"

"To Rotherham? Errrrr…" he thinks about it properly, "never say never in football. Yeah it'd be a nice way to end your career, going back to your old club, that's for sure," he says, cleverly slipping into third person, perhaps to distance himself from making waves. There's a glint in those eyes; I reckon he'll be back at Rotherham, you mark my words.

Gerry Forrest

In the north-east, I discover right-back Gerry Forrest living near Middlesbrough, on a suburban iced up street I slide down as though it's a travelling walkway. Once one of the most 80s footballers imaginable, Gerry's bushy moustache was everything you could describe about circa 1984. Forrest is best known for his Southampton days, when he was tashed, but played for the Millers 391 times across two spells, and after retiring, shied away from football. In fact, he seems pretty shy generally, as he sits nervously in the living room twiddling his thumbs. The only remnant of his years as a footballer is a photo of him in mid-action, printed on a canvas. Even the tash is gone these days, and he mumbles modestly as though in those days he was a different bloke from another time.

"I had nine years there. I left Rotherham for Southampton and had to retire through a knee injury. Luckily, I had a trade before I went into football, so I've just gone back into kitchen fitting and that type of stuff." This seems like a rare little jaunt back to football memories for Gerry, and he smiles fondly as he tells me about the old days. But he's moved on.

Martin McIntosh & Paul Hurst

Luckily, not far from Rotherham, I find defenders Martin McIntosh and Paul Hurst, the former an amiable Scot who's just been on an FA coaching course to get his 'A Licence' along with Ryan Giggs, Ole Gunnar Solskjær and Gary Neville. No pressure then.

"Were any of them really shocking at coaching?" I ask, slyly.

"Erm…" he looks away out of the corner of his eyes furtively. "No, none of them, they were all very good," he says, even more slyly, and with a grin the width of his head. I fail to get much more out of him on that score.

I find Paul Hurst in a car park just outside Rotherham. Not that he hangs out here, that would be weird, it's just that we arranged to meet here because it's near the school he works at.

"*You'll never beat Paul Hurst,*" he sings at me in the style of an early-stage *X-Factor* drop out, just to make meeting a stranger in a car park even more awkward than it naturally is. It's the song they sung at him when he played at Millmoor. Now, he's wearing a shirt with the top button fastened and a comfortable jumper to go with his chino trousers. He's *sir* now, a school teacher, and seems quite happy about it.

Alan Crawford & Dave Watson

Down near Nottingham, I find Alan Crawford, the winger who still works at the club as Chief Scout, having previously worked with Gary Megson as an assistant at Bolton and Nottingham Forest. Alan's a smart, shapely man for his age.

"I had one season that went particularly well, I scored 31 goals, which is what everyone remembers me for. Recently, I'd been scouting and I got a call from current manager Mark Robins, who asked me if I'd like the Chief Scout job. I jumped in with both feet, obviously."

"You two-footed Mark Robins?"

"Well, no," he laughs.

"What's your favourite type of pizza?" I ask, a little bored of having talked about nothing other than football all day.

"I don't eat pizza," he replies, in all seriousness.

Tucked away in a small quaint village near Nottingham – the type of village where hanging baskets prevail – I find a grubby little doorway with a little sign that says 'Dave Watson International'. The hallway up the stairs smells typically communal, a mixture of dust, damp and strangers, and as I stand outside a door that might not have been painted afresh since the 80s, it seems a little ironic that there's really nothing much 'international' about this remote piece of preserved office. Some research made me a little nervous of this encounter; Watson was big news back in the day. He was once the seventh most capped England player of all time. That's big bananas.

The door whines open and wedged into a corner of the office is a grey-haired man whose face looks like a collapsed version of the strong-jawed Adonis that wore the old skin-tight Admiral England kit alongside Keegan, Brooking and the lads. He was the first England player to be capped while at five different clubs, and this journeyman who hit heights with an FA Cup final win with Sunderland and played as far afield as Werder Bremen and Fort Lauderdale, along with his 65 England caps, perhaps doesn't see Rotherham as the stand-out football experience in his career.

"I quite enjoyed my time at Rotherham, it was a family club when I was there. We got relegated, but I enjoyed my time there pretty well," he explains, almost convincingly, a sun-baked face flexing its lines as he speaks; a dead ringer for Robert Kilroy-Silk.

"I went from Rotherham to Sunderland and won the cup in '73 against Leeds. After football I immediately set up an agency for former players. We get them work, whether it's on TV, after-dinner speaking or corporates … we're pretty busy." He says 'we', but there's only one desk in the office. It's strange that this football legend has sunk into a behind-the-scenes role outside of the game, while other players who haven't achieved even half of what he has end up running the game. I walk out of the office backwards, a gesture worthy of royalty, as Dave butters me up for Stan Bowles's mobile number.

That's ten players of the eleven.

Gerry Gow ... Gerry bloody Gow

I'm being eluded, evaded by a classic football tough guy, wild-maned midfielder Gerry Gow, a man whose tackling could be mistaken for manslaughter and who is idolised and adored by all the clubs he ever played for. As well as Rotherham, silver-permed Einstein-lookalike Gow played for Manchester City against Spurs in the 1981 FA Cup final. He was one of the players Ricky Villa wriggled and wafted past like a delicious football *Swan Lake*, yet more poetic, to score the goal that can never

ever be overplayed. And just like his defensive skills that day, Gerry's missing to me now. I can't find the bugger.

"Where's Gerry Gow, Ronnie? Please…" I asked Ronnie Moore, who burst out laughing at the very mention.

"Probably in a bar somewhere in Spain."

"Tony, where on earth is Gerry Gow?" I asked Tony Towner. He also giggles, like Crazy Frog, at the mere mention.

"Last time I saw him I think he was kicking somebody. As he normally does."

Gerry Gow … where are you?

Well, I nearly did it. Considering I've chugged the length and breadth of the country, I'm quite pleased with myself, in the way Laurence Llewelyn-Bowen is with himself, generally.

I proudly bundle up the signed shirt and stuff it in the post to Rotherham's Mr Press, who's agreed to send me another shirt, so that I've got one to wear in videos and for an end-of-season photograph. I've done my bit.

* * * * *

"What happened here, what happened here, what happened here? It were like a ghost. He chickened out like a chicken. Chicken and chicken. It's like chicken and sweetcorn, but I don't like sweetcorn anymore."

Nope, I've no idea what he's talking about either. But when one of your only friends at a football match populated by people who have promised to sing songs that give reference to you being a w****r wants to talk incessantly about chicken and ghosts, he's more than welcome. Even though one of the other fans threatens to clump him one at half-time for babbling. It's an unforgiving, straight-talking place this; and my perceived foppish Soho media tendencies poke out like an inappropriate erection at the swimming pool. It's strange, I've always thought of myself as a social chameleon, I can always find some way of fitting in even temporarily, but here it's different. We're just an ocean and a rock away.

Dave, the chicken and ghost peddler, or 'Reaction Dave', as I've come to label him, is one of those blokes who can attach an opinion or at least a running commentary to anything and everything that's happening, and then repeat it.

"That were a foul, that were a foul, pushed him off t'ball, off t'ball," he says in his gloopy-thick Rotherham accent, floppy hair flapping down in front of his eyes and tongue slithering through a curious triangle gap in his front teeth. You can't help but like Dave, especially as he's just lost his job and split up with his girlfriend, and reacting to all that is making him a little vulnerable. With his mate Sean, and the attached dads up in the stand behind us, I'm offered a little respite from this snowy Yorkshire wilderness, this wintry solitude I'm drifting around in. I suspect most of the fans are just as friendly, but I haven't cracked through the husk of Rotherham at all.

As Scunthorpe United ease to victory in the second leg of the JPT Trophy regional final, I get off the hook from having to try and break this tough nut open. I get to bid farewell to League Two, also.

I've been promoted.

"This is Reaction Dave, signing off. What a rubbish week I've had. Broke up wi' girlfriend, we lost one-nil; that means end of Reaction Dave, I'm sorry viewers, but that's it." Dave milks his final bit of garble.

Over the other side of Don Valley, the players are performing the archetypal 'going to Wembley' celebrations, and the claret and blue of Scunthorpe is being waved frantically in the away end. I am of them now. I am of League One. Suddenly, Dave isn't reacting now, as he watches the furore jealously; it could have been Rotherham heading to Wembley for a big day out. But now they've just got more cold nights at this wind-swept, brutally exposed bowl that's a trek away from their beloved Millmoor. Before I leave Rotherham, I take a little trip down to said Millmoor, to find it perfectly maintained. Mown grass and goalposts still up suggest that the rift between the club and the owners of the ground, despite rhetoric otherwise, perhaps isn't entirely over. But the Millmoor pub at the top of the red-brick alleyway leading down the side of the ground is boarded up and snow lines the path that would otherwise be trampled and slushed up by excited away fans. I imagine their echoes, while grabbing brief flashes of the inside of the ground through the gaps in warped wooden gates that have been bolted shut since the one-nil win at home to Barnet on the last game of last season – not much more than a hundred years since the stadium was built.

"We'd sooner not," says Ken Booth, the owner of the ground tersely on the phone. He also owns the adjoining scrapyard and sounds laced with bitterness about the whole deal – to the extent that he doesn't want me in there waxing lyrical in the stands about bygone triumphs they all shared together.

That seems to sum up my Rotherham spell; all my good intentions, just bouncing off.

The press guy at the club never did send me a replacement shirt, and only even confirmed receiving the signed one when I chased him to find out. I don't know if they auctioned it, or if they painted it pink and paraded around the living room in it. It's a shame; I wanted to use my airtime to do something for the club, the fans.

My memories of League Two, however, by far usurp this gloomy experience, and there's a tiny tug of loss inside me, when I consider that it's incredibly unlikely, virtually impossible that I'll work my way back down to this division this season. Walking around the barbed-wired walls of Millmoor, with all its doors locked, I hum *Drop me off in Rotherham* by local band The Tivoli as I think about my late-summer days at Grimsby and Brentford, my brief ingestion into Luton and all the miles and madness ever since. That's all over now; no return.

This adventure has just spliced itself in half, as despite the snow, the season starts spilling itself Spring-bound and the moods among fans of different clubs become wildly disparate – hopes, fears and mid-table boredom spreading out around the country ... some are already looking to next season for their dose of glory.

Leaving Rotherham, the radio plays a John Martyn song called *Spencer the Rover*, which I later find out is actually about a man called Spencer, leaving Rotherham. With Martyn freshly dead, this morose folk song rings around the car resplendent in melancholy and poignancy. Splatting through the now murky grunge of melting snow mixed with boot dirt and red gravelly salt, I hit the highway and look to the future.

Scunthorpe. Scunthorpe is the future. This may be the first time that sentence has ever been printed.

ROTHERHAM UNITED 2-0 GILLINGHAM
Clarke 25
Green 81
Attendance 2,757

ROTHERHAM UNITED 0-1 SCUNTHORPE UNITED
Hooper 74
Attendance 6,555
Johnstone's Paint Trophy Northern Area Final 2nd Leg

WELCOME TO SCUNTHORPE

I tear my way up to Scunthorpe, in North Lincolnshire, home of the country's finest cauliflowers (if there is such a thing), for a flying visit before heading back down for Saturday's away game against Swindon. I arrive at Glanford Park just as it's getting dark, and skid myself into the massive car park surrounding the ground. The club has been here since 1988, when they left the Old Showground because it didn't meet fire regulations after the Bradford City disaster. Their former ground used to be just down the road, where there's now a giant supermarket.

I'm late. But I find a door open that leads through to the offices. Taps drip and pipes crack and that's about all is going on. No-one's here. I wander around the dressing rooms, imagining rallying screams and half-time dressing downs. I can smell liniment, soil and sweat. I creep my way around to the tunnel and wander down it, out into the compact, squat little stadium that seems older than 20 years. A club flag flaps in the souring evening sky and a nip whips across the damp grass. I do my jacket up and squelch around the side of the late-season pitch; mud for touchlines that looks like chocolate custard, pierced with the stabs of linesman's studs. I settle into a stand and watch darkness blanket the stadium. And in this flying visit, I remain pretty much in the dark about Scunthorpe.

Although I do learn from the Wikipedia entry that the name 'Scunthorpe' is thought to have come from the old Norse name Escumetorp, meaning 'Skuma's Homested'. Whoever Skuma was. Those crazy, crazy Vikings.

I'm surprised I even made it to the game, having been passed through the deep intestinal experience they call Swindon's 'Magic Roundabout'. It's like being squidged through the cogs of a giant f****d clock, this thing. There's a big central roundabout, around which there are five mini roundabouts, each with their own treacherous swivelled-up steering-wheel-sabotaging nightmares. It has directional rules that I simply don't get; it's like being caught up in an A-road typhoon. I go the wrong way around one, straight over the top of another and then stop through sheer fear between two of the others. Magic? Bloody *Magic*? It's about as magic as

Paul Daniels; it's a f*****g nightmare, and now I've got a sore throat from the related in-car shouting (mostly at Emma SatNav, and the rest shared between other drivers and my own head). But the Magic Roundabout debacle – something they've been proud of in this concrete oasis since 1972, and which, believe it or not, features in the UK Roundabout Appreciation Society calendar – is a necessary evil you have to grind your teeth through in order to get to Swindon Town's County Ground. I dread to think of how many team buses have become wedged stuck on the Magic. But it seems pretty typical of a place like Swindon to have a concrete disgrace like this.

I park myself in amongst the travelling claret and blue Iron supporters in the away part of the stand, none of whom I recognise apart from, oddly, one of my teachers from college in London, who eyes me with a strange glint of recognition and I do likewise before we adjourn the cross-stadium eyeball frisson and get back to the game. I look across to the other side, and in amongst the shafts of winter sun haze, I see an arse. Not just a bit of arse, an entire arse, utterly out of its pant holster, as its owner runs up the stairs of the opposing stand with his trousers nearly at his ankles. Why would he do that? He *must* have known his arse was hanging out. Why would you do that? Arse-gate isn't something I can quickly rinse out of my brain; it'll probably be etched onto the inside of my eyelids for hours, despite the bursting of my League One cherry being easily the best game I've seen all season.

Scunny are fourth in the table, Swindon are battling like wasps in a tin of Coke to keep out of the relegation zone and when the Iron race into a 2-0 lead, I start thinking about a lengthy stay up in South Humberside, chasing promotion to the Championship with Scunny, just 30 miles from where I started in Grimsby. It's a no-brainer. Isn't it? I'm on the road to a new adventure, and the drunkest man alive sitting in front of me is giving a slurred commentary on what must be another game somewhere else, because it makes no sense whatsoever. His blinks are so long and laboured that I think they must be taking a good couple of minutes out of his viewing enjoyment.

Cliff Byrne is sent off for Scunthorpe just after half-time. Ten men; that'll be alright, won't it? With half an hour to go it's still 2-0.

Mirfin gets sent off. Thirty minutes, nine men, should be alright though, eh? 2-1. Don't panic.

Nineteen minutes left, an own goal, Swindon level, and in a whirlwind, blood-curdling last ten minutes, the Robins chuck home another couple and run out 4-2 winners to dump me in Swindon, somewhere off the M4, to continue this football slaggery at yet another club.

The home fans who like the needle of sitting on the cusp of the away section wave with gloaty smugness. I don't mind, I'm one of you now. And off I trot, over the other side, thankful that I don't have to wear my Scunthorpe shirt anymore – nothing against the club, it's just that it's too tight and gives me the cleavage of a 13-year-old girl.

SWINDON TOWN 4-2 SCUNTHORPE UNITED

Timlin 62	Hooper 26
Wright (og) 71	Lansbury 39
Robson-Kanu 82	
Peacock 85	

Attendance 2,757

---

* * * * *

WELCOME †O SWiNdON

Swindon (or in Anglo Saxon, 'Swine Dun', meaning 'Pig Hill') was used as a location in a 1994 Benilyn cough medicine commercial. Thank you so much for that, *the internet.*

An actually interesting fact is that while Noel Gallagher, the scrunched-up faced one in Oasis, was working as a roadie for 90s band Inspiral Carpets, they played at Oasis Leisure Centre in Swindon. Noel brought a tour poster home, and it was Liam who spotted the name, liked it, and so brought to the world a band named Oasis. Thankfully they didn't call the band 'Oasis Leisure Centre'. A swimming pool in Swindon is not quite as rock and roll as you'd have hoped from the Gallaghers.

To find some proper old Swindon, you have to get out of the bricky centre and into the villages, where it borders Wiltshire, slightly north of Stonehenge, that infamous concrete mess without a roof.

During my minute city-break-esque, three-day tenure at Swindon Town, that Magic Roundabout thing doesn't get any easier. I find it frightening that my brain simply does not have the capacity to process how it works. My hopes of becoming someone who can use creativity to contribute and make a difference to society are being obliterated by the stark reality that a mildly complicated roundabout has totally unravelled me, and that I'm not brainy enough for it. My confidence is in tatters over a silly pissing roundabout. Maybe I should sue, claiming it's caused confusion and subsequent depression; I could say it's turned me bi-polar, that's the trendy mental affliction these days – I should win a few quid with that one.

* * * * *

TUESDAY, 24 FEBRUARY 2009.
The County Ground, Swindon. Leaving, again.

Three days after becoming a Robin, here I am, walking away from another ground, having been handed over yet again without gaining any real purchase or insight into the club or area. The misty Magic Roundabout buzzes around me, like I'm slowed down in a pop video where everything else is speeded up, and the County Ground's floodlights glow, smearing through the rain in the distance. With six clubs in the last month, I feel like a problem child, constantly getting fostered out to different parents who couldn't really give a monkey's and might possibly interfere with me. Not a chance of getting interfered with here though, unfortunately; all I've got to grips with is that Swindon town centre is yet another concrete nightmare and that Martin Allen, manager of nearby Cheltenham (and of course part of the Allen family football dynasty), once practised corners by throwing bits of toast into the area for forwards to try and head in. That's a fact told to me by Clive, one of the journalists sitting morosely in the control box I decided to give a go for the drizzly Tuesday night home game against Hartlepool.

Whizz kid Gary also sits up in the archaic little wood and glass cabin at the top of the stand, tapping at a computer that controls the electronic dot-matrix giant scoreboard in the ground. 'Welcome new fan, ITV's Gloryhunter', he put up on the screen – the first time I've seen my name in lights since my ticket came up at Argos when I was buying a new Hoover.

"Come on Whizz kid Gary, I'll give you 50 quid ... just to start flashing 'goal' up on the screen right now," I offered, while the first half played out in abject dreariness, with no sign whatsoever of a real goal. It was one of those latter-season games that everyone wishes they didn't have to bother with. A senseless gathering of chilly reluctants.

"No chance," said Gary, most definitely. He's a plump lad, with glasses, exactly how you'd expect someone operating this sort of machinery to look. He sits at the Jurassic PC throughout the whole game, clicking on the names of players and sponsors and birthdays he wants to flash up on the board. I've always wondered who the Wizard of Oz that makes the boards say stuff is. Well, it's Gary. Whizz kid Gary.

"I upped my offer to one hundred and fifty. He laughed it off with incredulous disdain. Of course not.

"No way." He's the ultimate scoreboard pro. Why would he risk a cushdy number like this?

"One thousand five hundred?" A pause. His grin went all pensive and ditherish. I had him on this one. I haven't got fifteen hundred quid to pay a bloke to put 'goal' up on the screen, but I did achieve my goal of chucking a playful moral quandary up his throat.

"Don't put me under pressure," he complained, whiny and wanty. I hope that episode hasn't made him start questioning his entire moral set-up.

"Alright, how about this," I continued, too bored not to, "five thousand pounds, to put up on the screen 'a nuclear attack is imminent.'" This one was a straight off no. It's a good job I don't have a job like that. I just wouldn't be able to stop myself.

The game played out with the slightly dramatic twist of a late Hartlepool winner, which sent the handful of travelling fans into a flappy frenzy. I sat on my own in the stand, having decamped from the library-atmosphere control room, so that a Danish TV crew, who came all the way over specifically to shoot a story about me, point their camera at my nonplussed reactions. *Why are they here? Why am I here?* When I'm moving about so often, there's no way of investing any heart into these games. I enjoy the absurdity of being here, but it's just so singular. And the Danish crew could sense the glorious English melancholy that this whole evening was wrapped in.

SWINDON TOWN 0-1 HARTLEPOOL UNITED
Clark (pen) 90+1
Attendance 6,010

'*Please* can you help save our club' someone emails me from Darlington, like a distant war is occurring and the SOS call has just come through the wires. The news has just broken that the club have gone into administration. What a mess. But what can I do? Probably the worst thing I could do to my mates up there is become a fan of Hartlepool United...

15.

MY EYES HAVE SEEN THE GLORY

TUESDAY, 24 FEBRUARY 2009.
Stonehenge, Wiltshire.
Chilly and dark and knackered at Sunrise.

The dewy grass honks of wet dog on a fabric car seat, as the sun shifts slowly above the horizon; an immense yellow-golden spherical juggernaut rising with the grace of a helium balloon that's just slipped out of a child's hand. It ghosts glaringly, like David Platt, between the two vertical obelisks I'm leaning against, its piercing rays shooting light right down the throat of my pupils. I'm not sure you're supposed to *lean* on Stonehenge, for obvious reasons. 'Gloryhunter accidentally knocks over ancient monument' isn't a headline I'd like to slip into my press-pack. But I'm a bit tired, so I'll risk historical dominoes for a couple of minutes respite, after the last month of cross-country football whoring.

I'm here alone, stranded in these sparse green plains that are cut open only by B-roads that seem to wind off into frilly nowheres. Somewhere off in the distance there's a security guard in a jacket of similar luminescence to the sun, beadily eyeing me with suspicion and apathy blended into a curious half-stoned leer. Or maybe he's just a raver who's been lost here since the early 90s. I wander around this, one of the most famous places in the world, with it all to myself, chucking out some facts about the place to camera – about how it's 4,000 or so years old, about how Charles

Darwin came here to study earthworms, about how although no-one knows *why* it's here, that it was definitely here before that bloke called Jesus was around. I talk about the druids and the solstice, about how the Queen owns it and how I wonder why she hasn't put a roof on it. I think about all the people who've visited exactly this spot over the years, the good and the great, and how right now it's just me. Little me. I feel tiny, I realise that anything I've ever whined or worried about is *so* insignificant, in the grand scheme of history, *so* ultimately pointless ... but in a positive way. Suddenly the burdens of life, those stresses and concerns, evaporate. It's almost a form of therapy, a straightener putting me back in my place; my tiny place, my little dot in history that matters so little that I may as well grab every second of it for enjoyment. The stones tower over me like the first ever goalposts, and in their serenity, watch me working out everything I need to know, which, it turns out, is very little really.

Wise lunatic David Icke discussed the universal spiritual energy that the place apparently exudes, and I try to sense it, conduct it to somewhere tucked away in my gizzards. But all I can really feel is last night's falafel as it negotiates the last bit of colon.

Why am I here?

Well, because Hartlepool hate Darlington and Darlington hate Hartlepool, that's why I'm here.

I'm heading towards being stuck in the middle of a north-east battleground, risking being either hated by both, hated by one, or loved by both or loved by one, or ... oh gawd knows what's waiting for me up there. I just don't know what to expect from this, my first foray into sleeping with both sides of the enemy. And seeing as Stonehenge is in Salisbury – just down the road from my previous owners, Swindon – I thought I'd pop by before heading back up to the north-east, and try to harness some of that Icke-claimed energy (although apparently not through my not so conducive gizzards) in a spell to help Hartlepool win away at Colchester on Saturday.

It's essentially a licky gesture to plug across the local Hartlepool papers and radio in an attempt to curry favour among the fans. I am, after all, a former Darlo devotee who's about to appear in Hartlepool's home end – I need all the help I can get – and what better help than the all-consuming power of the universe, via a load of messy old rocks that belong to the Queen and a snide spell what I found on the internet?

I found it on one of those websites that someone's built themselves, which scrolls down for miles, has a crap font, pictures that overlap text, 'latest news updates' that haven't been updated since 2002 and much semi-insane inane babbling. But it does give instructions for a spell to put a jinx on the enemy.

So, here I am, on my own, at Stonehenge, at the crack of sparrow's ... cutting open an orange (as per spell instructions), inserting the name 'Colchester United' – written on a bit of paper – inside, then using nails to put it back together before placing the orange in a tumbler that has ash and salt in it.

It's not the first time over the last few months that I've found myself wondering what on earth I'm doing. Not even Icke would condone this sort of madness, and I get a feeling the security guard fancies reporting me for conducting a sort of satanic ritual on the property of the Crown. But he looks too bored to bother. So I conclude my 'spell', without any surge of power or a lightning strike disturbing the process, and wander around having the last gawps of my private close-up look at these old rocks. I touch every one of them in a sort of obsessive-compulsive attempt at being a part of ancient history, and then leave for the north-east; 308 miles, two overpriced Moto sandwiches and a belly ache away, feeling a bit weird that I did a spell featuring an orange in ash with nails at Stonehenge. *What a weirdo.*

* * * * *

I sheepishly bypass Darlington, feeling a bit guilty that not only am I not there to help in their hour of need, I'm also joining the enemy. But what can I do? I'm a Gloryhunter; I'm a rancid bastard.

Around six hours after leaving I find myself immediately wrapped in a Hartlepool United flag, sitting in the studios of Radio Hartlepool being interviewed by DJ Andy Booth. It's a little community radio set-up in the middle of a row of terraced houses that people can gawp in at when they walk past. And they do; mainly the out-of-work brigade who permanently have their mouths open and clutch a carrier bag full of nothing in particular. I didn't expect to be dragged into the fold and plonked in the middle of the table like a roast suckling pig quite so soon; I've just bloody got here. But I quickly find that although harbour town Hartlepool hasn't got the market town quaintness that Darlington does, there is a real sense of community and togetherness here. People call in and ask questions, and I'm sure Andy does a good job of filtering the abusive texts without telling me. He gives me a quiz on the local area, which I fail at with significant levels of humiliation.

Not long after the radio station tip me out, I'm on the phone to a Hartlepool fan called Ron, who the club have put me in touch with to help with my ongoing investigations into the area. The accent's a little more difficult to translate into cockney than Darlington's. The words that I can mainly make out are "Alreet", "kid" and "f**k". We're like UN delegates without the translations in our earpieces, but I do get the drift that Ron intends to put me in touch with a monkey ... a cheeky monkey...

WELCOME TO HARTLEPOOL

12 miles north-east of my old haunt and now rival club Darlington, Hartlepool sits on the coast. 'Curiously isolated – a remarkably fine race of men,' wrote Isambard Kingdom Brunel of the place. I'd love to be called Isambard.

The town got thoroughly trounced by the Germans in the First World War and after the Second, its shipbuilding industry saw a steady decline. However, these days, major regeneration has injected fresh hope into the area.

Wayne Sleep comes from Hartlepool.

Wayne Sleep. Just the name makes me laugh.

Famously, Hartlepool United have the nickname of 'Monkey Hangers', which, a Mr Stuart Drummond of Hartlepool tells me, comes from an old tale which goes that during the Napoleonic Wars, a French ship was sunk off the coast of Hartlepool. The only survivor was a monkey dressed in a French uniform (presumably to amuse the French sailors). Many of the locals had never seen a monkey before, and believed it to be an actual Frenchman. So, in a makeshift trial on the beach, they decided to hang the poor little bleeder. As we stand in the Hartlepool Marina, a wide open freshly renovated area full of bars and restaurants, the white poles of boats smothered in inexplicable ropes, new build flats and green shoots of hope for the area, Stuart explains to me that the monkey story is why there's a brass statue of one here beside us in the marina, and why the club have a monkey mascot called H'Angus.

Stuart used to be that mascot. Which is why Ron, in his torrid tsunami of an accent, told me he wanted me to meet a monkey; *a cheeky monkey*. Suddenly, the Hartlepool jigsaw is coming together, in fits and starts and clacky glottal stops and the word 'fook'.

Stuart's around my age; a lanky, almost awkward looking shaven-headed man in a suit, with podgy cheeks like Orville the Duck; although he carries a deep voiced, serious manner about him that doesn't quite match his background, nor that of poor flightless duck-twat Orville. "I started doing that [being the mascot] at the end of 1999. He was a bit of cheeky monkey, H'Angus." See, told you, a cheeky monkey. "He was always getting into scrapes. I was probably kicked out of about half a dozen grounds for fighting with the opposition mascots and things like that. I thought it would be good publicity to have H'Angus standing in the mayoral election, and I managed to persuade the chairman to lend us the £500 deposit. I'd never had any interest at all in politics or local government, so I had to actually find out what was going on in the town and take an interest, or at least pretend to take an interest at the time. I entered the election and somehow managed to win it. And I've been there ever since. I got re-elected in 2005 with an increased majority. It made international headlines all around the world." And it really did. A bloke in a monkey suit – a cheeky monkey suit – who gets thrown out of football grounds for fighting other mascots (and on one occasion for simulating sex with a female steward away at Scunthorpe) ... got elected into office – still wearing his (cheeky) monkey suit!

Is this a mockery of the electoral system, or is it the bullet up the arse it needs? Personally, I think the latter.

"I haven't tried to make a mockery of anybody – I believe that the mayor should be independent, as I am," Stuart said at the time. Labour chairman Charles Clarke said the monkey mascot's success was "a serious issue". I'd probably say invading other countries needlessly and screwing the populace is "a serious issue", Chaz. Peter Mandelson, the MP for Hartlepool at the time, was also apparently furious. Most people from other parts of the country, and the world, found it hilarious, and probably a one-up for the common man who wants action rather than pithy, political rhetoric.

Despite the gimmicky nature of his campaign and to the disappointment of the baying media, straight away the monkey suit was retired, and popular Mayor Drummond has continued to take his role very seriously. It's transformed his life, from a seemingly beer-swilling cheeky urchin to a respectable mayor, and in turn, much of his work has transformed the area. He's more evidence that local government should be run by people who care, who want to help; not by people who slavishly serve on behalf of a party or their own ego instead of the people they're responsible for. Both Stuart and Luke Kirton at Brentford have shown me how football has a greater role in the community than just balls; and both have exemplified that greater depth of humanity that I've been looking to poke through and find in this country. Stuart's story lifts me.

Although Stuart's an important cheeky monkey now, he doesn't mind taking a few hours to show me around Hartlepool. Out near the coast, he drives me around the surprisingly wide open spaces, full of expansive wild grassed plains you could mistake for Martha's Vineyard in the USA. I've not seen this sort of rugged, open coastline in this country before. He's proud of the place, even proud of showing me the former home of infamous 'missing canoeist' John Darwin – the bloke who faked his own death for the insurance dosh by canoeing into the North Sea and thereby whipped up a media circus for the local area.

Down at Hartlepool United, Victoria Park sits with squat white stands near the Marina, and Stuart wanders me around the place, regaling tales from his lifetime of supporting the club.

Up in the hospitality boxes, he tells me a story about someone I knew I hadn't heard the last of.

"It was a game against Darlington and Gabbiadini scored for them. After the game, a Hartlepool fan ran down and stuck one on him. George Reynolds was their chairman at the time." Here we go, welcome back Georgie boy. "He came running (well, running for George) along the corridor with a couple of his heavies, who were about seven foot, and started booting the door down of the box that these Pools fans were in. So I went over, dressed as the monkey, to try and protest. One of the heavies pushed me back and showed me the inside of his jacket and he had a gun in there. I though oh s**t." A man in a monkey suit being shown a gun by a chairman's mate is the sort of shenanigan that could only occur in the lower leagues. These clubs are the real wild west.

"OK Mr Mayor … a fist fight, between you in a monkey suit and George Reynolds. Who would win?" I ask playfully.

"Me," Stuart replies immediately, in all seriousness, with wide eyes – as though it's about to go off right here, right now. He actually looks up for it. George, if you're reading, shall we get this thing on? Call me. I'll put it exclusively on YouTube, it'll be an internet sensation.

We wander down to the balding, end of season-looking pitch, bogged up and supremely boot-stud torn. We stand by one of the goalposts, Stuart squidging his shiny shoes into the turf of his beloved club as the wind files clouds past so fast that one minute we're gloomed up and the next the sun shines like the flick of a switch.

"We were playing Cardiff quite a few year ago, and it were actually the game that Rob Earnshaw made his debut in. If I remember rightly, he scored a goal, an overheard kick, and a load of Cardiff fans behind the goal all got excited, as you would. One of the fans jumped over the fence in his frenzy and ran straight into the goalpost. Knocked himself clean out, and had to be carried out on a stretcher. I understand that when he got outside, he came round and the police were waiting there. He just jumped off the stretcher and ran down the street. They couldn't catch him."

We go over the other side of the ground, to the Rink End. In the blue away end seats, Stuart picks out and sits in a particular plastic chair at the front of the stand.

"This seat is usually occupied by a local guy called Laurence. He's well known to Hartlepool fans; in fact he used to *be* a Hartlepool fan. Now he just seems to support whoever Hartlepool are playing, much to the delight of the away fans, who quite often seem to adopt him. Sometimes he wears the strip of whoever we're playing, but more often than not he's dressed up in women's clothes. And he's actually the worst transvestite you've ever seen; he's more masculine than most blokes. There's a few rumours about his dad. Allegedly, without wanting to be sued, it was Robert Maxwell. But that's another story and one that I can't substantiate." Blimey. A big call, that one. And definitely one I wouldn't assert. I can't find any evidence to suggest that's true. On YouTube, you can find videos of Laurence, dancing in the street in full dress and high heels. It's not pleasant. Do *not* watch it when you're having dinner.

"Tell me Mr Mayor," I ask, mischievously. "Laurence … after a few pints … would you?" Stuart bursts out laughing with abject disgust, dismay and a look on his face like he's been pepper-sprayed.

"You're having a laugh." He pauses, clearly going over the scenario in his brain. I love it; I've got the mayor of Hartlepool sitting in front of me, considering the idea of having sex with a bizarre hairy transvestite dressed in a skirt and an away kit.

"Oh, no, I couldn't even stomach it. I'm just trying to think how much alcohol it would take…" Hmmm, so you're still in with a chance, Laurence. Call me. We'll get a load of booze, put it on YouTube, and we'll have ourselves another internet sensation.

* * * * *

SATURDAY, 28 FEBRUARY 2009.
Clacton-on-Sea, Essex.
A donut hell, near Colchester.

It's been 20 years since I last came to Clacton-on-Sea, one of the Essex seaside towns that East Londoners would flock to of a hot weekend when I was a kid. Back then, it was an exciting day out; chips, sweets and then more chips and sweets and then some chips and sweets to go with our chips and sweets. Oh, and the sea was usually there too, but that was merely an aside to the chips and sweets.

Now, it's half closed down; more shops boarded up than open-doored, and full of tracksuited nightmares; people with teeth like shards of smashed Caramac. The seagulls hover around, bereft, screeching what seems like a rallying call, 'Come on, this is supposed to be a f*****g seaside town', as they hunt for the bits of chips (and sweets) that used to supplement their diets. As soon as I get out of the car, I feel a languid sense of morbidity, my morale way below sea level. People walk slowly, shuffling on benefits, like they've just given up. I walk through the main high street down towards the deserted seafront. It is winter, I suppose, what did I expect? But then again, it was December when I was in Bournemouth, and the place hummed with energy and fresh, vibrant hope. Here, it's like someone's put date-rape drugs in the water, but can't even be bothered to follow through with the rape.

The empty amusement arcade places – which I find depressing enough at the best of times – clunk alone and spew out electronic melodies allergenic to the ear, crying a mechanical loneliness that needs but a two pence piece to put right. A woman stands by one of the machines, shouting down the phone, wearing purple velour tracksuit bottoms that plunge deep into her bum crack, creating an uncomfortably defined pair of cheeks with the classic dimples of cellulite like bin liners of offal round the back of the butchers. She's got a fag on, burnt right down to the filter, but she's going to suck every bit of smoky goodness out of the thing. I walk past and catch a lung of smoke, along with a whiff of donut fat and the words, "I ain't got no f*****g bank account." Don't worry, love, I'll just pay for you in my next tax bill.

Half an hour away near Colchester on the A12, things between me and Emma are getting a little bit tense. The Colchester United stadium is so new that postcodes don't work for it yet, and Emma SatNav wants me to do a left into some trees to get to it. The stadium sits shiny on the other side, as a parade of other SatNav slaves in front of me confusedly slow down and look for the imaginary turn off. An hour later, I reach the spanking new Weston Homes Community Stadium. It's an impressive replacement for Layer Road, Colchester's knackered old ground, which I was at just a few months ago, covering the auction of its fixtures and fittings for ITV. I bought a 100-year-old terrace gate for a tenner. Quite what I'll do with it, I have no idea. Another bloke bought the disabled toilets, although he looked fine. Maybe it was just in case he had an accident on the way home. Someone else had a turnstile, perhaps planning to start charging guests at his next dinner party. The whole affair had a slight lack of dignity about it, but this stadium hasn't. It's learnt from all the failings of some of the other less impressive, flat-packed new stadiums around the country. It's a crowded four-stand affair, piled high and glistening new in the middle of an A-road nowhere out of town.

"Well, we're comfortable at the moment. Am I allowed to swear?" asks Fireman Bob in the upper tier of the away end, during the first half.

"If you want," I reply, not quite sure why he needs to.

"Well, we're f*****g comfortable at the moment," Bob corrects himself, grinning with his eyes shining through milk-bottle-bottom glasses. They swear a lot in Hartlepool; so often in fact, that somehow the words don't seem as offensive. They just seem to replace 'and' or 'err' with a random expletive. The north-east patter doesn't have that spiky sharpness you'll find in us cockneys, and it just doesn't have a harshness about it to make you wince.

"There was a fire behind the football ground and *he* turned up," says Ron, the man previously on the phone who calls me "kid", which I sort of like, because it takes the pressure off adulthood for that nanosecond, "and Chief Fire Officer Bob went in, with his axe in his hand. He knocked the door in and went through the door. The lady said, 'What you doin' in here?' 'I've come to put the fire out,' he said. She said, 'Try next door, where the flames are.'" Ron chuckles with a big screwed up face and beer-drinker's ribbled hooter, his voice turning over like an engine full of spanners. These are good blokes. They don't care about me and Darlo's previous love affair, and, too be fair, neither do the Darlo lot – they've got other worries. I'm sure there are some of them who can't stand me, but the ones who've come forward get why I'm here and what I'm up to.

Colchester take the lead, and despite my activities down that supposed hub of millions of years of stupid universal energy, Stonehenge (what a rip off), it looks like I might have my seventh club in a month. At least I won't be too far from all the chips and sweets. Jesus, it's not as if my gut hasn't swelled enough with all the fizzy hops water. Do I really want to move around again? And do I really want to lose the opportunity to get to know these funny, kind, swear-monsters?

It doesn't matter what I desire, anyway. Madam Fate will always grab me by the scruff of the neck. In the second half, Hartlepool get an equaliser and M. Fate once again shoves me into the clutches of the monkey hangers. It's joy untold for this lot, who've driven for five hours to this Meccano stadium. And I'm chuffed for them. And for me. Until Tuesday, I've got a home, and a bunch of friends.

COLCHESTER UNITED 1-1 HARTLEPOOL UNITED
Vernon 45   Nelson 71
Attendance 5,158

---

* * * * *

"What? Are you serious? *Your daughter was conceived on this terrace?*" I ask, with astonishment painted all over my face. I've never heard one like this before.

He giggles and points to a little corner at the back of the Town End home terrace, nodding.

"Aye, me daughter was conceived in that corner there."

On a dark, wet Tuesday night, with a coastal wind that's more of a violent mugging than a breeze, the dank corners of Hartlepool's football ground have a touch of the Jack the Rippers about them. And the thought of this grinning little fella claiming his conjugal rights during a football match here is a shivery, sobering thought. But the weather and the football mean little to this lot when it comes to using the games as a diversion from the drudgery of life. Sex in a corner of the terrace isn't the norm, I must point out. There isn't a queue of amorous couples waiting to get into the courting corner. But they do have a good laugh on this terrace.

I'm not sure how much of a welcome diversion 'Ben the Bowels' is though. It seems his diet is geared largely around a matchday unleashing of gases from his backside that are probably outlawed in the EU. Here with Ron, who looks a bit like Ricky Tomlinson anyway, and Fireman Bob, who looks like a Reeves and Mortimer character they haven't invented yet, it becomes like a very low rent, fart-soaked Royal Variety Performance.

"Hold on lads," says Ron after the ball's been gusted out of play yet again. "Round of applause for Ben's arse…" The whole behind-the-goal brigade break into a respectful ripple. "If anything son, you're consistent," adds Ron, who then continues with his routine. "The lad who's in the H'Angus the Monkey suit is the best player of that Geordie computer console, the Nintendo 'Wye Aye'." Meaning, of course, the Wii.

If I thought it was rowdy enough when the game was trundling itself into dreary dead-ends and wind-forbidden long balls … when Hartlepool score in the second half it turns into a zoo of jubilant gargoyles, as I'm slung up, down, horizontally and worryingly vertically all over the home terrace. Faces flash in front of me in the dark like a hectic nightmare, kids screaming like banshees and pulling faces I've only ever thought were possible under the influence of heroin and depression. Big Bob, Ron's nephew, a lovely, friendly bloke who's, well, quite big, bulges his eyes three inches out of his head and roars an unfeasibly loud vocal engine fuelled by cider and bile. The camera catches him front on; an image that to me, says everything about the momentary perfection of that second of complete peace amid the frenzy that football can give us. The glory drug is being dealt, and Big Bob just jacked up on it big time. I take a freeze frame of Bob's footballgasm, and decide right there and then to use it on the cover of this book.

And it happens again; Tranmere had managed an equaliser, but the Pools nab an 83rd minute penalty. A decisive moment; not for me – it looks like I'm here to stay another day – but for these fans who in truth don't get too much opportunity to celebrate.

The home end falls deathly quiet for the first time tonight. Ron's one-liners cease and Big Bob's jowls hang still. From behind, I catch a sight of the pitch through Fireman Bob's glasses, and the green grass fizzes off into an unfocussed nothing. With the tension hanging off a cliff, through Bob's glasses I drift away for a moment. I pop back into myself and dwell for a few seconds on something that's been nagging away at me…

…I've been battling with myself over it for weeks. When I gave Spurs up for the season, I was determined to stay true to my word. But suddenly another equation has popped into the fray. We've got through to the Carling Cup final. *Wembley.*

Could I? Should I? After all, it was last season's final, viewed on some poxy screen on an island in Vietnam that coaxed me back to England in the first place. It was the beauteous spectacle of that packed stadium, the sea of blue and white, that convinced me there's something here for me after all. That match is the reason I'm here in this writhing, reverberating, gloriously united home end in Hartlepool. Having spent months and months making new friends, bringing to life the visions I'd foreseen in hope, albeit with slips and slides, wouldn't it just be poetry that one year later, with my landscape changed so dramatically, my outlook shifted so poignantly, I go to the corresponding fixture, I join that sea of glory at Wembley?

I'm supposedly a Gloryhunter, wouldn't this be the ultimate, final act of the 'Gloryhunter' character?

I just can't decide what's right and what's wrong and what's bang out of order and what's actually my true, righteous rite of passage…

Fireman Bob's glasses spin out of view and my eyes focus pin-sharp back on the pitch, just as the razor-sharp penalty kick slots into the back of the net and suddenly, here I am again, being thrown and grabbed and screamed at like an inverted horror movie; riding the crest of their wave, hijacking their glory and getting it on film for all else to witness. But while the frenzy unfolds, dies down and Big Bob's eyeballs pop back in, and we relax back to the Corner Flag Bar – that the fans built on the corner of the ground with their own hands – I'm preoccupied, just a little confused as to whether I should indulge in that selfish, indulgent glory of my own. Wembley feels like that last delicious chocolate that belongs to someone else.

HARTLEPOOL UNITED 2-1 TRANMERE ROVERS
Nelson 69   Chorley 70
Clark (pen) 83
Attendance 3,033

The Pools fans continue to include me in their little group, with warmth and honesty and swear words guaranteed. Big Bob proudly shows me the dedicated beer fridge in his living room, I get texts from the mayor on a regular basis and it's starting to feel like I could settle in here.

But just four days later, like the Gloryhunter police, in march the raiding army of Peterborough United. They smash and grab both three points and my affections.

"Are you really Jeff Stelling's cousin?" I ask a giant of a man, who literally looks like a stretched out version of the Sky Sports presenting genius, who supports Pools and also hosts *Countdown*. And yes, he is Jeff Stelling's cousin.

"Can you set me up with that Rachel Riley, the Carol Vordeman replacement?" I attempt to get at least a bit of positivity from the jaws of defeat.

"We'll see what we can do," he replies. We all know it could never happen, but just the idea of it gives me a springier step to the Corner Flag Bar.

Although I'll miss this bunch of monkey-hanging reprobates ... sorry, I mean f*****g reprobates ... Peterborough are sitting pretty, six points clear in the second automatic promotion spot. With six games left of my ultimate season, will it after all end in the glory of promotion? Will this be my last upheaval?

I say my goodbyes to the Bobs, Ron, Ben and his bowels, Mr Mayor and H'Angus, and slip conveniently south ... conveniently 80 miles from North London ... *Hmmmm, Wembley anyone?*

* * * * *

HARTLEPOOL UNITED 1-2 PETERBOROUGH UNITED
Monkhouse 38   Keates 11
                                       Boyd 48
Attendance 3,722

I don't know why I'm crying. *Crying at the football? Pull yourself together, you're a wreck.*

The last time I came to Wembley Stadium was when Spurs beat Leicester in the League Cup final in 1999. *I cried then, too.* It was back at the old stadium, the big, bold, beautifully ugly twin towers were still in attendance, and Robbie Savage got Justin Edinburgh (the Brentwood Pelé) sent off by diving his socks off. That old Wembley stadium meant so much to me. I went on the stadium tour, first with my grandad in the mid-80s, and then at least 20 times as a kid, teenager and football coach with the community scheme at Orient; I probably went into those old dressing rooms and up those old stairs more times than any player in history. To me, it *was* football. That those towers weren't in some way preserved when the old girl got torn down is a crime to football ... although I'm very much in favour of the new stadium. And as I walk in through the vast beer-court (which has predictably run out of beer), the memories flash by me; I'm behind the same goal I was when Gazza scored that free-kick against Arsenal in the 1991 FA Cup semi-final. When the ball went in, I went so deranged that I eventually found myself on the floor five rows down, minus a programme and a flag. To my left is where I sat when Gazza twatted his knee all over Gary Charles in the final of the same year, and from where I saw Brian Clough for the last time in the flesh, sitting on the Nottingham Forest bench. To my right is where I saw Alan Nielsen score the winner in '99, and from where we subsequently taunted Robbie Savage so beautifully comprehensively. Further to my right is where I saw England score eight against Turkey in 1987. Oh, this place is steeped in me, in all of us.

As I walk out into the steep new stand, the full power of its awe smacks me right in the middle of the eyes. Whatever people say about it, I don't care, it's awesome. It's remarkable. And everything that I saw back on that screen in Vietnam is here, right now – the flags and the faces and the sheer sparking electricity. It's a bit much for me. I don't blub, mind; the tears simply drop down my cheek. I hope I look dignified and stoic.

"Are you crying you f*****g poof?" says my mate Alan. Maybe not so dignified and stoic, then. And yes, I am crying Al, and proud. I'm overawed. This is England. This is my country. This is Wembley. Here are my Spurs. These are my mates. I love it.

I f*****g love it.

Spurs go to penalties against Manchester United, despite the force of the man who I believe is everything that's wrong about our game at the top level – Cristiano

Ronaldo, prancing around half in brilliance, half utterly disgracefully in the shadow of his persistent cheating. I admire and despise him. He's a revolting genius. I find myself genuinely wishing ill of him, which isn't an attractive way to carry on, but that's what he evokes in a man.

We lose on penalties.

But I'm not sure that dampens the experience for me one little bit. Wembley has been a beautiful, cacophonous bubble of glory; a rousing, rallied bunch of England, showing the world our metal.

"*My eyes have seen the glory…*" we sing, in defeat, but in glorious unity.

I'm home.

16.

FABIO CAPELLO IS MY LODGER

> ⊠ TEXT MESSAGE
> FROM: PERRY BRENTFORD
> Fraulein's pregnant!

Oh. My. God. What? Nooo. *Oh. My. God.*

Smiffy's only gone and put a baby up her.

They've only just started mixing their CD collections together (there's now two copies of *The Best of Genesis* in the rack), and now they're mixing their genes up, *already?*

I feverishly rush out garbled text messages to the pair of them, asking for clarity on the status of Fraulein's ovaries. I hope Perry wasn't joking, because without context it could appear a tad pervy. But they both confirm the allegation, with as much gusto as can be conveyed in a text message. I'm not sure whether to congratulate them or commiserate with them. Did they mean it? I mean, I'm sure they didn't accidentally get his thing stuck in there, but do they really want a baby? And should I take some of the blame for muddying the Brentford gene pool, because I helped fuse them together in the first place?

Well, it seems the answers are yes, yes and no.

Yes, they meant to collide egg and sperm, *yes* they're chuffed – they are engaged to be married after all ... and *no*, blame isn't necessary, people are responsible for their own ovaries thank you. Unless of course it grows into a monster, and then I'm sure blame will be sought. 'Available for blame', says my CV.

I offer astounded congratulations, which must come across so breathily on the phone that they probably suspect I'm engaged in something wildly unwholesome. Where I was jealous before, perhaps I'm not so now. Sod that. All that crying and buying buggies and nappies and then college ... *oh no no, not yet.* I've too much gloryhunting to do. But for them? I couldn't be happier, if not a little weirded out.

* * * * *

TUESDAY, 10 MARCH 2009.
Ebeneezers Club, Peterborough.
Amid a sea of anti-Barry Fry sentiment.
Before Peterborough v Scunthorpe United.

"FRY OUT!" insists tubby mastiff Adi Mowles, with pug-faced venom, for the hundredth time in the last minute. Adi runs the Peterborough Independent Supporters' Trust, or PISA if you fancy, and has an almost identical face to that of the scaredy lion from *The Wizard of Oz* (without the make-up). He really is quite adamant about his and his organisation's belief, that Barry Fry shouldn't have anything to do with the club. Meanwhile, I can't stop myself from imagining Adi singing about lions and tigers and bears, with Barry Fry done up as Dorothy. It turns out, in my bizarre daydream anyway, that Barry Fry is quite the dancer.

WELCOME tO PEtErBOrOUGH

Peterborough is 80 miles almost directly down (that's my cod geography terminology) from where I started in Grimsby. It sits on the east of England, in Cambridgeshire, and is amid the famous Fens; which are essentially low, flat, characterless fields in which stuff grows.

Even more characterless is the industrial estate car park I've arrived at to meet author Simon Potter, who said he'd give me some titbits from his book, *Weird and Wonderful Peterborough*, which he's written to raise money for the Sue Ryder Care Thorpe Hall Hospice. So outside his office in a windswept nowhere, Simon gives me the stranger highlights of Peterborough, so I don't have to bang on with facts you don't want to know:

The last person to be executed in Peterborough was David Myers in 1812; for exhibiting signs of homosexuality in a public.

Bob Geldof lost his virginity in Peterborough – he was a 16-year-old kid who came over looking for work and lost his virginity to the daughter of an RAF sergeant. He had to escape out of a window when the sergeant caught them at it.

There are only two clubs in the whole of the Football League and Premiership that have never beaten Peterborough United … Arsenal and Liverpool. It's true …

This Barry Fry thing is a big surprise to me, and probably would be to most neutral onlookers. I assumed he was a much-loved 'colourful character', a sharp-tongued chancer, a big wibbly-wobbly lovable rogue whose turn of phrase could never be predicted and always infinitely quotable. There are, after all, not too many of such characters left in football. But no, there are large sections of Posh fans who don't buy into all that, and blame him for failures in the club on and off the pitch down the years.

Fry started his career at Manchester United – never actually playing for the first-team – and ended it early due to injury while with Dunstable United. But really he's best known for his lower league antics, eccentric witticisms and unusual styles as a manager, rather than a player. He arrived at Posh in 1996, managed them until 2005 when he relinquished his chairmanship of the club to Irish multi-millionaire real-estate businessman Darragh MacAnthony, and was installed not quite out of meddling reach as Director of Football. Whatever 'Director of Football' actually means. I always imagine someone organising 'rehearsals' and shouting, 'Right darling, if you could run over there, and you love, yes you sweetie, if you could kick the ball thing to him and … oh yes luvvie! What a pretty goal …'

Adi Mowles started going to London Road in 1973, and so has seen much more than just the rocky tenures of the Fry. He definitely doesn't include some of those Fry episodes, which have charmed much of the rest of the football world, as among his personally favourite years. Hence, 'FRY OUT!', every time I turn the camera on. They've protested and boycotted … but these days, with Alex Ferguson's son Darren at the managerial helm and the new owner providing a sturdy framework, it looks like the Barry Fry blues are more or less yesterday's gripe. Posh are going for promotion again (they got promoted from League Two just last season), and I seem to have jumped on that rocketship at just the right time.

Meanwhile, I ask the club for an interview with Barry Fry, so I can reflect both sides of the coin. The press officer agrees heartily, but after charming me into doing a video interview for their own website, he consistently, conveniently, doesn't get around to setting up something for me with Barry. Eventually, he stops even replying to my emails and phone calls and remembers not to leave me press passes on the door. I'm beginning to think that after an initial flourish of love, the club have gone off me, monumentally. I'm starting to like press officers so much more – or at least I'm liking the idea of them being smacked around the mooey with a shovel.

I arrive with a hot-pan-splash into London Road, thrust from the just-poking-above-relegation pessimism of Hartlepool, into the simmering world-thumping optimism that's prevailing right now at Peterborough. If these fans were boxers, they'd be Muhammad Ali. The London Road end is packed with anticipation as thick in the ether as an airborn fruit cake. But with such cake-slicing atmosphere comes laced a tense paranoia, conditioned over decades of 'nearlys', a nagging doubt congenital in all football fans, that no matter how good your team is, it's all going to go wrong.

When my old club Scunny (although I doubt a single fan will remember or know I was ever even there) take the lead, a few trembly hands start leafing through programmes, nervously checking the league table to see how close MK Dons are creeping up behind. The helplessness of a football fan is almost unbearable. All you can do is will them on, but sheer willpower just doesn't seem enough. People around me twitch their legs with every kick, strain their backs upwards with every header, appeal for every free kick vehemently, whether they saw it or not. I wonder what it would be like if you *could* directly influence the game, and if so, how far you would be prepared to go in doing so?

"Would you have a toe cut off to get your team promotion?" I ask those around me.

"I'd have me knob off," says a bloke called Paul Donnelly, probably not joking.

"No," says another, "it's not the question of the toe, it's the question of would they stay up." He's got a point. What a waste of a toe if they come straight back down again.

"If it grows back on relegation, then yeah, go on," refines Keith, trying to negotiate the terms.

"Absolutely ridiculous question," snaps a sensible one, before adding, "of course I would."

But no toes are required tonight. Apart from those of Craig Mackail-Smith, who after Posh equalised, grabs a winner and turns faces in the home end into caricatures of caricatures of themselves. A father and son leap up and down next to me, grabbing at each other like grandad just rose from the dead; the older one going more mental than junior, looking like a little bearded tidal wave, an epileptic Catweazle on gin.

Posh are still marching towards promotion, and with Adi and the gang, I might well be following them on that Yellowbrick Road to glory; *because because because because because, because of the wonderful things they does...*

PETERBOROUGH UNITED 2-1 SCUNTHORPE UNITED
Whelpdale 63   Lansbury 39
Mackail-Smith 86
Attendance 5,637

---

* * * * *

┌┄┄┄┄┄┄┄┄┄┄┄┄┄┄┄┄┄┄┄┄┄┄┄┄┄┄┄┄┄┄┄┄┄┐
☒ TEXT MESSAGE
FROM: ADI MOWLES POSH
Are you coming to our cultural evening tonight?
7pm down Ebeneezers. Adi
└┄┄┄┄┄┄┄┄┄┄┄┄┄┄┄┄┄┄┄┄┄┄┄┄┄┄┄┄┄┄┄┄┄┘

Could be interesting, I think. Not quite sure what he means by 'cultural evening'; whether it'll be a spot of jangly Morris Dancing or weaving together clumps of heather collected from the Fens to make a nice local basket ... but I've just got to the area, so I'll show willing and give the 'cultural evening' a go.

Ebeneezers could easily be the Pheonix Club, as created by Peter Kay. An almost day-care centre feel to it; plain, function-room chairs not designed to be sat on for longer than half an hour and tables dotted around the place with sheeny, plasticcy, non-stain tops to repel dribble and beer. It has a stage in the corner, which in contrast to the white walls in the rest of the place, has been painted in a sort of purple glitter, which gets caught in the lights when you swivel your head round and makes you constantly double-take in error because momentarily there's what appears to be a sequined dance troupe lined up in the corner. There never is though. When I arrive for the cultural evening the room has a darker, more scarlet hue than normal; it feels like an approximate act of seduction. The chairs have been rearranged into a crescent shape around the stage.

Ohhhhh...

... I seeeeee. 'Cultural evening' is a 'Gentleman's Cultural Evening'...

'Gentleman's', as in *not* a night of discussing Renoir's influence on the local reverend who paints in oils, but one of goggling at some droopy-titted, orange-tanned nightmares whopping their jugs out on the tables as blokes sit in silence with stony sex-faces and strategically placed beer glasses resting over their crotches to hide the offending articles.

I suddenly wonder how relevant the plastic tablecloths are.

To prevent non-paying gawpers peering in from the outside, the windows on the doors are covered with kitchen towels, taped across them. Classy, and useful, because they can also soak up any unaccounted for fluids floating in the air of what's about to become a spray mist sauna of testosterone soup. Some of the lads in the half-empty room are already parked down the front row, legs spread, ready for the impending localised personal growth and intent on getting as much for their tenner as possible. I get myself into the furthest possible corner and make a chair barricade to prevent any attempts to include me in the 'participation' sections. No way. Just no way. As much as I enjoy private interaction with females, I'm not about to have one prod me with a strap-on, atop a purple glittery stage that itself could be miscon-strued as the inside of a stripper's wotsit. Plus, I'm intrinsically scared of any woman who has breasts larger than my head. I have a large head as it is, and breasts bigger than it make me start to imagine that they both have brains inside, and are either plotting to suffocate me, or will try to take remote control of my thoughts and make me do a perpetual Frank Spencer impression for the rest of my life. Come on; don't tell me you haven't had the same concerns?

The tone in the room is sex-club shifty; forbidden, quiet and masturbatory. Furtive whites of eyes flash around the room, to check if the missus's mate's husband is here, or one of the kid's teachers. On comes the comedian. I don't think I even need to describe him. He's not famous, but you know exactly the bloke. Silver hair; very close to gaining wig status but apparently real, and a showman's style glittery jacket and tie that both clash with the backdrop like a gay test-card. Within the first few seconds he mentions lady parts and the insertion of members therein. I'm not sensitive like that, but really.

A slightly off and tinny drum-roll shudders around the walls, followed by a cymbal that sounds more like a dropped saucepan. On come the girls, and one of them actually looks like a dropped saucepan, the other in the region of a collapsed camel. And there they are, exactly what I feared; the *giant* head-breasts. Humongous things dangling like sacks of pound coins. I start imagining that the girl closest has a human face on each breast ... *No, it's not them*, is it? It is! I'm bloody seeing Hoddle and Waddle's faces in her tits; I'm actually hallucinating two legendary footballers' heads are attached to her chest. I begin unconsciously humming *Diamond Lights*, to comfort myself.

One of the girls pulls up a kid who's just turned 18 for the 'taking part' bit, which I would have fought a bloody battle not to get dragged into. Poor little sod. The whole thing goes incredibly moody when she puts a strap-on around him and then actually gets him to do a full-on sex simulation, missionary, on the floor. This flabby stripper, with legs that could each be a fully-grown sea lion, with boobs like the heads of my two favourite ever footballers, is having sex with a dildo attached to a boy. *Help. Me.*

I drink myself through the rest of the night, most thoroughly, and get back to the travel tavern after a subsequently raucous spell out at a club; stinking of Malibu and other people's sex.

* * * * *

"Arrrrrrrggghhhhhhhhhhhhhh," is the general consensus among my tonsils. But then what did I expect of being popped on the back of a speedway bike and dragged around the circuit as part of a high-speed Peterborough Panthers victory parade?

I've decided to get out and see some actual culture around Peterborough, rather than just its mammaries. And also, as a change from just skanking around the town centre and shaking my head self-righteously at the chain stores converging on the beautifully gothic Cathedral Square like a corporate *Day of the Triffids*, I decide to inspect some other things that contribute to the town's persona, and one of which is its proud tradition of speedway.

Just blokes going round and round on motorbikes? Well, yes. No two ways about it, Speedway has a touch of the geek about it, with the greasy-haired brigade in attendance, pencilling their programmes with the most minute of statistics and eating sandwiches necessarily containing piccalilli. But then there's the smell of the engine oil, the bits of dust flying at you when you get close enough to the side, and the stomach-rumbling noise that can dislodge bits of colon debris without the use of a jet pipe up your jacksie. There is something exhilarating about speedway that goes beyond the leggy girls who stand gratuitously on the starting line before each race.

"It's like a drug," the team manager tells me, and I can sort of see why. The bikes have no breaks on them, and there's no doubt that part of the thrill is watching these blokes tempt fate with their bodies almost adjacent to the ground as they lean into full throttle bends.

"So you're number one, does that mean you're the goalkeeper?" I ask one of the adrenalin-loopy riders in the cockpit, a little Scandinavian, standing in his leathers that have the 'number one' badges on them. Many of the racers these days are from down Scandinavia way. He laughs patronisingly at my faux football-based mistake.

"What's going on with you then, I've heard there's an issue with your leg?" I ask him; he's apparently one of the star racers.

"Yeah, I broke it, but it's pretty well now."

"So it's not broken any more?"

"Well, it takes about a year to heal, so maybe it's a little bit broken." The head-case has been racing these death-traps round and round with a plaster-cast on his 'little bit broken' leg. That's why the folk of Peterborough have been coming out to the showground to watch speedway all these years; it's essentially watching nutters nearly crash, and I for one condone it.

And then the press guy, Mick – himself a Posh fan who gave up going a few years ago because of what he calls the 'Barry Fry factor' – puts me on the back of one of the great growling beasts (I mean a bike, of course). *Not so gobby now, Gloryhunter*. I doubt I've screamed so much since the day of my actual birth. My life, and probably enough life for two or three other people, flashes in front of my eyes every time we lean over on a corner, as my front teeth nearly scrape lines in the gritty track.

Exhilarating, yes. But *never* again.

I therewith end my investigation into what the people of Peterborough get up to. After having octane that high, I doubt anything else will measure up. So I start looking at the actual people of Peterborough instead. *Who are you, Peterborough?* Hopefully they won't all want to put me on the back of a brake-less motorbike and give my hair a permanent wind-shoved quiff...

PETERBOROUGH UNITED 1-0 NORTHAMPTON TOWN
Lee 33
Attendance 8,881

---

* * * * *

Posh are still in second place, five points clear of MK Dons, who've got a worrying three games in hand. With just seven games to go, will Posh stay unbeaten and take me with them to the Championship? Or will the Dons catch them and send me to maybe a guaranteed Wembley play-off final? I'm at the season's nubbin, the sharp end of the stick, nearly at its very wire ... it's all or nothing for me now, my glory is in sight.

Derby day, Posh against Northampton at London Road, all the jibes about the away fans having six fingers, all the neighbourly hatred that's in duplicate all over the country. I can't say it's quite got the venom of a Spurs-Arsenal war; it's more dismissive than it is fuelled with abject revulsion. But yet there's still that extra kick in the air – a game which Posh play for 83 minutes with ten men after Zakuani gets sent off – I spot Fabio Capello up in the stands. Interesting. *I wonder who The Don is here to look at?* I think. And from a distance, it looks like he really celebrates the Posh winning goal. Confusing.

After the match, after the obligatory beers and the bar room rhetoric about how after beating the six-fingered Cobblers we're going to win the league, I get back to the travel tavern and sit luxuriously in my pants, poring over the forthcoming fixtures and my path to glorydom.

There's a knock on the door.

The door never knocks. Who's knocking on the door? I haven't ordered pizza or curry ... oh, please tell me Adi's not arranged for old Hoddle/Waddle tits from the other night to turn up, please...

"Fabio?"

It's Fabio Capello, all dressed in his instantly recognisable suit, coat and glasses. He doesn't say a word. He's alone. He just walks in and starts looking around the room with a snooty air about him. What does he want? Why is Fabio Capello in my bedroom? Surely he's not going to try it on with me?

Actually, Fabio is really a bloke called Howard. Howard from Peterborough. Which is why I saw him in the stands at London Road earlier on, vigorously supporting the Posh. And actually, I've invited him over as part of my investigation to meet the real people of Peterborough. And while we're being honest with each other, I'm actually wearing more than just pants, for the record.

It turns out Howard (whom you can see at www.howardisfabio.co.uk) is a former engineer who was made redundant just before Capello was installed as England boss. Can you imagine, you're a normal bloke, working a normal job in Peterborough, minding your own business, when suddenly you lose your job and the new England manager looks almost exactly like you? Howard's world has been turned inside out. He can't go anywhere without being mistaken for the wide-jawed Italian, until he opens his mouth, that is, and reveals a two-feet-thick Peterborough accent. But he's no idiot, Howard. He's taken the bull by its horns, or the Fabio by its chin, if you like, and has become a fully-fledged Fabio Capello look-alike. He's the same age as Capello and he's been married to his childhood sweetheart for over 40 years, just like Capello; it's astonishing.

Howard's been doing corporates, adverts, events, even stuff for the Football Association. The other night he was at an England game giving a public performance through a window to a congregation of screaming England fans. He even fooled Harry Redknapp into believing he actually was Fabio Capello and has become the face of a major pizza chain's new pizza. He's been having the time of his life; suddenly thrust into fame by proxy, by sheer fluke, by weird coincidence.

But what'll happen when Capello eventually leaves the post? Will you find Howard off his tits in some sleazy bar, drinking the post-fame blues away with the Sven Goran Eriksson, Steve McClaren and Bobby Robson look-alikes? Does this look-alike world leave a trail of failures by proxy too?

The next day I wander back down to the ground to meet a bloke called Mick; another person of Peterborough. Mick's one of the two club mascots; they've got one of those big silly ones in a hairy suit, a rabbit called Peter Burrow, and then there's Mick, who plays the traditional, elder statesman of mascots, 'Mr Posh'. No sign of a big animal costume here. 'Debonair', the Peterborough website calls him. He's basically a sort of Willy Wonka – with top hat, coat with fancy rosettes pinned on, tails and a monocle.

"It started around 1935, 1940." The date's a little bit sketchy for Mick, who might be getting on in his 60s, and he certainly wasn't around at the time the whole 'Posh' thing started. He stands on the edge of the pitch, having come all the way down to meet me, and has gone through the rigmarole of getting his Posh costume on unceremoniously in the toilets. He's a very slight man, Mick; ginger and lean with a lined, weather-battered, sunken-thin face probably formed through the window cleaning business he runs outside of all the Poshness. He's also known in the local area for singing in a band that does the pubs; he's quite a popular local face, old Mick.

"They had these maroon shirts on and somebody said 'oh they look posh don't they', the national paper got hold of it and we've been called Posh since then." Well, that's not quite the full explanation – sorry Mick, don't mean to burgle your heritage, but the stories also go that the previous tenants at London Road – Fletton United – had a player-manager called Pat Tirrel, who announced in the pre-season of 1921 that he was looking for "Posh players for a Posh team". Fletton United folded some ten years later, Peterborough United formed to occupy the ground and it was then that the first cries of "Up the Posh" were heard, and have been ever since. Although, in 2002, when the club applied to patent their nick-name, it was opposed by the lawyers of Victoria Beckham, who objected on the grounds that the name 'Posh' is inexorably linked to her. Lawyers; I love them almost as much as press officers.

Sorry Mick, carry on.

"So, they invented a Mr Posh, and I've been doing this 20 years. I've actually been coming here 50 years, man and boy." He drifts off into a mental highlights package of 50 years of supporting his local club, and as he describes one particular goal, pointing out with misty romance the exact bits on the pitch where it happened, I notice a little glisten form into a droplet in the corner of his eye; and it's not just the monocle digging in. He genuinely loves this club. He tells me how the current owner asked him into his office a while ago and offered him a bit of money for carrying on with the Mr Posh thing. Mick politely refused the money and carried on anyway.

"It's a big honour. One of the players once said to me, ''ere Mick, I reckon you're more famous than us'. Matchdays I come out here about two o'clock and get changed." (In the toilets.) "I come out here, give sweets to the children, say to everybody 'thanks for coming, we can pay for the nets now'. The away supporters give me a load of stick," (I'm not surprised, if you're handing out sweets to their kids, dressed up like the child catcher), "but I can take it. It's a family here, you see." He interlocks his fingers to exemplify the family-ness. "Of course, the monocle has to have no glass in it these days, for health and safety, you know."

"So I could, if I wanted to, poke you right in the eyeball?" I put my finger a little bit through the frame of his monocle.

"Yeah, well, you could do," he says, a little bit put out.

I decide to test Mick for poshness. I've brought along with me a packet of proper premium quality biscuits you daren't dunk in fear of missing its full biscuity crunch, and a packet of crappy Value biscuits you wouldn't even let the dog eat; because in my eyes, you can tell straight away how posh someone is by the biscuits they serve.

"You've got to tell me which biscuit is the posh one, Mick."

"Well I don't eat biscuits," he replies, with a face that won't budge.

"Oh for Christ's sake Mick, I've just been down Marks and Spencer's all special for this." I eventually persuade the skinny old sod to chew on a couple of biscuits for the sake of the cameras, which he does so with his bony jaw clunking up and down and a face that doesn't want to be here.

But Mick gets it right; he correctly identifies the expensive biscuits from the biscuit-offal. He is, after all, Mr Posh. Suddenly, his enthusiasm returns and he goes running off into the middle of the pitch with his hands aloft, shouting like, well, like he's just won a biscuit competition. A grown man, dancing around, over biscuits. Brilliant.

But that seems to sum up Mick; an example of a man who's taken the plunge and willingly put himself up for community consumption. He breathes the place and his enthusiasm runs out in front of him.

* * * * *

Saturday, 4 April 2009.
A pub, in Rochdale.
No idea which one, no idea what time.

"I used to fancy you when I were young, but I *really* don't anymore," the barmaid reassures me. Well, it's not actually *me* she's saying that to; it's David Gray. But seeing as the entire bar staff think I actually *am* David Gray, then I suppose I'll just have to take it on the chin.

Inviting my mates Matt and Huw to join me in Gloryhunting at Posh's away game at Oldham has delivered unusual results. This is the third pub at which they've successfully convinced the staff and various punters that I am the successful singer/songwriter David Gray.

"What are you doing up here then?" The barmaid, who fancies neither me nor David Gray anymore, asks.

"Well, it was Friday night, I was going nowhere and all the lights were changing green to red, so I stopped here." She looks at me blankly, not detecting my not-so-subtle crowbar of David Gray lyrics. "So I thought, if I wanted it, I'd come and get it, for crying out loud." She gives up trying to get what I'm on about, and asks for a photo with me/David Gray. A steady queue forms, and I supply a number of others with evidence of their fake David Gray experience.

I don't even look like him.

Meanwhile, the Peterborough bandwagon is screeching along at such speed it's in danger of hitting 88mph and ripping the space-time continuum. It's unstoppable; a late winner today away at Oldham's three-sided ground, Boundary Park, on the edge of Manchester, sent the fans around me into outrageous dimensions of delirium, a parallel neverland of ecstasy. Steve next to me looked like he'd just popped a whole packet of Pro-plus and washed it down with Red Bull, as his son Ashley jumped up and down so fast I thought his face had actually stretched into a permanent three-feet-long g-force mutation. The win leaves Posh five points clear in second place with only five games to go. This is going to be a doddle. I'm surfing my way to a victorious end to the season.

Leading up to today's game, Posh have continued their run. Last weekend at home to league leaders Leicester was the day the Posh faithful really started to *believe* promotion is properly on. No messing around, this is the real deal. Leicester came down for arguably the biggest game of the season – for them, Posh, and me – and London Road was packed to the rafters; 14,000 fans waving flags, twatting balloons, throwing clouds of bits of paper into the air that drifted in the harsh wind also driving hailstones in fury, eventually settling on the turf together. There was a cup final atmosphere in the ground, woven into a confidence in their team that can only really happen among two or three sets of fans in any division each season.

This is it; this is why I signed up for this. Fans with their arms around each other, strangers or not; songs of unity and pride. When former Spurs man Charlie Lee scored a scorcher to give Posh the lead a minute before half-time, the season seemed to jolt onto the next level, and the fans celebrated as though this was the very confirmation that promotion will happen. It was a giant carnival; it felt as though this dog had finally got on the other side of the door.

At half-time, I got talking to one of the fans about goalscorer Charlie Lee, the squat midfielder who's made himself a favourite among many fans. Maybe not all of them though.

"When we went up last year," the skinheaded teenage fan tells me, while his mates grab his arse from behind to put him off in front of the camera, "we went out with the players, just in town. It got a bit messy, a good few beers. Charlie Lee decided to come up to me and put a kebab in my face." He finishes the sentence with the customary student rise in tone that they seem to have borrowed from *Neighbours*. "I wasn't too happy," he confirms, unsurprisingly. "*He* thought it was brilliant but I got absolutely ribbed for about two weeks after as well."

"So is he your favourite player?"

"He wasn't at the time, but he is now." Oh how a simple stroke of genius can rinse a man of sin. There's David Beckham, getting sent off against Argentina and then healing the wounds with *that* free-kick against Greece, and now, here's Charlie Lee, with the thunderbolt against Leicester, striking off any wrongdoing associated with the incident with the kebab in the face.

* * * * *

"Look Joe, I really need to apologise to you," I slurred to a man who seemed at least three feet taller than me after the game. Joe Lewis plays in goal for Posh, and came out to celebrate with the fans at the smallest sports bar in the world after finally doing Leicester over 2-0. Chris Whelpdale got a late second goal and launched the roof off London Road. Those less frantically engaged in celebration – such as me with my camera duties – also got to enjoy Leicester's Paul Dickov having a to-do with his own team-mate. Dickov. What a lovely man. Anyway, the bar we were in is much hyped locally, but might as well be someone's living room done up really nice with lots of tellies. It's tiny, which makes big Joe Lewis look like even more of a freak-boned giant alien.

"What do you mean?" he replied tentatively, looking at me as though I was a complete blabbering drunk. Which I was, I was out of my box. He's only 21, and at a chisel-jawed 6ft 6in and with the jet-black stubble of an Italian lothario, he seemed to look and have the presence of someone a lot older. I'm not sure if it was my incongruous apology that perturbed him, or whether he generally has a slightly per-turbed way about him – as though the world is, and will continue to be, an utter mystery.

"Do you remember getting a load of stick from the Hartlepool fans when you played them away?" He looked into the distance, as though you can see the past, somewhere over there.

"Yeah, sort of, why?"

"Well, that happened because when you let a goal in, I whispered to someone next to me 'I reckon he's a fruit', just as a joke." It was mainly because he's so gangly and upright that one could detect a smidgen of essence-de-camp about him. But only if you're cynical and looking for it, and I discovered as he towered over me in the bar that he's not really camp at all. "And you see that whisper got whispered further, and lead to the song 'Lewis takes it up the arse'. And although I didn't sing along, that's why I want to apologise. Even though I didn't start the fire, I might have been holding the matches." Joe looked at me even more perplexed, trying to work out why I was in the away end and why I felt the need to apologise right at that moment and why I had some matches.

"Oh. OK then," he said quietly, before edging away and being accosted for more photos with teenage fans who probably shouldn't have been served their blue WKD.

Apart from disgracing myself in front of the players, and accumulating stories about them kebabbing fans, this Peterborough experience is becoming the high-light of my season, the promotion-hunting pinnacle, and people like Adi Mowles and the gang have welcomed me into their glory.

But can they really stay undefeated for five more games?

BRISTOL ROVERS 0-1 PETERBOROUGH UNITED
McLean 70
Attendance 7,103

PETERBOROUGH UNITED 2-0 LEICESTER CITY
Lee 44
Whelpdale 79
Attendance 14,110

OLDHAM ATHLETIC 1-2 PETERBOROUGH UNITED
Taylor 43   Mackail-Smith 26, 86
Attendance 5,083

* * * * *

Millwall? I can't really go to Millwall, can I?

Oh Jesus, I'm a Spurs fan; they genuinely will rip my head off. And stamp on it. Properly. I can't have that, I like my head. They'll destroy me. As it is, the club haven't allowed me into the New Den to watch the match against Posh due to safety reasons. So here I am, down Ebeneezers with Boozy Baz and a big bunch – who either couldn't get tickets or couldn't get there. Boozy Baz looks a little bit like a worried Tony Curtis, with a perfectly formed silver quiff, like a freeze-frame of the sea in a surfing video.

"We will win. Full stop. End of story. We will win," confirms Boozy, with his slow Peterborough drawl that's intoned like a robot. But just 45 minutes later, he's changed his tune.

"I'm f*****g speechless," he says with his eyebrows so raised that they've nearly joined in with his quiff, as everyone else in the room shouts at the screen with their arms outstretched and faces like they've been the victims of a senseless and violent crime. This is all very ominous. "I cannot explain what just happened there. Take it away." Baz waves his hand at the camera dismissively and turns away to the bar to fume privately. Once the blue mist has settled, he turns back around to further lament his seemingly now various predicaments, "I'm downstairs again tonight, as well. She chucked me out again."

Millwall got a penalty, you see. Joe Lewis saved it, but apparently came off his line. They took it again. He saved it again, but apparently came off his line, again. They took it again, Joe Lewis definitely came off his line, but the ball went in and the goal stands. I've certainly never seen anything like it. Conspiracy theories fly all over the room, along with promises to take this to the High Court and further. In the heat of the moment, this feels like something Kofi Annan needs to take up with all the world powers. This is the wobble everybody has been worried about, the jitters just as the prize emerges. And when Millwall score another, I know I should have seen it coming when Posh drew at home with bottom club Cheltenham on Good Friday. They've stuttered their way back into uncertainty, and whether or not they recover to get back on the course to promotion, I won't be here. I'm Millwall bound.

PETERBOROUGH UNITED 1-1 CHELTENHAM TOWN
McLean 36   Hutton 66
Attendance 9,817

MILLWALL 2-0 PETERBOROUGH UNITED
Martin (pen) 25
Price 58
Attendance 10,518

The vicious Easter Bunny has torn apart my hopes for automatic promotion; nibbled them to shreds, and now, because of any permutations of Millwall's fixtures, or their potential conquerors' fixtures, the most I can hope for is the play-offs. But at least if I get to them, I'm guaranteed to be a Wembley winner, which in some ways might be more exciting than straight promotion. But it's a shame, I was hoping to see this through with Peterborough; it's been two months, and I feel a real part of their push for the Championship.

And with all the die-hards down at Millwall, I don't even get a chance to ask Adi for one little rendition of the *Wizard of Oz* medley he's so far refused to take part in. Glory at Wembley with me and Millwall? *How on earth is this going to work?*

17.

HOME

WEDNESDAY, 13 APRIL 2009.
Isle of Dogs, Millwall, East London.

The rain drives rudely into my face, digging at my pointy features and slapping my chins as I stand with hands clutching pathetically at the rusty railings, grabbing at the sort of metal that stinks on your hands afterwards. I'm drenched, wearing the same dirty old trainers, faded jeans and knackered jacket I've been wearing for nine months, and now the wet's drawing out the musty odour of all those spilled pints and faded curry stains. I look, half longingly and half not quite sure, at what used to be me.

There's my flat, over there. All my stuff; the pots and barbecue on the balcony, along with ghosts of parties I've had; my ex sitting out on the deckchair in summers gone. But I can't go in; it's someone else's home for now. I have no home, except on a night-by-night basis. I know though that in a few weeks I'll be back on that balcony, looking out at the spot I'm standing in now. I'll be home, having chewed on England and its football world. From here though, it's hard to imagine who I was, or what sort of a life I was leading when I was living there. And it's hard to imagine what sort of life I'll pick up when I return. It's strange how this journey, with three games to go, has dispatched me as close to my home, no matter how distant that may seem at this moment, as football possibly can.

You see, just about 300 yards along the Thames Path from my flat is another set of nondescript purpose-built flats. But the ones up there are exactly on the spot where once stood Morton's Factory. Now home to Canary Wharf and so many developments of luxury apartments that it's too thick and fast to keep track, this area of the docks was once the preserve of factories, many of which were of Scottish origin (as was Morton's, which made a variety of tinned foods for ships). It was the workers at the factory – some Scottish, some English – who decided to form a football club, Millwall Rovers, and from then on they shifted grounds all over various bits of the small Isle of Dogs until 1910, when the club made the move over the river into South London, to the now infamous Cold Blow Lane. I had no idea that I was living amid the very origins of the football club, and all those months ago when I started I had no idea that at some point, this football journey – to anywhere in the country – would bring me 300 yards from my home.

WELCOME to MiLLWaLL

As you've read, the name 'Millwall' these days is confusing, because the club isn't in Millwall anymore. It's in Bermondsey, South London – which, need I say, is probably most famous for being where the late Jade Goody was from. Perhaps more inspiring former inhabitants would be Tommy Steele, the singer, and David Haye, the boxer.

The discovery of a spring in the area in the eighteenth century lead to it becoming a spa leisure resort, which when you traipse around the New Den, is somehow hard to imagine.

I wander south, feeling displaced, bereft and grubby like a smack addict, down the path. The Thames is misted into a Dickensian gloom and waves slap against the walls after the latest boatful of disappointed looking, half-drowned Japanese tourists in plastic kagools drift by on their alleged 'pleasure cruises', half-heartedly taking pictures as though it's not something they can stop, even when it's s**t. Somewhere in Osaka, there's a photo of me in an album; a homeless man in smelly clothes, sneering at the rain like a dog does at invisible stuff in the corners of rooms. Seagulls scream blue murder, probably over a misplaced bit of worm head, and the cormorants huddle around a stooped heron, plotting against me, I expect.

Around the bulb of the clitoris-shaped island, I walk through the Greenwich foot tunnel, a worryingly tight, white-tiled and dripping Victorian passage that takes you from Millwall out to the currently burnt-out Cutty Sark mess in Greenwich, South London. It smells different in South London; sort of gassy. The Millwall faithful who decided to continue supporting the club after its move to Cold Blow Lane would walk through this claustrophobic tunnel to get to matches, and as the water leaks drip down gooey tracks on the walls, I imagine their boisterous echoes as they made their way under the Thames, straight from the factories. I wonder how different a football crowed felt back then, without the replica shirts, over zealous stewards, replays on screens or people conceiving in the corners. I wonder if anyone did what I'm doing for their own amusement.

A bit of a walk away I arrive at the New Den, which sits among scrap yards and puddles and tight roads that send grimy London spray up your legs as huge lorries squeeze down with raucous diesel roars. Cranes and the clunking of huge chains on the side of skips … this is real *man* territory, and with me a lily-fingered writer, I feel like Quentin Crisp prancing around here, skipping across the deep troughs of murky puddle – in comparison, at least, to the savage hulks loading up vans with a fag on and swearing for fun, with voices so much deeper than my own that I'd have to slow down a recording of mine by three to get anywhere near. I walk through underpasses, the gloomy guts of the area. These are the sulky, unlit and dank orifices of London where indiscretions are compulsory, fighting necessary and shiftiness a behavioural must. The rain intensifies as I get to the reception of the club, the sky as dark as night and my mood matching the whole scenario. I feel like I'm in the film *Seven*, but less cheerful.

This late in the season, and having been through and done what I've done, my only real concern about Millwall is whether or not I want to be here. The fans will have much more to worry about than me; this time I'm not going through the head-pelting worries that plagued me earlier in the campaign, even though if ever there should be a time to worry, it's upon landing up at Millwall. But my scars are deep; I've seen it all now. I'm like a well worn break pad; a used condom.

I receive a warm enough welcome from the press guy, Deano Standing, whom I remember as a match reporter from the days when Jonathan Pearce would scream himself rancid throughout a Saturday afternoon on Capital Gold radio.

Right now, though, he's my Brad Pitt in this Millwall version of *Seven*. Deano's fought so many fires at Millwall, with its allergy to the press, that it seems to show on his face; a generally concerned looking, ruddy man who's shell is impenetrable to the likes of me, almost like an emotionless, macho cowboy. Deano puts me in touch with a few fans ahead of Saturday's game at Bristol Rovers and then sends me off into the ground to do all that grass-eating nonsense I do. 'The hell I will,' I go to say in a cowboy drawl, before realising that my imagining him as a cowboy hasn't been mentioned out loud.

I wander around the New Den. It's smart if non-descript; relatively new, tall and shiny, practical and fresh, if lacking the gritty, brutal charm of the old Cold Blow Lane. They moved here in 1993, a wrenching switch from the old Den a quarter of a mile away. I squelch around pitch-side in the grit, trying to make out distinguishable features to write about, but there's little to pick out other than it's *quite* nice. So I reluctantly eat a bit of grass, like a kid being forced to finish the cabbage. No idea how many I've eaten now, and in the soaking wet everything seems like a stupid idea; everything, including breathing (but excluding gorging a metre of pizza in bed while watching *Countdown*, simply for a feelgood fix of Rachel Riley, who, incidentally, hasn't been in touch yet).

I leave a little note under the dugout bench for Millwall manager Kenny Jackett, just saying good luck, hoping it'll be found in a hundred years time and I'll become this mythical Gloryhunter character, akin to a football version of Jack the Ripper. Probably.

I leave the Den cold, wet and pissed off, dreadfully pissed off, wishing I could just pop home, turn the world off and wake up in Summer, smothered in women.

* * * * *

"I won't be able to swim, will I? Can I swim on one side?" muses Chris Bethell, after I've asked him whether he'd have an arm off to save the club – a game I like to call 'Administration or Amputation'. Chris is a Millwall fan who came to meet me for a drink before kick-off at the away game with Bristol Rovers. He only came, really, because when Millwall play away, all the pubs in the local area shut their doors and board up windows as though a hurricane's about to sweep through it and rape everybody. Subsequently there's nowhere for Millwall fans to enjoy the righteous path of beer infusion that other fans do. It makes me feel a bit bad for the vast majority of them who behave themselves, that they have to be shepherded in and out of the local areas, in big police-chaperoned convoys of coaches, and then whipped straight out again afterwards. Chris knew that with a press pass, I could get him into the bar, so he's grabbed onto that with both hands, irrespective of my camera or what I'm doing, which is fair enough. He's a likeable character; short, round and chirpy with a cheeky grin you'd invite to Christmas dinner. (That's not an actual invite Chris, sorry, it's just too soon.)

While I was waiting for Chris, the Bristol Rovers 'Pirates' bar – essentially a working men's club that issues plastic glasses, overlooked by a scrag-assed, glass encased waxwork of a pirate – started to fill up. Darlington away to Rochdale was on Sky and I recognised nearly everyone in the shot of the away fans; Woody, Darlo Pete and the gang. It was weird to see them up there, thinking that months ago I was a part of that. Just in front of me in the bar, a group decked out in army gear clutching collection pots came and had a quick drink and I overheard one of them telling an anecdote, recounted in that Bristolian twang that makes you want to drink a litre of cider and join him on a year off in a squat being an artist or something. The story was about how one of his army colleagues was drunk and utterly naked while away somewhere – how, I have now idea – and as a mother and young daughter approached, he scrambled around and reached for the nearest thing he could find in the park to cover his gems. It turned out that all he could find to grab was a dead duck. So, there he was, covering himself with a dead duck. I bet the old pirate in the corner has heard many a cider-fuelled story like that, so many in fact that he's probably gone teetotal these days.

"An arm, yeah definitely an arm," confirms Bob Asprey of the Millwall Supporters Club, a slightly younger, cockney version of Captain Peacock from *Are You Being Served?*, who's here with Chris. I get talking to them about the reputation the club has, and although they seem to feel as though they're picked on a bit by the press and the police and the general population of football fans, they're under no delusions that there isn't *some* smoke without fire. Some of the latest high jinks included 47 injured police officers and 26 injured police horses after a play-off game against Birmingham. Whenever you meet a Millwall fan it seems a shame that the conversation always falls back into the rut of their reputation, which is probably what perpetuates the trouble in the first place, like a very aggressive chicken and egg situation.

"Both arms? Well I won't be able to wipe my arse now, so there *is* a problem. My tongue's very short," Chris replies to the next level of 'Amputation or Administration'. I wonder what the wider reaching implications of a short tongue are? Could you say 'Totally Tutankhamun'? How about 'Taxi to Titicaca'?

"Both legs, both arms? Yeah yeah yeah, I'll just keep me head," Bob concludes, confident that he would donate pretty much any limb available to keep the club going.

As we walk outside, Chris tells me about his son, who's on the ground staff at Chelsea. He was caught in the centre of a bit of a storm when he had, let's say a *tussle*, with Manchester United player Patrice Evra. It sounded like handbags to me, one of those when both parties appear to want the fight more after others have arrived to hold them back. Apparently, after that, the players at Chelsea started saying hello to him and the club paid for him to go to Moscow for the ill-fated Champions League final.

Bob points out the numbers of police outside the ground here, and the way they're looking at everyone. This is the second time I've been here this season, and there's definitely a more vigilant presence than I remember. No s**t Sherlock, it is Millwall – their reputation arrives long before they do. But there's certainly no sign of trouble, nor even an atmosphere that may induce such, but then given that this is my first game, I don't know if that's because the police are here in such numbers, or if Millwall do genuinely go away from home without fuss most of the time.

Inside the ground, I'm not allowed into the away end. Again, it's for safety reasons, although it's not made clear exactly whose safety. So, they park me next to a photographer on the side of the pitch near the away fans.

"At least it's not bloody raining," he says miserably, as though he's just turned up for a shift at Asda. I soak up the emerging Spring sun while the Millwall fans make untold noise to my right. "*No-one likes us, we don't care, we are Millwall, super Millwall, we are Millwall, from the Den,*" they sing. I look around them, wondering whether these will be the bunch I'll end my season with, maybe at Wembley Stadium. There's certainly an energy about them that I haven't experienced elsewhere. It's a latent buzz, a clouds-a-brewing feel, like the moments just before a custard pie hits your face.

"Oi, come and film me you slag," shouts a ginger kid down the front who's been gesturing to anyone who'll look and mouthing off at the stewards over nothing in particular. I swing the camera past a bunch of them, including him, and they unleash a volley of as many swear words and hand signals as one can within the momentary sweep of a camera pan. The mood in the enclosure starts to simmer up and approaches boiling point as police arrive like stormtroopers and line the edges, refusing to crouch, which inflames the Millwall fans. It's like a stand-off. I get the feeling, just a feeling mind, that the police *want* to get in the way, *want* to wind up the fans – and the fans aren't slow in taking the bait. The whole time, the orchestral soundtrack to *Star Wars* plays over and over in my head. I often find that underscoring thoughts helps make a situation more interesting, although I don't know why *Agadoo* pops up during job interviews.

Much of the discord among the Millwall fans is to do with the recent death of fan Ian Tomlinson, the newspaper seller who got caught up in the May Day riots. He died shortly after being pushed over by the police, and now the fans are singing for justice and upping the tension with that as the fuel.

It gets even more intense as Rovers take the lead. As does the impending destiny of my season. This could be it; if Millwall don't draw or win here, the possibilities for me are a series of closing doors – one of which being a door to the Championship play-offs, a door to Wembley that could be closed within a couple of hours.

When Millwall equalise, the away end erupts into a wriggling mass of upstream leaping salmon, the promotion valve pops open and out spurts fresh hope. Some of them stand up on the edge of the hoardings, one fan even runs onto the pitch and on being chased by police and stewards, sprints back and flips himself over the fence and back into the anonymity of the crowd, like the end of *Escape to Victory*. But my relief is momentary.

Suddenly, this dog is trapped on the wrong side of the door.

Rovers go 2-1 up, then 3-1 up, and their fans start doing cut-throat gestures to the Millwall lot in mockery. *Come on Millwall.* I never thought I'd be whispering those words to myself. *Come on you Lions…* But as the tension self-perpetuates like feeding dark chocolate to a migraine, my whole quest for glory seeps out into the ether, just wisps off into the clouds with all the other evaporated dreams. It's like pouring a vintage wine down the sink – so much hard work, gone in seconds.

Rovers fans jig around in dreamland, having never expected to trounce promotion-hunting Millwall. I spot Chris in the crowd behind the goal, mouthing off at a policeman who refuses to get out of the way.

"I ain't paid all that money and come all this way to look at your helmet."

Even sitting virtually on the pitch, the amount of coppers filing past is making it impossible for me to see Rovers knock home a fourth.

It's over. No Wembley. No glory.

BRISTOL ROVERS 4-2 MILLWALL

Disley 12   Abdou 28, 78

Lambert 32

Kuffour 37

Lambert (Pen) 45

Attendance 6,618

---

* * * * *

SATURDAY, 2 MAY 2009.
Last game of the season.

As I dangle my feet in the clouds, one thousand feet above the typically English, undulating, moist-green countryside of the Sussex Downs, spotting the peak that Delboy actually unwillingly hand glided from in *Only Fools and Horses*, I wonder who's in the specks of cars down below and where they're going. Some of them are probably on their way to the game at the Withdean, which I'll also be at if I make it through this precarious lofty dangle.

Looking down at it all from the great height of this paragliding experience – that a Brighton fan's cajoled me into despite my rampant vertigo – I realise with the objectivity of height and enough time up here to process my thoughts away from the earth upon which they're fuelled, that actually, I have, after all, reached my cup final, of sorts. And it turns out that it didn't need to be at Wembley for it to be glorious.

I've to some extent disengaged with football fans over the last couple of weeks – Bristol Rovers and now Brighton (after Albion did them over only three days after the Millwall game) – but not through disinterest, more through feeling as though my work here is done, I've learned all I needed to learn, and with a sense of wanting to take a step back and begin to rejoin the anonymous masses, I've felt the need to meld back into society instead of sticking out like a great throbbing penis, with a camera on a stick and dirty jeans that smell of old beer. I've reached the end of the journey and now the games are petering out, soaked in the nascent glares of early-summer sun, just as it baked us to a gallop ten months ago in Grimsby and Brentford. What went around came around; I've stuck at it through all the seasons, and now I can smell home.

The end of season malaise is here already and I've just been enjoying the sense of relief, that I've made it unscathed – although this paragliding expedition isn't perhaps a guaranteed way to remain so. From up here I look down at the tiny people whose lives seem so large when you're down among them, and I imagine – however difficult it is to step outside of your own dilemmas and minimise them for a moment – how small I'd look, too. Similarly, from the stand at the away game with Huddersfield, I looked objectively across to a travelling battalion of Brighton fans as they tried to gee their team on to stay in the division; each of them a complex mine-field of worries and triumphs and tragedies.

Subsequently, the cup final I've reached is Brighton versus Stockport. Brighton *have* to win to stay in League One. Simple as that. For these fans, it's as big as any cup final that's ever been played. *I may yet get my glory*. From up here in the sky looking down at the ickle cars, and looking across as an outsider to the Albion fans at Huddersfield, I can really see that glory is utterly relative, and totally arbitrary. You can set your standards however you want, because happiness and glory is in your own hands, it's up to you. Therefore, I decide, my cup final is not only this game, it's this entire season. I realise that I can set my bar however high or low I like, to whichever highs or lows are going to make me happy. After today I can go off and live in a now that suits me, that's relative to my own expectations and no-one else's. This constant searching, chasing, needn't be.

I hit the ground and go looking for my glory. The streets around the stadium are awash, smothered in fans with regalia, fans excited and addled with hope, despite the thoroughly dismal campaign they've limped through. But they've adjusted their expectations, their remit for glory is simply *today*, a virtual cup final, a chance for the hysteria and mania that they'd have found in equal measure had they been walking out at Wembley. "Seeeeeaaagulllllsss" they sing, tins of beer and huddles of anonymity as they climb the steep hills in joyous mobs, to *their* Wembley.

Here I am, the last day of my amazing season, the final act, a very last glimmer of glory and I'm going to grab it, this is my complete now...

4.53pm
On the pitch, Withdean Stadium, East Sussex.

When empty, this athletics stadium (not built for football), surrounded by huge trees and family homes, can feel like a tranquil oasis in a dense Canadian forest.

But right now, the temporary stands are empty because the pitch is covered with their contents; jubilant fans in blue and white, celebrating the saving of the end of the world; hugging in relief, in joy. There are tears and screams and whoops. People are grabbing at bits of turf, swinging on the goalposts and taking pictures that'll be all over Facebook in minutes. And the sun shines down on it all. Spring is here and another season of thrills, spills, beers and cheers is over. Meanwhile, a bald man is being held aloft, on the shoulders of fans in the old fashioned way you've seen Bobby Moore balanced in pictures from 1966 (and all that). Manager Russell Slade has guided Brighton into the arms of League One safety. They've not won anything – no cups, no promotion – they've narrowly avoided relegation to the bottom league. After a desperately unsuccessful season, here he is lapping up the praise for only just avoiding doom. He's enjoying his relative glory.

And me too.

Glory? I *did* get my glory.

This sun-baked carnival was the dramatic climax I'd envisioned, although in vastly different circumstances than I'd thought. I had no idea I'd get my glory at this end of the table, on the pitch at Brighton and Hove Albion. It didn't even occur to me.

I love the fact that a man calling himself 'The Gloryhunter' ended up in a relegation scrap in League One, that even when you decide to cheat at being a football fan, it bitchslaps you back into order. Football and Madam Fate have rightfully slammed me back in my place, and now I really ought to scurry off back to where I came from, back to Spurs, with renewed vigour, fresh hope and a deeper appreciation of what the football means to all us fans. We can't always win, but if only in our minds. And I know that this journey has reached way beyond football for me; the game is merely a microcosm, just a practice for the game of life, which is something I should really get back to working on playing.

I decide to leave the Withdean while it's still buzzing, wanting my last vision of a football ground on my ultimate season to be one of unrestrained celebration.

BRISTOL ROVERS 1-2 BRIGHTON & HOVE ALBION
Lambert 28   Owusu 43
                       Andrew 52
Attendance 6,193

HUDDERSFIELD TOWN 2-2 BRIGHTON & HOVE ALBION
Booth 16   Andrew 38
Collins 57   Owusu 66
Attendance 4,740

BRIGHTON & HOVE ALBION 1-0 STOCKPORT COUNTY
Forster 73
Attendance 8,618

* * * * *

SATURDAY, 9 MAY 2009.
White Hart Lane, Tottenham.
Numb, awestruck, speechless...

A week later, I find myself sitting in the dugout at an empty White Hart Lane; the bowl-like stadium wrapping itself around me like a warm hug. I'm home. I've come *home*.

They've let me in to film my very last ITV episode, and as I sit moist-eyed in Harry Redknapp's luxury car-seat style chair, I think about the managers who've sat here before, on probably less luxuriant benches, and what they saw while I was up in the stands. Keith Burkinshaw at the 1984 UEFA Cup final sticks out furthest, the penalty shoot-out against Anderlecht and the ensuing frenzy of goalkeeper Tony Parks's celebration after making the winning save. Just thinking about it makes me feel like I'm having my stomach tickled by a claw. I've got the tingles here in a way no other ground has given me, or could ever give me.

I sit and drift off into a headspace far away, thinking back over my season, all the months and adventures that have lead me back to my North London bosom.

Over the last week, however, I've gone further than just a dream with a gooey face; I've been out on the road, on one last tour of some of the clubs I was with during the season, just to see how they got on, to see my friends again, and to give me a sense of closure...

* * * * *

Up in Grimsby, I meet Jon, the narrow-faced boy who welcomed me so warmly to the club. We stand outside the ground, looking in at the pitch – as I did ten months ago, with my first tentative steps into the unknown. Now, I peer in with a familiar fondness.

"We went through a really bad, bad phase, but we've turned it around now and things are looking up for the Mariners again. We're looking forward to next season, which hasn't been going around the town for a good few years. We'll be looking to challenge next year," says Jon with a twinkle of hope. But then that's what he said this year.

Grimsby stayed up by the skin of their teeth, finishing 22nd in League Two.

* * * * *

Further north in Darlington, I meet Woody for a pint or seven and perhaps a curry – to be honest, through the beery haze I can't remember much of it. He's just had his head shaved, put a couple of curry pounds on and seems to have missed having his 15 minutes of being on camera. With the backdrop of the Darlo clocktower looming, we lament what's happened since I left.

"It's been an emotional time. We had a few bad results after you'd gone, but we got it back on track. But then we went into administration and lost ten points. There's not going to be a football club if we can't find a buyer. It's just an emotional time, at the end it was like ... if this is the end ... me record of not missing a home game in nine years and an away game is six years is gone..." He looks away morosely, until the clock starts chiming noisily in the background. His demeanour reverts back to cheeky. And maybe a little pervy.

"I like the ladies, and the ladies like me. That clock is going ding dong, like my schling schlong goes, ding dong." Christ knows what that's all about.

But **Darlington** did keep themselves going and although those ten points would have put them in the play-offs, they ended up 12th in League Two.

* * * * *

North-east further, in Hartlepool, I meet Ron and Big Bob, along with Scott, who dons the H'Angus the Monkey costume these days.

"It's all gone pear-shaped since you left. We were doin' alright 'til you went," says Big Bob with a playful look of blame. I seem to have been accused quite a lot of leaving a dreaded curse behind me. "We were that poor, we got dragged into it [the relegation battle]."

"For our centenary season, it's been poor," adds H'Angus with his lesser-heard voice not currently inside the monkey.

"It's been garbage for a centenary season," concurs Ron, glumly, with the souring backdrop of a chilly Hartlepool Marina evening dipping into darkness.

"We stayed up by the hairs of our chinny chin chin."

Hartlepool finished 19th in League One – one point off relegation.

* * * * *

In Rotherham, I meet Reaction Dave and Sean at a local pub, where they become progressively and agreeably drunk.

"Sean should eat more chicken and cheeky pizza. Chicken and cheeky? I mean chicken and chicken pizza," blurts Reaction Dave in his customary nonsensical manner.

"I'm quite happy to stay up this season, we've done quite well," adds Sean, before we continue to make my week of visits an official bender.

Rotherham finished 14th in League Two, and I still haven't heard about my signed shirt, or received a replacement.

* * * * *

Unsurprisingly, it's raining in Macclesfield. Profusely. In fact, I sometimes feel that the Macclesfield rain comes down with an element of sarcasm. Inside the ground, I catch up with Andy 'the voice' Worth and his mate Jon Smart.

"Well we survived," says Jon, in a grim monotone that matches both the season the Silkmen have just experienced and the weather, as the cigar-shaped chimney thing up on the hill winks at me one more time. It's watching me; I know it.

"But it got worse," Andy adds gruffly, with less sex in his voice than last time I saw him. "Why did it get worse, Jon?" he asks, impotently.

"Well, we didn't play great. We had some fun…"

"Did we?"

Macclesfield finished 20th in League Two.

* * * * *

Down in Peterborough, I wander the main street amid flags and scarves emblazoned with bombastic words of triumph and victory. An open-topped bus wafts past, with manager Darren Ferguson and all the players waving like royalty.

Peterborough United survived their wobbles and got their just desserts – automatic promotion to the Championship after finishing second behind champions Leicester.

"This season's been a very very pleasant surprise," shouts Adi Mowles with a rare grin, above the sound of cheers and foghorn hooters. "At the beginning of the season I would have bit your hand off for play-offs."

"Oh God, no, I just can't think," says Boozy Baz, looking fresh as a daisy, as though he may have been allowed back into the marital bed. "I never wanted it to end…" (The season, not the marriage.)

* * * * *

Down the Percy pub in Bournemouth, tucked away in the warren of sordid boozy booths, I find John and Steve and the rest of the gang.

Bournemouth pulled off a great escape down the bottom of League Two despite having started with 17 points deducted.

"Fankewww, Eddie Howe," says John.

"He may be the youngest manager in the league, but he's the best," Steve gloats. John starts talking about previous managers of the club in comparison to Howe.

"Jimmy Quinn, he was wonky. And Kevin Bond, he was wonky." And then he starts telling me a story about how he once drank his sister's breast milk.

"It was fantastic going into the last game of the season and not having to worry..." Steve interrupts appropriately, and we drink swiftly towards my last curry of the season, as I'm embarking on a diet to un-Gloryhunter my stomach.

Of the fifteen teams I spent time with, the bottom five of the entire football league were among them. I didn't have time to catch up with the fans from **Chester** – relegated to the Conference, and **Luton** – relegated to the Conference. **Swindon** finished 15th in League One, **Bristol Rovers** 11th and **Millwall** lost in the play-off final to my other former club **Scunthorpe**.

* * * * *

Walking down the tunnel on the way out of White Hart Lane and out into the world away from Gloryhunting, I remember my re-visit to Brentford. Actually, it was on that last day of the season when the sun was shining over the Withdean. Straight after the game, I drove back to London and popped into the Griffin, where celebrations were not so much in full swing as hanging off, all over the streets...

* * * * *

...It's as ragged and raucous as a Victorian brothel on absinth. Each corner of the pub, inside and outside, there's singing of different songs, although all of them making reference to the word 'champions'. They're clambering on walls, on the furniture and all over each other. There's smeared lipstick and mascara, and the women look bedraggled as well. Johnny M incoherently accuses me of being a white witch, while others just drag me as close to their faces as possible and scream unintelligible glottals. I'm given the shocking news from Tim/Top Cat that Sven of the Swebees is no longer *of* the Swebees. He's left them to start up his own clan, The Viking Bees.

Brentford went up as League Two champions.

"We shall no longer be a big fish in a small pond," laughs Councillor Kirton in the nippy late night pub garden. As the night draws to a close and my bleariness, exhaustion and sheer lack of vitamins takes its toll, Smiffy and Fraulein emerge and ask if they could have a quiet word. *Here we go*, I think, *what have I gone and done now?* They can't bar me from the pub on the last day of the season, can they?

"You know how Fraulein's pregnant?" says Smiffy proudly, but obviously I know that, seeing as she's standing in front of me in the packed pub and her bulbous belly is almost propping up my sagging chin.

"Well, we were wondering if you'd like to be the Godfather?"

Tears somehow find their way past my internal efforts to keep them in. What? *Godfather*? It's punched me right in the face, a total shock. I'm flattered, I'm touched; I've never been asked something like this before, but then, I've never put myself in a position to be.

I've been wandering the planet, wondering where I belong, and right now it hits me that it's not *where* you go, it's *who* you're there with.

Hello England.

We toast a new season, a new start, a new life.

ACKNOWLEDGEMENTS

The people who I met along my ten-month glory-scavenge are what made this ridiculous journey what it was for me, and rather than write an all-encompassing *thank you* to cover any and everyone, I'd rather make a big fat list of those who I think deserve the credit of a name check for affecting the course of my story, however big or small their input. Of course, there were some major players in my stories, but in this list I'm including almost anyone who's touched my path, even in the remotest fashion. You might have just sent a brief message of support through Facebook, and you might be shocked to see your name, but when you're away, on your own, it's the little things, and even a nod in the street can change a day. So here we go, club-by-club and in no particular order therein (and sorry if I've still missed you, there are a lot of names to remember and remembering isn't my favourite … erm … thingy. But those beyond this list's recollection, rest assured, I'll be kicking myself as soon as it's printed and your face randomly pops into my head while I'm on a train or on the toilet or something. So *thank you* anyway!).

Thank you to:

Grimsby
Steve 'Ghandi' Moore, Jon Spurr, Josh, Andy Murray, Sarah Griffiths, Mandy Woods, Matt Newton, Katie O'Neill, Nutty, Bruce Fenwick and the gang, 'Jesus', Swanny, Mr Groundsman, Alva, Dale Ladson, Marilyn Monroe, Dean and Rachel and the Trust, Leon Harding, The Queen of the Pontoon, Craig Stoddart, Jane Stolworthy.

Brentford

Richard 'Smiffy Wilf' Smith, Fraulein Edmonds, Perry Fogden, Nicky Fogden, Johnny M., Luke Kirton and his mum, Sarah Faulkner, Alex Brown, Nick Bruzon, Steve Tidy, Bradley Bates, Mads Tarrant, Ralph+Mark+Betty+the girls down the Griffin, Angela Hagaman, Annette Curran, Ashley Levy, Astra Seibe, Ben Hamer, Andy Scott, Peter Gilham, Dave Appanah, Dave Carter, Callum Taylor, Catarina O'Mahony, Chris Kennedy, Claire McNicholls, Dan Suh, Jonesy and Stu, David Ilett, Gaz Evans, Gayle Sheldon, Gemma Teale, Glenn Joyce, Jason and Natasha Judge, Jim Finnigan, Justin Kempton, Laurie Hicks, Lucy Woms, Mark Burridge, Mark Fuller, Mark Sallis+Piers+The Naughties, Martin Sexton, Matt Davis, Nick Hester, Ricky Simon, Tim Collinson, Ronan Gay, Russell Barker, Mark R. Harfield, Simon Hoyle, Steve Brent, Stuart Heavens, Sven Aasen, Terry French, Spencer Cox, No Coat, Nick Logan, Greg Dyke, Greg Dyke lookalike fan (the mouthy one), Tom Moore, Stan Bowles, the 91/92 Promotion team, Jon Gosling, Steve Hedge, Tim Street, Jacob Murtagh, Twiggy and Nick, The Brentford Tandoori, Carl Hutchings, Dave Merritt, Antony Lock, Pudsey Bevan, Andrew+Jack+Dawn+Olivia Daniels.

Luton

Jeff Thomas, Jane Ledsom, Gary Sweet, Nick Owen, Liam Day, Kev Rouse, Vivienne Murray, Justin Cerri, Graham Brazier.

Darlington

Nick Woodward, Ted Blair, Andy Park, Deano Browne and Anthony, Hayley McDaid, Becky Ackrill, Cheryl Parttison, Chris Coates, Chris Swinton, Dave Adamson, Jack Huscroft, Jonathan Cimmerman, Lucas Brooke, Michael Dowson, Roland Winder, Sam and Dave, Sandra 'puddle soup', Simon Hawkins, Dee-Jay, The Laughing Policeman, Jeff Winter, George Reynolds and Stuart, Marco Gabbiadini, Darlo Pete, Cockney Darlo, Dave the Drummer, Misled Icons, Claire Robinson and the north-east Ghost Hunters, all at West Auckland FC, Tina Raynor at Killhope Mine, Phil Cornforth, Chris Jackson.

Chester City

Little Alan Carr, 'Shaun Ryder', Chas Sumner, Mike Poole, Sue Choularton, David Mitchell.

Bournemouth

Steve Brown, Serena McClelland, Carey Paton, Chris Manning, Clarissa Mills, Danie Papeguay, Dave Jennings, Dave Stone, George James, James Swyer, John Garard, Katy Muncer, Matt Maybury, Mick Cunningham, Paul Williams, Sandra Jones, Terry Sowle, Tom Dowthwaite, Vinny Goodfield, Paz Simpkins, Mild Mannered Mike, Phil at Burley Villa School of Riding, NOT Darren Anderton.

Macclesfield Town

Andy Worth, Jon Smart, Moose, Chris Wilcock, Ciaran Perks, Nicole Byram, Tina Lawrence, Patrick Nelson, Big Jim, Boris Johnson, Roger Boden, Matt Beresford.

Rotherham United

David 'Reaction' Besley, Sean Thompson, The Greatest Ever XI.

Scunthorpe United

Craig Parker.

Swindon Town

Nigel Bennett, Whizz kid Gary.

Hartlepool United

Ron Harnish, Bob Harnish, Fireman Bob, Andy Booth, Stuart Drummond, H'Angus the Monkey, Ben the Bowels, Jimmy McKenna, Ian Lowry, Dave Walls, Jeff Stelling's Cousin.

Peterborough United

Adi Mowles, Paul Donnelly, Boozy Baz, Craig Matthews, Dawn Livingstone, Jayde Baxter, Neil, Sam Baines, Lee Jackson, Andrew Linnett, Andy Mills, Anthony Lickerish, Keith, Chris Dowson, Craig Lyons, Isaac Lodziac-Green, Nick Prince, Nick Warrick, Paul Mitchell, Steve Thorpe, Simon Alexander, Rob Graves, Mick Bratley, Howard Brown, Nilesh Patel, Mr Posh, all at Flag Fen.

Millwall

Chris Bethell, Bob Asprey, Deano Standing.

Brighton
Paul Camillin, Steve Purdie.

Other thanks...

Everyone at KTS: Richard Roper, Simon Lowe, Gareth Stringer, Tony Lyons.
Everyone at ITV.com: Richard Northen, Mark Segal, Luke McLaughlin, Ben Ayers, Phil Timm, Marc Webber, Becki Burrows.

Those who came to the original draw: Ben Stevens, Ben Russell, Tamara Gilder, Patrick McMahon, Matt Smith, Huw Slipper, Tom Thostrup, Dave Winnan, Frank Winnan, Ged and Tina O'Shea, Shirley Jones, Chris Rushton, Nick Cochrane, Alan Williams, Rui Alho, Andy Thomas, Dan Wright, Steve Marsh, Catherine Mann, Alix Fairbairn.

Miscellaneous thanks: Adrian Swift, Gareth Collett, Chris Nee, Leigh Francis, Keith Lemon, Steff Wright, Mr Poopoo, Patrick Mascall, Keith Hall, Paul Ross, Bill Wheatcroft, Spoon Newell, Lee Sweetman.

Special thanks: Mum and Dad, for putting up with the random, occasional drop-ins.

And finally, thanks to the beautiful game, for giving us balls.

Spencer Austin
September 2009

†HE CLUBS

After making the draw in the Freemason's Arms pub in Covent Garden, birthplace of the Football Association, Spencer 'supported' 15 clubs, plus Brentford on two occasions. For ease of reference, in order they were:

Grimsby Town
9 August 2008 – 16 August 2008
3 games – 1 win, 1 draw, 1 defeat

Brentford
16 August 2008 – 7 October 2008
9 games – 4 wins, 4 draws, 1 defeat

Luton Town
7 October 2008 – 11 October 2008
1 game –1 defeat

Darlington
11 October 2008 – 25 November 2008
11 games –6 wins, 3 draws, 2 defeats

Chester City
25 November 2008 – 6 December 2008
1 game – 1 defeat

Bournemouth
6 December 2008 – 26 December 2008
4 games – 1 win, 1 draw, 2 defeats

Brentford
26 December 2008 – 24 January 2009
4 games – 1 win, 2 draws, 1 defeat

Macclesfield Town
24 January 2009 – 31 January 2009
2 games – 1 draw, 1 defeat

Rotherham United
31 January 2009 – 17 February 2009
2 games – 1 win, 1 defeat

Scunthorpe United
17 February 2009 – 21 February 2009
1 game – 1 defeat

Swindon Town
21 February 2009 – 24 February 2009
1 game – 1 defeat

Hartlepool United
24 February 2009 – 7 March 2009
3 games – 1 win, 1 draw, 1 defeat

Peterborough United
7 March 2009 – 13 April 2009
7 games – 5 wins, 1 draw, 1 defeat

Millwall
13 April 2009 – 18 April 2009
1 game – 1 defeat

Bristol Rovers
18 April 2009 – 21 April 2009
1 game – 1 defeat

Brighton & Hove Albion
21 April 2009 – 2 May 2009
2 games – 1 win, 1 draw

about the author

Spencer Austin is a television producer who spent his formative years in Walthamstow (going to school with East 17 and playing for the same football club as David Beckham are small items of trivia he churns out at dinner parties). In his teens he won the *Waltham Forest Guardian* Young Sports Journalist of the Year and subsequently worked for Leyton Orient Football Club.

At 21 he fell violently into stand-up comedy and ended up performing as part of a double act on stage and screen with very little applause. But it did result in being offered a job as a TV researcher at LWT, where he worked closely with Jeremy Beadle and legendary writer Denis Norden for a few years. He wrote and produced a number of TV pilots featuring talent such as Leigh Francis and Edgar Wright before Nasty Nigel Lythgoe noticed and took him under his wing.

From there he went on to devise and/or freelance produce shows (*Celebrity Stitch-Up, Your Face or Mine, Gagging For It, RI:SE, Rajan and his Evil Hypnotists*) that have been sold in the UK and internationally. He formed Hideous Productions and very quickly created a show called *24 Hours With...* for ITV1, as well as selling it to 13 countries all over the world.

He now lives on the Isle of Dogs with no-one but himself.

Praise for *Chasing The Eighties*

A p**s-funny book about living the 80s celluloid dream and enduring the cinematic nightmare. Part stalker-fanboy-diary and part Jackass-Rough-Guide-to-movie-America, Spencer Austin faked an orgasm in Harry and Sally's favourite deli, got drunk in the Tom Cruise singalong bar from *Top Gun* and attempted some nut crushing dance shapes at *Dirty Dancing*'s Lake Lure. The Time of His Life or What? And he'd never felt this way before. *Paul Ross*

By visiting the real-life locations of those 1980s films and doggedly tracking down and interviewing the frequently bemused and now unknown stars, Austin hoped to fuse his memories of film and TV with more recent memories of real people and places, finally curing himself of wistful nostalgia. The results are often hilarious and surprisingly poignant. *Waterstone's Books Quarterly*

Also by the same author

CHASiNG THE EiGHTiES

The Ultimate North American Movie Location Adventure

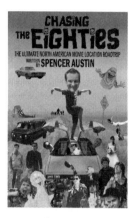

Spencer and his two friends Tom and Luke were sick with youthful nostalgia – the plague of the modern generation. Unlike those before them, there were videos, photos and the internet to help them wallow in how good the past was and how crap the present is. It was so bad, even watching *Back To The Future* had become a painful reminder of what was no more. The only way to cure nostalgia, it seemed, was to say goodbye properly. So, they threw in their jobs as TV producers and hit the road on a three month, 30,000 mile romp around North America in search of the heart of their eighties; chasing new memories to replace the old.

From the Police Academy building to breakfast with The *A-Team's* Murdoch to beers with Chunk from *The Goonies* – they did the lot. They ate omelettes with Louis Gosset Jnr after shaving their heads and spending the night at the *Officer and a Gentleman* barracks, met Bubba Smith (Hightower in *Police Academy*), played football against a vampire hunter from *The Lost Boys*, were taught the *Karate Kid* 'crane kick' by its creator and recreated 'that' moment in the very seats Harry and Sally lunched in.

Chasing the Eighties is a journey of cure and healing: a trip under the skin of what the eighties mean to not only those who grew up in them, but those from other generations who've likewise been snared by the *Goonies*, the *Ghostbusters* and The Guttenberg. Surely, over one hundred locations and twenty-five interviews with film and TV stars will dampen those nostalgic twinges once and for all!